JUNIOR COLLEGE DISTRICT

of St. Louis - St. Louis County

THEODORE SEDGWICK, FEDERALIST

THEODORE SEDGWICK
A Portrait by Gilbert Stuart

Theodore Sedgwick, Federalist:

A POLITICAL PORTRAIT

BY

Richard E. Welch, Jr.

WESLEYAN UNIVERSITY PRESS

Middletown, Connecticut

Library of Congress Catalog Card Number: 65–14054
Manufactured in the United States of America
FIRST EDITION

For My Parents
HPHW *and* REW

Contents

Acknowledgments

I AM indebted to many persons and institutions for assistance in the preparation of this book. I am under obligation to the directors and staffs of all the libraries and historical societies listed in the bibliography, but most especially to those of the Massachusetts Historical Society. Mr. Stephen Riley, its director, has been most helpful, and my debt to Miss Winifred Collins and Mr. Warren Wheeler will be instantly recognized by anyone who has worked at the society. They stand as living proof that patience can indeed be inexhaustible.

Professor John Gilchrist Barrett, a former colleague at The Virginia Military Institute, Professor S. H. Brockunier of Wesleyan University, and Professor Jacob E. Cooke of Lafayette College have read and criticized the manuscript during its various permutations. They are not responsible for either its organization or its style; they are responsible for diligent efforts to improve both.

Mrs. Wilma Benka, Mrs. Hazel Bonnell, Mrs. Eileen P. Ricketts, and Mrs. Sally Scott gave essential help in typing various drafts and portions of the manuscript, and Mrs. Jean Gordon Cooke, editorial assistant for *The Hamilton Papers,* kindly traced the repository of several Sedgwick-Hamilton letters. Mrs. Arline Bishop of Windsor, Connecticut, prepared the index.

Two obligations, however, stand out above all others: that which I owe my teacher, Frederick Merk, Professor Emeritus of History, Harvard University; that which I owe my wife, Christina Marquand Welch.

RICHARD E. WELCH JR.
Lafayette College

Easton, Pennsylvania

THEODORE SEDGWICK, FEDERALIST

Introduction

On the eleventh of March, 1796, a tall gentleman possessed of a prominent nose and New England accent rose in the House of Representatives and launched into a full-scale defense of presidential authority, national honor, Federalist principles, and the Jay Treaty. Despite the fact that the intent of this long oration was to limit the prerogatives of its immediate audience, it was received with great acclaim. Indeed, the orator—with typical immodesty—reported that he had gathered an embarrassing array of compliments. In the midst of his speech, he had received from a lady in the gallery a delicious sweetmeat of orange, neatly folded and accompanied by a note; from Vice-President John Adams, Rufus King, Oliver Ellsworth, and Robert Morris there had come the warmest of praise for his masterly eloquence; and from the editor of a Massachusetts paper an ode, wherein the speaker's strength was compared favorably to that of the "unshaken Andes."

Though this oration represented one of the more dramatic moments in the career of Theodore Sedgwick, it by no means stands alone as witness to his contemporary prominence. Consequently it is somewhat surprising that historians of the Federalist period have largely relegated Sedgwick to the category of a footnote figure in their accounts of the early years of this nation. Acknowledgment is made of his role in the funding debate and his loyal support of Alexander Hamilton and that gentleman's financial system; occasionally there is a reference to Sedgwick's animosity towards Frenchmen and Jeffersonians, but the index seldom points further than this. The great struggles and decisions of the formative years of the Republic continue to be described almost exclusively in terms of the great figures and contending champions. It is possible, indeed, to gain from some accounts the sensation that all the crucial establishment of legislative precedents, all the in-fighting and struggle, all the defeats and victories of the Washington and Adams administrations were the exclusive concern of Thomas Jefferson and Alexander Hamilton. Mention will be made, of course, of the valiant support lent by a Madison or King, Burr is counted on to provide a sinister note of color, and the noble Washington hovers uneasily overhead. But what of the crucial leaders of the second rank? They usually receive short shrift. This is unfortunate, not because the careers of such men necessarily serve to revise the existing picture of the Federalist period but, rather, because they provide essential and illuminating details as to the day-to-day operations and practices of their party, its formation and organization, its evolving philosophy and basic divisions.

Only the boldest of romancers would claim for Theodore Sedgwick a place at Mount Rushmore. His chief significance lies not in the fact that he was a leader; rather, that he was a follower. Sedgwick was typical of the Hamiltonian Federalists who made possible the Federalist régime as they eventually helped divide the Federalist party and assure its defeat. In his opinions as in his conduct Theodore Sedgwick personified the party and program of New England Federalism. To recount his political career is to explain the contributions and limitations of New England Federalism, its strong points and its weaknesses.

A man whose nationalist sentiments and democratic antipathies were fashioned in the fires of Shays' Rebellion, Sedgwick's political progress was not marked by dramatic metamorphosis nor even marked growth. Inspired by a dread of mobocracy and anarchy in 1786, he died in 1813 decrying democracy and demagogues. But whether he labored to fund the debt or damn the Embargo, Theodore Sedgwick usually bespoke the fears and hopes of the Federalist majority.

Personally he was a man of rather paradoxical character. He loved his wife with sincere devotion and by his long absences from home contributed largely to her occasional attacks of insanity. Convivial and popular with his equals, his conduct towards "inferiors" was occasionally something more than autocratic. Greedy for fame, he was a man of the utmost probity in all business dealings. Hated by his political opponents with a degree of personal animosity unusual even in a time of factional bitterness, he was held in the highest esteem by George Washington.

There have been more attractive historical personalities than Theodore Sedgwick, but few men have labored more zealously in behalf of state and nation. As commissary agent in the Revolution and proponent of the Constitution, as congressman, senator, and judge, Sedgwick contributed significantly to the welfare of his country, despite a lasting distrust for a majority of his countrymen.

REVOLUTIONARY LIBERALISM

I

Boy and Lawyer

I remember how painful was my prospect when I was
making my entry into life, without friends from whom
I could expect anything, without any property, young,
and with a most diffident opinion of my own talents
the prospect exhibited a settled gloom. I did all but
dispair. To this I did not submit. On the contrary, I
determined, if possible, to succeed & I did succeed.
                                   Theodore Sedgwick [1]

THE Sedgwicks arrived in the New World in the person of Robert Sedgwick, staunch Independent and loyal comrade of Oliver Cromwell. A
descendant of a family which can be traced back to the Sedgwickes of
Dent, Yorkshire, in the reign of Henry VI, Robert emigrated to Massachusetts Bay in 1635.[2] Settling in Charlestown, this devout Puritan felt
called to advance the true faith by exhibitions of business acumen and
military valor. His military record encompassed the command of the
Massachusetts militia in 1652, a sortie against the French at Castine (in
the Penobscot region), and finally the post of Commissioner General of
the recent British acquisition of Jamaica. Arriving in Jamaica late in
1654, Sedgwick found it a place of pestilence and misery. After fighting
a losing battle against tropical disease, disintegrating morale, and dissension between the military services, he contracted yellow fever. There
in Jamaica he died May 24, 1656, disheartened and tortured by unwarranted self reproach.

1. To Theodore Sedgwick Jr., February 16, 1801. *Sedgwick Papers,* Massachusetts Historical Society. (The institution will henceforth be referred to as M.H.S.,
and Sedgwick Papers as *S.P.*)
    The spelling, punctuation, and capitalization of all quoted material has not been
altered, except to bring all superscript letters down to the main line and to replace
the dash with the period when the latter is clearly indicated. Attention is called to
misspellings (by the insertion of *sic*) only in cases where confusion as to meaning
might otherwise result.
    2. *New England Historical and Genealogical Register,* XLII, 85.

The General's elder son Robert died childless, but his younger son William, a less religious or admirable individual, managed to extend the family line in the person of Samuel Sedgwick (1667–1735). Samuel and his mother drifted about New England for a time, finally settling at Hartford, Connecticut, where Samuel subsequently married the young daughter of Stephen Hopkins—a prominent Hartford citizen and descendant of the Pilgrim Father of that name. In 1716 Mary Hopkins Sedgwick gave birth to a son Benjamin, father of the subject of this biography.

Benjamin Sedgwick married Ann Thompson (1719–1793) of Wallingford, Connecticut, and was for a number of years a moderately prospering Hartford merchant and storekeeper. Coming upon hard times, however, he decided to better his fortune with a new start and scene. With his wife and four children, Sarah, John, Benjamin, and Theodore, he removed in 1748 to Cornwall Hollow in the northwestern corner of the state.[3] Theodore, born May 9, 1746, was but two at the time.

Settled only ten years earlier, Cornwall in 1748 still bore unmistakable traces of its Mohawk history. The surrounding white oak, chestnut, and hickory forest was in many places practically unbroken, and the mode of life virtually pioneer. Benjamin Sedgwick quickly built a small farmhouse, erected a sawmill on a nearby stream, and commenced the arduous task of clearing some of the six or seven hundred acres of farm land he had claimed in Cornwall and its Litchfield County neighbors of Goshen, Canaan, and Norfolk.

After encountering a succession of difficulties inherent in pioneer farming in poorish soil, he was on the verge of something like mild success when he fell victim to a fatal attack of apoplexy. His epitaph expresses in concise fashion his sudden end:

In Memory of Dea. Benjamin Sedgwick, he died of Apoplexy Feb. 7, 1757, AE 41.

> In an Instant He is Call'd
>   Eternity to View;
> No time to regulate his house,
>   Or bid his friends adieu.

His eldest son John, not yet fifteen years of age, inherited two-sevenths of his father's property, and the total responsibility of caring

---

3. Theodore S. Gold, *Historical Records of the Town of Cornwall.* . . . (Hartford, 1877), 181.

for his mother, brothers, sisters,[4] and the property that had fallen to their share. Possessed with more stamina and drive than his father, John, by herculean exertions, kept the family together, operated for a time a small tavern, and enlarged and improved the Cornwall farm. By his efforts he enabled the pride of the family, the promising young Theodore, to receive at Yale a college education.

Theodore's childhood was relatively uneventful. A farm boy in a community not long since reclaimed from the wilderness, he applied himself dutifully to the countless chores that were the fate of that occupation, and though exhibiting no particular athletic prowess was respected by his contemporaries as a fair swimmer and a persistent, if somewhat clumsy, skater.

There is a temptation to theorize that Theodore Sedgwick's later ambition and success were forged by youthful hardship and poverty, but this is doubtful. He suffered no particular privation during childhood, and if his family was neither well-to-do nor socially prominent, neither were their neighbors. Indeed, these attributes were hardly to be expected in that region and time. If one can judge from the scant documentary evidence available, probably more formative than his days in Cornwall was his stay at Yale. At New Haven—as in any college, at any time—there would be talk of money and social position, glory and honor.

Young Theodore very early had revealed a bent for learning and an aptitude for literary and oral articulation that amazed and delighted his older brother. Through the agency of the latter, he was presented at the age of fifteen with the opportunity to become one of the colonial élite, a learned man. He matriculated at Yale in the winter of 1761–1762, and, contemplating the ministry, pursued the usual classical course of instruction. For three years he studied zealously and behaved meticulously. In his senior year, however, he committed his life's one verifiable act of needless frivolity. No record survives of the actual deed, but for some "boyish gaities" Sedgwick was abruptly dismissed.[5]

Chastened and repentant, he began to study for the ministry under

4. Two daughters were born to Ann and Benjamin Sedgwick in Cornwall: Mary Ann (1749–1826) and Lorraine (1755–1823).

Ann Thompson Sedgwick married as her second husband, Captain Timothy Judd (Yale '37) of Waterbury, Conn. After a short period of much unhappiness she secured, July, 1771, a legal separation. See *S.P.*, M.H.S.

5. His daughter Catharine Maria dutifully observes in her *Recollections:* "I received the impression . . . that he [President Clap of Yale] was a compound of pedagogue and granny." Mary E. Dewey, ed., *Life and Letters of Catharine M. Sedgwick* (New York, 1871), 23.

Seven years later, Sedgwick received his degree, as of the class of 1765.

Doctor Bellamy. It took but a few months, however, for him to decide that metaphysical theology and genteel poverty held little allure for one who craved a life of active power and worldly success. Having rejected the ecclesiastical, being unattracted by the military, and yet strongly desirous of engaging in a career that presaged his eventual acceptance in the best and most comfortable social circles of the day, he turned, naturally enough, to the bar.

Sedgwick had the excellent good fortune to be accepted as a law student by his second cousin, Colonel Mark Hopkins of Great Barrington, Massachusetts, one of the few professionally trained lawyers in western Massachusetts in 1775. After a single year of earnest apprenticeship, Sedgwick, not yet twenty years of age, was admitted to the Massachusetts bar (April, 1766).[6] He opened an office in Great Barrington and commenced with the September term to practice in the Berkshire County courts. A year's efforts at Great Barrington brought him but few clients and a debt of seventy pounds, and Sedgwick determined to move. Travelling about five miles to the southeast, he began life and law anew in Sheffield, Massachusetts, in 1767.

In Sheffield Sedgwick's luck quickly changed for the better. It was a promising region and a most propitious time for a young lawyer determined to climb the legal ladder. There were in the late 1760's few attorneys and but a pair of barristers in western Massachusetts. With the advent of the Revolution and the emigration of certain leading members of the bar,[7] opportunities would further expand, and Theodore Sedgwick was before long the busiest lawyer in the courts (Common Pleas and General Sessions) of newly incorporated Berkshire and its neighboring counties to the east.

A close student of English law, Sedgwick was early noted for his ability to pepper his court pleas with citations from *Holt's Reports*, *Viner's Abridgement*, *Sayer on Damages*, and other such works. By these learned references, he would by intention bedazzle and convince the farmer-jurymen of what was still a frontier area. The nonexistence of American law reports and law books made it impossible, of course, to have in the eighteenth century any distinct body of American law. Con-

6. Before 1787 there were no statutes or rules prescribing the period of study for candidates for admission to the bar in Massachusetts. Neither was there a written or formal examination.

7. A list of 1779 indicates only ten barristers and four attorneys for the whole of Massachusetts who were such before the Revolution. William Sullivan, *Address to Members of the Bar of Suffolk . . . March, 1824* (Boston, 1825), 201, 204–239.

sequently, the ability of a lawyer to produce analogies to English cases or to convince the jury by superior lucidity or charm was crucial to his success. Sedgwick possessed such abilities in large measure.

By his very appearance, Sedgwick demanded attention. Tall, broad-shouldered, and sternly erect, he was the possessor of a countenance more dignified than handsome. His hair was brown, and his rectangular face was distinguished by ruddy cheeks, a large, rather Roman nose, and a firm, square chin. His most outstanding features, however, were his large black eyes. By all accounts, he used them rather like an actor, conscious of their size and expressiveness. Often his face would remain immobile and only by his eyes would he register for the jury the desired emotions of scorn, pathos, and heartfelt conviction.

The relatively rapid growth of Sedgwick's law practice and legal reputation was naturally reflected in his social and economic status. Arriving in Sheffield in 1767, an impoverished bachelor, he possessed by 1771 not only a growing law practice but a house and garden by the village green, a half part of thirteen acres of farm land, twenty-three acres of pasture and wood lot, horses, a Negro house servant (Caesar), a cook (Ann Olds), and the title of Gentleman. He grew flax, sold logs, lent out his farm hand at a profit, and bought a dressing gown costing 3½s. and shoes costing 4s. He purchased books such as *The Progress of Darkness* and *The Fortunate Country Maid,* participated in a two team squirrel hunt, and fast achieved his aim of becoming an accepted member of the still amorphous town aristocracy.

Sedgwick was greatly aided in the latter endeavor by his marriage in 1768 to Elizabeth (Eliza) Mason (1744–1771),[8] daughter of Deacon Jeremiah Mason and Mary Clark. The Masons were a highly regarded family in Franklin, Connecticut, and the match delighted Theodore's mother. After less than three years of a most happy marriage, Sedgwick and his Eliza were tragically separated. Just a month before she was to have given birth to their first child, Eliza died of smallpox. She probably contracted the disease from her husband, for Sedgwick had earlier suffered a severe attack. He had been removed to the pock house outside of town, where he had undergone kill-or-cure treatment at the hands of a Dr. Hillyer. Recovered and certified as being non-infectious, he had then returned to his wife. Within three days she was stricken ill; within a week she was dead.

Sedgwick cherished tender recollections of this, "his first love," throughout his life. Though he remarried in 1774, he continued to enjoy

8. She was the aunt of Senator Jeremiah Mason, LL.D. (1768–1848), friend of Daniel Webster and lion of the New Hampshire bar.

annual visions of Eliza. These instances of intimate spiritualism were subsequently and lovingly described by his youngest daughter, Catharine Maria:

> Not long after her death, he was lying upon the bed he had shared with her (a "field bedstead," with a bar across the two foot-posts), and unable to sleep; he said to himself, "If I could but see her as she was, in her everyday dress—see her once more, I should be comforted." . . . till suddenly the room filled with a light,—not like the light of a lamp, nor like a thousand, the brightest—not like the light of the sun, but a heavenly radiance, and his wife—his young wife, her face lit with love and happiness, stood leaning over the bar at the foot of his bed looking on him. He . . . remarked the buckles on her shoes; he sprang forward to embrace her—she was gone—the light was gone—it was a dream. . . . Through his whole life he had once a year a dream that was like a visitation of this girl-wife. She always came to return to him those days of young romantic love—the passages of after life vanished. I can well remember the sweet, tender expression of his face when he used to say, "I have had my dream!" [9]

If Sedgwick's marriage and growing prosperity aided his entry into the town élite, his prominent part in the country's Revolutionary activities secured it. A period of political revolt is often conducive to social change. The young and ambitious become impatient at their exclusion from the charmed circle, and by supporting the new political order of things quickly achieve greater importance in the social sphere.

Though there were not many out-and-out Loyalists in western Massachusetts, the great conservative families (the Punchons, the Stoddards, the Partridges, the Dwights, the Williams) tended to think more of established position than of natural rights. Quite early they saw the danger that the "common folk," once utilized to help combat the distressing exactions and regulations of George III, would not be content to retire subsequently into their respectful shells. There were exceptions, of course, but on the whole the would-be aristocrats of western Massachusetts dragged their feet in the Whig cause.[10] Patriots of a non-radical complexion, such as Theodore Sedgwick, were ready to take advantage of this quasi-abdication of leadership.

9. Catharine Maria Sedgwick's *Recollections* in Dewey, *Catharine M. Sedgwick,* 25–26.

10. A notable exception was the Congregational clergy. To some extent, however, they were driven into supporting the "popular" side by their fear of Episcopacy.

II

Property and Liberty: Sedgwick in the Revolution

The cause for which we are now embarked had pro-
fessedly for its object the preservation of our Property.
think you that a lawless Violation of that Property
can tend to support such a cause?

Theodore Sedgwick [1]

In the period between the Boston Massacre of March, 1770, and the Boston Tea Party of December, 1773, Sedgwick's political opinions were those of a stouthearted Englishman who wished only to knock a little sense into the heads of the stupid colonial advisers of the best loved of sovereigns, George III. Such was the stand of the Sedgwick-drafted Sheffield Resolves of January 12, 1773. These resolves were the product of a convention held in Sheffield to protest "the design of Great Britain (which is too apparent to every virtuous lover of his country) gradually to deprive us of invaluable rights and privileges which were transmitted to us by our worthy and independent ancestors," and to declare unconstitutional the late acts of Parliament "for rating and regulating the collection of revenue." Professing "the most amiable regard and attachment to our precious sovereign and [to the] protestant succession," and freely offering "that deference and respect due to the country on which we are and always hope to be dependent," Sedgwick and his colleagues resolved that man had certain inalienable rights, exempt by nature from governmental destruction or modification. They solemnly declared that the great end of political society was to secure in a more effectual manner, "than was possible in a state of nature," the right to "undisturbed Enjoyment of their lives, their Liberty and Property . . . privileges wherewith God and Nature have made us free." [2] The various resolves,

1. Sedgwick to Samuel Johnson, May 31, 1777. S.P., M.H.S.
2. These little-known resolves were perhaps the earliest protest of their kind in colonial America. The full text of the minutes of this meeting can be found today in the Town Hall of Sheffield.

which made mention of most all the grievances later itemized in the
Declaration of Independence, were read twice at town meeting and
unanimously adopted. It was one of the few instances in Sedgwick's life
where he was in complete agreement with the popular temper of the
time.

When Britain in 1774 abrogated the Province Charter and declared
that all offices, executive and military, should be appointed by the governor, Sedgwick advanced another pace towards advocating outright independence. In the existing political spectrum, he was now a Radical.
Firmly ignoring all aspects of internal class conflict in the oncoming
contest with Great Britain, Sedgwick, a strong opponent of British interference in the *domestic* concerns of the colonies, was shocked by the
"unconstitutionality" of the Intolerable Acts and the "illegality" of parliamentary attempts at direct taxation. On July 6, 1774, he rode over to the
Red Lion Inn in the neighboring town of Stockbridge and took his place
with John Ashley as one of Sheffield's delegates to the Berkshire County
Congress, called to protest the late actions of the Mother Country.

Elected Clerk of this Congress, Sedgwick kept careful minutes of its
day-to-day proceedings.[3] From them we learn that he was a member of
Mark Hopkins' committee "to take into consideration the act of Parliament made for the purpose of collecting revenue in America," and most
probably served, too, on the final drafting committee. The convention,
after piously recommending that July 14 be set aside as a day of fasting
and prayer—"to implore the Divine assistance that He would interpose
and in mercy avert those evils with which we are threatened," resolved
upon two main lines of action. They expressed their sympathy and support for the "distressed inhabitants" of Charlestown and Boston, sufferers
under the recent Boston Port Act, and vitalized that sympathy with the
promise of certain "fat cattle" in the fall. Secondly, they voted to refer
to each town in the county a covenant for the non-importation and non-
consumption of British manufactures.

This covenant, after cataloguing the just grievances of the citizens of
Massachusetts, specified five lines of attack whereby Britain might be

3. A signed, original copy of its resolves of July 8, 1774, is to be found in *S.P.*,
M.H.S. It is not, however, in Clerk Sedgwick's handwriting. The minutes of the
convention may be found in full in *The Journals, of Each Provincial Congress of
Massachusetts in 1774 and 1775. . . .* (Boston, 1838), 652–655.

These resolves, and "the non-consumption of British manufactures League"
which they attempted to establish, were perhaps the first act of economic warfare in
Massachusetts after the occasion of the Boston Tea Party. They stand with the Suffolk
Resolves and The Association (adopted by the First Continental Congress on September 17, 1774, and October 20, 1774, respectively) as illustration of the Radical
position in the year 1774.

forced, in peaceful fashion, to mend her sinful ways. 1) No one was to import, purchase, or consume any British goods, wares, or merchandise which arrived in America after October 1, 1774. This resolve was to remain effective "untill our Charter, and Constitutional Rights shall be restored or untill it shall be determined by the major part of our Brethren in this and the Neighboring Colonies, that a non-importation and non-consumption Agreement will not have a Tendency to Effect the deserved End." 2) All were to agree that they would pay the most strict obedience to all constitutional laws, and would exert themselves for the "Discouragement of all Licenciousness, and Suppressing all Mobs and Riots." 3) Everyone should exert himself to promote peace and unanimity amongst each other, "and for that End . . . engage to avoid all unnecessary Lawsuits whatever." 4) To forestall shortages which would arise from the non-importation agreement, all should agree to "take the most prudent care for the raising and preserving [of] Sheep, and for the Manufacturing [of] all such Cloaths as should be useful and necessary." 5) Persons refusing to sign or who should refuse to "adhere to the real interest, and meaning . . . [of this Agreement, were to] be treated . . . with all the Neglect that they justly deserve." With the firmness if not the eloquence of Patrick Henry, Berkshire County was making sharp protest against the British Parliament, "who have, of late, undertaken to give and grant away our moneys without our knowledge or consent." The lines of battle were being slowly drawn. A year later a liberty pole would be erected in Sheffield; [4] another year and national independence would be proclaimed.

To judge from his correspondence, Selectman Sedgwick, never one to exchange loyalties lightly, entertained hopes for a peaceful settlement of colonial grievances as late as the spring of 1776. When it appeared, however, that all-out war could be avoided only by the sacrifice of principle, he accepted the inevitable. If British restrictions on colonial territorial and industrial expansion had not greatly disturbed him, those on the rights of local government assuredly had. He heartily concurred in the Declaration of July 4, 1776.

A steady and persistent adherent of the Patriot cause throughout the war, Sedgwick seems to have had but two brief tours of military duty.[5]

4. Not all Sheffield residents were Patriot in their propensities. There is record of the town's liberty pole being chopped down, and the culprits, when caught, being obliged to pass before a line of the town inhabitants, abjectly begging the pardon of each.

5. There is a strong possibility that he served as a volunteer aide during the Burgoyne campaign of 1777, but this is not capable of definite verification. There

The first was in the capacity of military secretary, with the rank of major, to Major General John Thomas, during that gentleman's ill-fated expedition to Canada in May, 1776. Sedgwick was one of the staff who advised the abandonment of the Quebec investment in June, 1776. After the death of Thomas, and the withdrawal of his expedition, Sedgwick resigned his commission in deep discouragement.[6] In the first years of the war, Aaron Burr, at this time a good friend of Sedgwick, pressed the latter on several occasions to accept the office of secretary and military aide on the staff of General Israel Putnam, but with no success.[7] Sedgwick's only other military post was a short tour of duty as temporary, or acting, brigade adjutant at Peekskill in the late summer of 1776.

The only battle exploit in which he is recorded as participating was his courageous rescue of his patron Colonel Mark Hopkins, when the latter was badly wounded at the battle of White Plains, New York, in October, 1776. Catharine Maria describes it most vividly:

> My father went to him at great personal risk, for the British were advancing, and our people retreating. He procured a litter and soldiers . . . and Mr. H[opkins] was placed on the litter and hastily carried off. They heard firing; Mr. H. . . . implored my father with tears to leave him to his fate, and save himself. My father of course resisted, cheered and sustained him, and conveyed him to a place of safety.[8]

Sedgwick by no means suffered from any lack of physical courage. His period of active military service was short and his contribution as a soldier slight, but as a family man without military training or experience he probably felt he could make his best contribution in the more com-

---

5. (cont.)

is a notation by a Colonel Burrell, of Connecticut, to the effect that after the battle of Saratoga a Major Sedgwick met him "with verbal orders from Gen. Lincoln" to stop the militia on the road leading to Bennington. *Trumbull MSS.*, as cited in Henry P. Johnston, *Yale and Her Honor-Roll in the American Revolution 1775–1783* (New York, 1888), 244.

6. Sedgwick had written his second wife, Pamela Dwight Sedgwick, May 14, 1776, of his "Extream Hurry of Spirits" and his despair that "the Troubles the Follies of Villainy with which I am surrounded remain altogether unimpaired." S.P., M.H.S.

7. See letters from Burr to Sedgwick of June 29, 1777, and July 4, 1777. S.P., M.H.S. The rank was to be that of major; the pay, fifty dollars a month. It would serve to introduce Sedgwick to some post "more adequate to his abilities."

8. Dewey, *Catharine M. Sedgwick*, 24.

fortable capacity of the civilian.[9] In this capacity he contributed significantly on several counts.

Sedgwick probably considered that he best aided the causes of victory and liberty by his wholehearted struggle against the "tyranny of the Mob." There were, of course, many residents of Berkshire County who welcomed the Revolution as a means of propagating doctrines of political and social equality. Not content to consider the conflict solely as a struggle for nationality, they insisted on taking Jefferson's Declaration at its face value. These under-represented citizens early gained control of many of the town committees of correspondence, and, as the war progressed and the near vacuum of civil government became more evident, turned them into extra-legal governing bodies. These safety committees, as they were sometimes called, disrupted the teaching profession and the ministry by a suspicion of certain of their practitioners, refused to allow any state court to sit within the county from 1774 to 1780, and declared the colonial charter no longer in effect. In the eyes of Sedgwick, possessor of two nankeen coats, three broadcloth waistcoats, and a set of silver shoe and knee buckles, these "men of lower sort" were embarking on a disastrous and most stupid course. He considered that all of them and especially the Berkshire Constitutionalists—those Radicals who demanded a new and ultra-democratic state constitution—were as bad as the Tories themselves.[10]

There was published in Hartford, Connecticut, in 1778, a short tract addressed to the inhabitants of Berkshire, "Respecting Their Present Opposition to Civil Government." [11] Published anonymously, it was, if

9. In 1781 Sedgwick was delegated by General Benjamin Lincoln to serve as liaison between Congress and the new "state" of Vermont, and to investigate the charges that Vermont was carrying on a treasonable intrigue with the enemy. Though working under a military command, Sedgwick served in a purely civilian capacity.

Concerning this "mission" see Lincoln to Sedgwick, August 24, 1781 and May 29, 1782, and Sedgwick to Lincoln, April 19, 1782, S.P., M.H.S.; *Misc. Papers*, M.H.S.

10. Quite obviously the present writer is convinced that in western Massachusetts there did exist a distinct radical *versus* conservative division within the Patriot ranks. A quite different interpretation will be found in Robert E. Brown's stimulating study, *Middle-Class Democracy and the Revolution in Massachusetts, 1691–1780* (Ithaca, 1955), especially pp. 365–400.

11. *Anonymous Impartial Reason, An Address to the Inhabitants of the County of Berkshire Respecting Their Present Opposition to Civil Government* (Hartford, 1778).

Sedgwick's own copy of this now virtually unknown pamphlet is among the S.P., M.H.S. The style of the writer is very similar to that of Sedgwick, but other

perhaps not the work of Sedgwick, in his possession and perfectly expressive of his views on the conduct of his neighbors. Its main theme was the regret that all good men must feel at seeing the noble exertions and warlike achievements of Berkshire "most shamefully tarnished by occasion being given for this base reflection, *That their struggle has not been for the establishment of a free and equal government on the ruins of tyranny, but rather that they might introduce a state of total anarchy and licentiousness, on the ruins of all government whatever.*" Begging the people not to despise lawyers and formal modes of justice simply because certain members of the bench and bar had unaccountably taken part with the King, the writer insisted that reforms in the laws concerning collection of debts, fee bills, deed recording, etc., could best be achieved by orderly methods still freely available in Revolutionary Massachusetts. There was no reason to think that the Declaration of Independence had annihilated the "constitution" of the colony of Massachusetts Bay, and, even granting that it had, it could not in any sense have materially affected the social compact existing among the people. It was absurd for men to cry out for a new state constitution, while claiming all the liberties of man in a state of nature. Man could not belong to any political society until he resigned certain alienable rights. This was "the necessary condition on which men entered into civil society." Ridiculing the threats of secession which had been made at certain town meetings in the county, the spirit of conservative Berkshire ended by castigating:

> These shocking inconsistencies, in which you have gone on for several years past . . . pretending to belong to the community of Massachusetts Bay by sending representatives, or rather spies to the general court, and at the same time, refusing to obey those laws and rulers which they prescribe, unless in some particular instances, wherein they happen to coincide with your fancies! [12]

---

11. (cont.)

evidence points to some resident of Great Barrington, Massachusetts, as its author, possibly William Whiting.

An excellent analysis of the Berkshire Constitutionalists is to be found in Fred Emory Haynes' unpublished doctoral thesis, *The Struggle for the Constitution in Massachusetts, 1775–1780*, 111–181. This thesis is in the Harvard Archives, Widener Library, Harvard University.

12. James Truslow Adams, *New England in the Republic* (Boston, 1887), 86–87. Perhaps the most forthright of "the threats of secession" was that authored by a county convention at Pittsfield, August 26, 1778. See Massachusetts Archives, 184, 196–198, as cited in Harry Alonzo Cushing, *History of the Transition from Provincial to Commonwealth Government in Massachusetts* (New York, 1896), 272.

Armed with such a well-organized sermon, Sedgwick must have considered the unregenerate behavior of Parson Allen's Berkshire Constitutionalists and the committees of safety, in general, as little short of treasonous. In Sedgwick's eyes these Constitutionalists were expending more animus and energy against the assembly and council of the Province of Massachusetts than against the red-coated forces of His Brittanic Majesty. As agent for the Continent and as spokesman for the forces of reason and order, Sedgwick felt doubly aggrieved. Rallying the frightened Conservatives of Berkshire, he attempted to follow every pronunciamento or convention of the "mobbish, ungovernable, refractory people" with a clear rebuttal and restatement of the true Patriot position.

In one instance, especially, did Sedgwick take the offensive. In the spring of 1779 "subversive elements" in Sheffield attempted in town meeting to establish a committee of inquiry "to see whether [the] present mode of Government . . . as is now Practiced . . . in the Easterly part of this State is binding [on us]," and to see whether the town would not authorize the Convention which was to meet at Stockbridge "to petition the General Court that the County of Berkshire may be set off to a neighboring State," providing no new state constitution should be formed in the meantime. Sedgwick, outraged by the invasion of radicalism into his personal bailiwick, vigorously attacked the suggested resolutions and quickly secured a decision "not to pass on either point." [13]

This year of 1779 was a most critical one in the struggle between the forces of order and reform in western Massachusetts. Appreciating the crisis at hand, Theodore Sedgwick was fearful of its resolution. He wrote James Sullivan, May 16, 1779: "Affairs grow worse continually, the gentlemen who have principally distinguished themselves as friends of order live in perpetual danger. . . . What will be the result, I know not, unless we are to be protected every measure will be attended with danger. Something decisive must be done or we shall be reduced to the dilemma of leaving the country or making the best terms we can. I tremble for the other parts of the state." [14]

Repeated and unsolicited acts of amnesty from the General Court did nothing to soothe the troubled spirits of the Berkshire Constitutionalists or to reopen the courts of justice in that county.[15] Displeased by

13. Sheffield Town Records (*MSS.*), April 27, 1779, as cited in Haynes, 169.
14. S.P., M.H.S.
15. The opposition of the debtor farmer to courts and lawyers is the connecting theme between the Berkshire dissidents of 1775–1780 and the supporters of Captain Daniel Shays in 1786–1787.

The lawyers appreciated their growing unpopularity and at a meeting of the Hampshire and Berkshire bars at Springfield on May 18, 1781, attended by Sedg-

the lack of a Bill of Rights in the legislatively-conceived Constitution of
1778, these eighteenth-century Populists were yet incensed by the rejection of this Constitution by such aristocratic easterners as the authors of
the *Essex Result*. Giving the state rulers one more chance, they demanded that the legislature take the sense of each town on the advisability of calling a special constitutional convention, the product of which
would be submitted to each town for popular determination in town
meeting. The legislature consented. The inhabitants of Massachusetts by
a five-to-two majority declared that a constituent convention would be
advisable, and the Constitution of 1780 resulted. This constitution was
only adopted after some rather sharp practice and it surely provided a
much less democratic form of government that the Berkshire Constitutionalists had in mind. Having gained the form of their demands, however, they were temporarily pacified, if not completely content.

These Constitutionalists did not, however, comprise all the Berkshire
Radicals. Many of the members of the safety committees and "the
mobocracy," in general, had been more interested in social equality in
local terms than with the organizational structure of the state government. These men remained "trouble-makers" throughout the Revolution.[16] Sedgwick wrote his good friend Caleb Davis, May 25, 1781, of
the continued danger they offered:

> I know too well your Generosity and Goodness, to doubt your
> warm and benevolent regard, to a number of Gentlemen, in this
> Country, who have done much and suffered more; for their attach-
> ment to the Cause of Order and Government. . . . if Government is
> to be administered by a Faction and the road to Preferment is to be a
> relinquishment of the Character of a Freeman and a servile adulation,
> aduration and bending the knee to those Characters which good
> Fortune, whim, Caprice have rendered most popular and all this,
> is apparent on a first Election. if these are the rewards and the only
> rewards acquired by our struggle in the Cause of Freedom, I think
> (to speak in the mercantile stile) the balance is greatly against us.[17]

15. (cont.)

wick, promised to use their influence to "prevent any kind of unnecessary Expence,
and especially that which originates from the Commencement and prosecution of
unnecessary and vexatious suits at Law." *S.P.*, M.H.S.

16. During the winter of 1779 a deputation of thirty self-appointed Tory-hunters
visited Sedgwick and began to castigate him for attempting to secure for suspected
traitors a fair and impartial trial. Rebuffed by his scorn and "resolution," they
quickly retired in search of lesser prey. See various Sedgwick letters of January and
February, 1779, *S.P.*, M.H.S.

17. *Caleb Davis Papers*, M.H.S.

The thread of Loyalist persecution runs throughout the pattern of the Conservative-Radical struggle in western Massachusetts, and the basic and fundamental antagonism between Sedgwick and the Radical "mob" is nowhere more marked than on the issue of legal safeguards for the accused traitor.

Neither Sedgwick's belief in the rightness of the American cause nor his ardent desire for political independence and military victory is liable to question. Because of his conservative temperament, however, his professional training, and a certain compassion for the badly treated underdog, he opposed unnecessarily harsh treatment of the passive Loyalists and decried the illegal trials given suspected "traitors." He was buttressed in this stand by a lifelong admiration for the able and educated, and by a strong belief in the value and perpetuity of old friendships. Old friends and men of worth should not be hounded like criminals merely because they clung to former loyalties, nor should Loyalist prosecution serve as an instrument of political factionalism.

Massachusetts had treated the supporters of the Crown with a distinct and understandable lack of charity. On the accusation of but one Patriot in town meeting an individual could be arrested as a Tory sympathizer. If convicted, he was deported. In 1778 an act was promulgated banishing all who refused to take the oath of allegiance to the Revolutionary government of the new state.[18] Death without benefit of clergy was their announced fate if they had the temerity ever to return. The Tory who kept his opinions strictly to himself usually was annoyed but little; the Tory who felt compelled to express his opinions or give aid and comfort to the enemy was warned, quarantined in detention camps, banished, or stripped of his property, as the occasion demanded. The

18. Sedgwick doubted the efficacy of oaths and other forms of "political catechism." As he explained in an undated letter to Timothy Edwards of Stockbridge, he wanted to see emphasis placed on a man's actions rather than on his alleged beliefs:

> I really think that we can't by any means so soon put an End to *disaffection*, as by doing good to all who have broken no Laws. . . . I am fully of opinion that all out *political* catechism will never make one political Conversion to Whigism, but if persued will make thousands of perjured villians and disaffect many weak persons.
>
> It may be asked whether I would have no Restraint. I answer, yes; Restraints upon Actions but none on Thought. I would punish without Distinction every Person, who was guilty of any Crime, against the state, I would admit none to the Honors & Emoluments of Government, but those who fully approved of the Independency of the Country, and of the Government established.

Papers of H. D. Sedgwick, S.P., M.H.S.

last punishment became more and more popular as the bitter and financially-exhausting struggle developed. Notification to the confiscatee could be made by a quiet insertion in some local paper, and suit consequently not contested. It was the usual procedure, too, to have judgment given by a single Patriot judge, without the troublesome delay of assistance from a jury of the defendant's peers.

The proportion of Loyalists to Patriots in Berkshire was very small, but perhaps because of this the former were for the latter a source of great irritation. The amount of property actually confiscated by the county's committee of safety does not seem to have been large—and much of that consisted of wild lands owned by non-residents—but threats of confiscation were numerous and the war-burdened farmers very noisy. A man of more integrity than tact, and a firm believer in the orderly processes of English law, Theodore Sedgwick proved a thorn in the side of the *ad hoc* popular bodies with their vigilante methods and extemporaneous rules of evidence. Certain men, such as William Vassall, Levi Allen, and the brothers Peter, David, and Henry Van Schaack, Sedgwick considered "honest loyalists." These he tirelessly aided in obtaining their release from decrees of banishment and in recovering their property.

An interesting example of such efforts by Sedgwick was the case of Colonel Elijah Williams, arrested under suspicion of treasonably aiding the enemy. Williams attempted to exempt certain of his cows and oxen from confiscation at the hands of the West Stockbridge committee by selling these cattle to Sedgwick. Sedgwick, a commissioner of supply for the northern department of the Continental Army, had purchased them in his public capacity and at a price considerably lower than that which many money-hungry farmers were asking. The committee, headed by Samuel Johnson, incensed at being thus thwarted, questioned Sedgwick's right to take chattel for the use of the Continent, and sequestered the cattle and certain horses of Sedgwick's until he should make restitution. Sedgwick, whipped to a fury by this action, took up his pen. Declaring that the committee was intermeddling in a matter foreign to its jurisdiction, he warned that any body of men which assumed powers not delegated to them by the constitution or government under which they lived were little better than tyrants:

> The cause in which we are now embarked had professedly for its object the preservation of our Property. think you that a lawless Violation of that Property can tend to support such a cause? does the guilt of Colo. Williams authorise injustice towards him, me & the publick? does not proceeding with him as manifestly guilty prejudge

the Cause. . . . is it not strange to detain my Property & my security
for it likewise? this may seem free language, it is so: but remember
that Freedom of Speech is one of the Liberties for which we are
contending. . . . I desire to ask one more plain Question whether
we are contending for a system of Law—legal security or a System
of arbitrary Power? if for the latter I have done for I would as soon
submit to British as American Tyrants.[19]

Perhaps the most pathetic of Sedgwick's Loyalist clients was Peter
Van Schaack of New York. This gentleman, almost totally deprived of
his sight, had lost six children in eight years. He was, moreover, nursing
a dying wife when in 1778 he was ordered by a New York Board of Commissioners to give up a flourishing business, quarantine himself in New
York City, and prepare to leave the country. He had not committed any
overt acts, but would not recant his belief in the indestructibility of the
British Empire. Sedgwick, who had tried over many a bottle of Van
Schaack's fine old Madeira to convert the latter, compared him to "a tall,
noble pine, perfectly straight," only it inclined a little at the top towards
England.

Sedgwick attempted to influence the New York commissioners to be
lenient and forbearing, but without success. When it became certain
that Van Schaack would have to quit his home at Kinderhook, Sedgwick
helped him dismantle its furnishings, making, it must be said, some
rather advantageous purchases. He also took Van Schaack's library
into his own safekeeping and promised to supervise the education of the
deportee's eldest son. Finally he wrote Aaron Burr, then stationed at
West Point, and asked him to see that all permissible aid and comfort
were given Van Schaack and his brothers on their journey to the detention camp.

In one of his letters to the unhappy Van Schaack, Sedgwick gave
excellent expression to his current views on political toleration:

It is with extreme pleasure I reflect, that during the *turbulency* of
the times, I have preserved entire my friendship and esteem for the
worthy, who have been opposed to me in their political creed; nor do
I imagine it is possible to select from the *aggregate* of human follies
and bigotry, a more sure and incontestable evidence of the weakness
of head and depravity of heart, than that narrow and confirmed
policy, which has for its end a uniformity of opinions, whether political or religious. I wish my country happy, great, and flourishing;
I wish her independent; but that she may be happy under the law,
it is necessary that she become wise, virtuous, and tolerant. This is

19. A copy of this letter of May 31, 1777 is in S.P., M.H.S.

the way most certainly to know whether a state is or is not actuated by
a spirit of freedom: let the constitution be violated, in the person of a
subject obnoxious to popular resentment, or let his happiness be in
any way sported with; if *this* gratifies popular malignant malice, and
no murmerings or disturbance ensues, it is a sure indication that not
only the flame, but that every spark of liberty is extinct. . . . We
now ought to make even our enemies know and feel, that we had
valuable ends in view, in opposing the pretensions of Britain; by
rendering our government sweet, it would become palatable; in this
way we might, we may have a great and glorious revenge; and all
men, almost, will wish for the salvation of that . . . which is a constant source of happiness to them.[20]

As the war came to a conclusion, Sedgwick continued his fight for
political generosity in the state legislature. On many occasions he took
pains to point out the financial and stabilizing contributions "truly re-
formed" Tories might make. Sedgwick in his later career was very decidedly not noted for charitable treatment of his political enemies.
During the Revolution, however, he can be so characterized—as respects
the Tory enemy if not the Berkshire Constitutionalist.

Another aspect of Sedgwick's Revolutionary activities, and by far
the most important, was his work as a commissioner of supply for the
northern department of the Continental Forces in the years 1775–1778.
Working but part time and in a civilian capacity, he bought and saw
transported thousands of pounds worth of provisions and material for
the military commands of Gates, Lincoln, Schuyler, and others. These
supplies he secured in good weight and full measure, at the best price
possible in a period noteworthy for its inflation-bred cormorants and
war profiteers.[21] Taking but a small profit for himself, he performed a
necessary service in a persevering and efficient fashion. Sedgwick had a
five-county territory in western Massachusetts and New York, and
worked under the direction, at one time or another, of the Boston con-

20. August 12, 1778, cited in Henry C. Van Schaack, *Life of Peter Van Schaack,
LL.D.* (New York, 1842), 116–117. See, also, Henry Van Schaack to Sedgwick,
September 4, 1778, and Sedgwick to Henry Van Schaack, March 24, 1783, S.P.,
M.H.S.

21. Sedgwick's brother John forwarded him a bit of doggerel in a letter from
Mount Independence (December 15, 1776), a part of which ran as follows:

Its not Right for a Soldier to Grumble I know
but there is one Grudge that I Lawfully owe
    those Damnable Sutters how Slighly they'll Come
and Charge us one Dollar for a Qrt. of Rum.

tractors Otis and Andrews, Collectors of Clothing for the Continental Forces; the young trader Oliver Phelps; and Colonel Trumbull, Commissary General. Except for uncertain state loans and town gifts, the general government was largely dependent for army supply on the purchases and requisitions of private individuals such as Agent Sedgwick.[22]

Sedgwick operated what was in effect a large wholesale business. He purchased wheat and commissioned its conversion to flour; bought cattle, clothing, blankets, horses, pork, hay, fodder, nails, salt, etc., at continually rocketing prices; saw to a variety of services connected with the transport and storage of these supplies; and organized and inspirited a fluctuating host of subordinate purchaser-agents. Perhaps his main effort concerned the purchase of meat for the troops in the field. Buying usually in small lots of from three to six head from scores of private citizens, and arranging for fodder, pasture, and drovers enroute, Sedgwick would forward anywhere from 25 to 160 steers, sows, "young creatures," bulls, oxen, and sheep at a time. During the three months May–July, 1777, he shipped livestock to the total amount of £3379, 9s., 9d., receiving a personal commission of less than 2.5 per cent. Cattle cost that year, in Continental currency, from eight to fifteen pounds; oxen from eight to thirty-two pounds; and sheep from one to two pounds.

Grain was another major commodity of purchase. Sedgwick's papers contain countless letters from his agents and customers haggling over the price of wheat, corn, bran, and oats. He attempted throughout most of 1776 to keep wheat to six shillings (one dollar) a bushel, and flour at two pounds six a cask, but with varying success. Shipments of six hundred bushels of wheat or two hundred casks of flour were usual, and their purchase and transport often made possible by cash advances from Sedgwick himself. For purchases of foodstuffs and "sundries for the Continent," he charged and received as his own payment a percentage commission; for securing and supervising a long array of services—collecting, crating, sorting, transporting, hiring—he asked nothing.

Actually considering the large volume of business he transacted, his "profiteering" seems to have been slight. There are in Sedgwick's papers receipts from sellers of foodstuffs and services totalling over seven thousand pounds for the year 1777 alone. His total commission on this sum seems to have been less than £140. His largest running account was that with Oliver Phelps, state superintendent for army purchases. A com-

22. Sedgwick was one of the first to advocate a system of private contracts, rather than public requisitions, as the main basis of troop supply. See his letter to the Honorable Committee of Supply of Watertown, July 26, 1775, in MSS. *Collections* of the Historical Society of Pennsylvania.

plexity of loans, advances, and authorizations, a variety of monetary mediums, and a constant fluctuation in the worth of these mediums make it difficult to evaluate the exact extent and value of their transactions. Their gross volume, however, from 1775 to 1778, totalled almost £ 27,000.[23]

As Sedgwick charged the Continental Congress for all personal expenses incurred in the performance of his duties as commissary agent, he cannot be said to have suffered any pecuniary loss while serving in this capacity. Because of the usual difficulty and delay in obtaining payment, however—and this while all forms of paper currency steadily depreciated—his commissions, his profits, were larger in theory than in fact. There would often be vouchers lost or verifications mislaid, and a corresponding decrease in the commissaries' notes, Congressional bills of credit, or much preferred interest-bearing loan office certificates that were Sedgwick's due. The Commissary Department's system of bookkeeping was uncoordinated and elemental at best, and resulted in increasing the work and riling the tempers of such honest but independent agents as Sedgwick. The military would occasionally interfere, red tape multiplied constantly, and the general impracticability of the civilian operation of a military function became ever more apparent. Amazingly enough, however, supplies did arrive, an army was kept in the field, and a war was won. To that end, Theodore Sedgwick, in several capacities, made a distinct contribution.

23. In 1782 Sedgwick was again associated with Oliver Phelps, this time as a partner in a Massachusetts company which had a special contract "to supply all the flesh necessary for the moving army." Sedgwick's chief contributions were: 1) to persuade Generals Heath, Lincoln, and Washington to accept the substitution of fish for meat during part of the summer of 1782; and 2) to purchase beef on his personal credit when that of Massachusetts was very slow in being authorized. See Sedgwick to Heath, April 19, 1782, in *Heath Papers,* XXIV, M.H.S., and Lincoln to Phelps & Sedgwick, June 16, 1782, S.P., M.H.S.

III

Legislative Apprenticeship: Sedgwick in the General Court and the Continental Congress

> *Delay and procrastination under our circumstances will I seriously believe prove ruinous to us.*
> Theodore Sedgwick [1]

WHILE Sedgwick was serving his country in various war posts and capacities, he was also serving his state as an inexperienced but industrious legislator. Sedgwick's career in the Massachusetts General Court is of interest both as a facet of state history in the "critical period" and as the apprenticeship of a future leader of the Federalist party.

There is reason to believe that Sedgwick served in the provisional state legislature in 1779, but his first ascertainable election to public office occurred in the spring of 1780, when the inhabitants of Sheffield and its small neighbor Mount Washington chose him as their representative to the first General Court held under the new state constitution. Sedgwick's main occupation at this term seems to have been as a member of various *ad hoc* committees considering and reporting various private petitions. Of more importance, however, was his assignment as one of General Warren's Committee to consider "what Instructions are proper to be given to said Delegates respecting the State of Vermont." [2] This assignment gave Sedgwick excellent background for his mission in 1781–1782 to investigate the imbroglio created by Vermont's claims to independence and her consequent flirtations with the British.

Between May, 1780, and May, 1781, popular elements evidently gained added political strength in Sheffield; for Sedgwick, self-proclaimed opponent of "frenzy," was not re-elected. Samuel Allyne Otis consoled him with the cheering thought that "Callumny is the tribute of eminence, you are not surprised at being called upon for your quota

---

1. Sedgwick to Caleb Davis, October 14, 1785, *Davis Papers*, XIII–B, M.H.S.
2. *Massachusetts. Journal of the House*, I, 118.

surely. . . . Do you think a man of Sentiment would not sicken, at least with apprehension of wrong conduct should such birds sing his praises?" [3]

The "birds" were in better tune after a twelve-month span, for Sedgwick was then again elected as a representative to the Massachusetts House of Representatives. The first of three sessions held by this Court was devoted, so far as Sedgwick was concerned, to the drafting of a bankruptcy bill and a bill establishing a uniform system of weights and measures. He was also made chairman of a committee to consider reports of insurrectionary activities in Hampshire County. This appointment was a portent of Sedgwick's later absorption with Shays' Rebellion. The committee never published a formal report, but it is probable that Sedgwick studied with considerable detachment Hampshire's economic grievances and objected strongly to various projects for restricting its zealous courts. Certainly, as a member of the newly formed Finance Committee he favored strong measures to force delinquent towns to contribute their just share of beef, men, and revenue, and proposed additional taxes upon polls and estates. An economic conservative, he wished to reduce the mounting war debt by means of a "pay as you go" tax policy.

It would, of course, be a mistake to try and fit all the votes and actions of the Massachusetts legislature in the early 1780's into a set Conservative versus Radical pattern. It was faction, not party, that dominated Massachusetts politics well down into the next decade. There was a shadowy alignment between like-thinking conservatives, but no organized party with a recognized platform or concerted course of action. With the proscription of the Tories during the Revolution went the basis of original party divisions. A perverse lack of tidiness was the outstanding characteristic of Massachusetts politics in the two decades after 1775. Consequently, when one speaks of Sedgwick and the "conservative position," it must be understood as more a descriptive phrase than a hard-and-fast classification.

There were, however, during Sedgwick's next term of legislative service several struggles reflective of a sharp division of economic interests in the General Court. In these struggles Sedgwick was almost invariably to be found on the side of "property" and "good faith." Various thorny problems connected with the aftermath of war now began to converge on the Massachusetts legislature. The leading issues in the fourth General Court were: 1) the payment of Massachusetts' proportion of the debt of the United States, with the aggravating side issue of

3. July 8, 1781. S.P., M.H.S.

commutation of pay owed army officers; 2) the treatment of returning Loyalist refugees. Sedgwick figured prominently in the debates on both these issues, and on both was usually to be found with the minority, his position reflecting his growing concern for "continental" needs and obligations.

Discussion over the bill "for levying certain imposts and other duties upon foreign goods . . . and for granting the same to Congress" was long and bitter. The main debate centered about a motion that a clause be inserted to the effect that no part of the money granted Congress should be applied to the "half pay for life, or the commutation thereof which the United States . . . have agreed to give the officers of the Army." The motion reflected popular animus and fears of militarism. It passed, July 8, 1783, over Sedgwick's strong objection, but was later quietly dropped. Another struggle concerned the provision that the act was not to go into operation until Massachusetts had been informed by Congress that all the other states had granted Congress similar duties, appropriated in the same manner and for the space of twenty-five years. Sedgwick and thirty-six other members attempted to delete this restriction, and to replace it by a simple statement to the effect that the money was to be applied "for the purpose of discharging the interest or Principal of the Debts contracted on the faith of the United States for supporting the War." [4] He argued that the original provision was the deceitful equivalent of making no attempt to pay the state's just portion of an honestly contracted debt. His efforts were to no avail; the bill with its vitiating proviso passed, 72–65.

The assistance Sedgwick gave certain Loyalists in the courts of law has been mentioned. Equally noteworthy were his labors in their behalf in the Massachusetts legislature. On July 24, 1783, there was brought to a vote on the floor of the House a bill to carry into execution the Act of 1778 which aimed to prevent the return of Tory refugees to Massachusetts. The enacting clause of this bill was the issue in point. It stated:

> Be it further enacted that when any such person [a returned refugee] shall be committed by two justices of the Peace or taken into custody by order of the Governor to be sent out of the State,

4. *Massachusetts. House Journal*, IV, 165.

See, too, Merrill Jensen, *The New Nation: A History of the United States During the Confederation, 1781-89* (New York, 1950), 63–76, 261–270; Jackson T. Main, *The Anti-Federalists* (Chapel Hill, 1961), 84–88. Professor Main has an excellent discussion of the significance of the debate over the impost in illustrating the desires of the federal creditor interest in Massachusetts as well as the strength of state's rights principles.

no writ of replevin to replevy such person shall be served, nor shall any action on such writ be prosecuted. . . . And the officer who shall prosecute to execute the same, shall be liable to a fine of one hundred pounds,—and be incapable forever hereafter of serving or executing any other Writ or Percept.[5]

Sedgwick, with others, tried to replace this harsh procedure with a milder enacting clause; a clause that would have been more in keeping with the spirit of the recent peace treaty and would have secured legal guarantees and a fair trial to rash Loyalists who dared return to make application for their confiscated property. They were submerged in a vote of 107–30. The Sheffield representative and certain of his colleagues felt so strongly about the injustice and unconstitutionality of the measure in its present form that they drew up a formal dissent.

Their declaration was the product of no little courage. Advocacy of fair treatment for Tory refugees was considered almost traitorous, and the labels "time-serving Whig" and "trimmer" were easily acquired. During the debate there was secretly distributed about the House a number of handbills containing the resolutions of the town of New Haven protesting even the deliberation of the question. Sedgwick, opposed to the exertion of any outside pressure on duly elected legislators, was outraged at this sinister bit of lobbying. More especially as it originated from the foreign base of Connecticut.

The Tory-baiters seem to have overplayed their hand; for the very end of the session found the General Court, in a more charitable frame of mind, repealing two previous pieces of anti-Tory legislation. Their repeal was accompanied by a simple declaratory act asserting the *right* of the sovereign Commonwealth to expel such aliens as were dangerous to the peace and good order of her government. Description of method or form was not essayed.

Sedgwick's activities during this Court brought him to the attention of the whole of Berkshire County, and for the next two years he served as one of that county's two state senators.[6]

5. *Ibid.*, 114.

6. Under the Massachusetts Constitution of 1780, to be properly elected as senator one had to obtain the suffrage of one half the voters, each voter casting two ballots. If the vote was so scattered that no two candidates had a majority, the General Court, in joint session, filled the vacancy or vacancies itself. In 1783, no Berkshire candidate for senator obtained the necessary majority, and the choice was thrown to the General Court. Sedgwick received, on joint ballot of the two houses, 99 out of 162 votes, but refused the appointment. His victories in 1784 and 1785 were both elective.

Sedgwick's change of seat did not presage any change in the leading issue facing Massachusetts in these years—the mounting public and private debt. But a week after his arrival in Boston for the fifth General Court he found himself on a joint committee ordered to consider how to arrange collection of that portion of Massachusetts' quota of a recent Congressional levy which could be paid in indents, and to consider the expediency and necessity of providing additional funds for the Continent.

The two acts passed at this session which brought forth additional revenue were a new navigation law and a new state-impost law. The navigation act provided that after August 1, 1785, goods of any one of the leagued states could not be exported from Massachusetts in a British ship and goods imported in foreign vessels were to pay double the duties paid on goods imported in American ships. The concurrent tariff or impost act imposed various duties on a long list of manufactured articles.[7] These laws are interesting as a reflection of the divergence of sentiment in the General Court and of the lobbying power of certain economic interests in Massachusetts. The merchants demanded the exclusion of foreign shipping; the artisans said that would raise the price of all imports to a prohibitive figure. The artisans wished protection from certain of the cheaply manufactured goods of Europe; the merchant said that commerce would completely die if there was any harsh discrimination against foreign manufactures. The acts in question attempted to please both sides, with the result that neither was particularly pleased.

The Senate was not totally occupied with problems of finance. Sedg-

---

7. Sedgwick disapproved of impositions on commerce such as regulations, heavy tonnage duties, and burdensome imposts. Though a back-country man, he appreciated the dependence of maritime Massachusetts on international trade. On October 14, 1785, he wrote Caleb Davis, questioning the revenue-producing qualities of certain impost and exise acts:

> The acts of the last session designed to aid the commerce of the State, it seems to me must eventually prove its destruction. for this reason I am sorry it was not in my power to attend the General Court. . . . trade will be diverted, the revenue defrauded, a spirit of smuggling introduced. these are among the consequences which must result from a perseverance [in the over-taxation of importers]. . . . I believe not a member from this county but will heartily join in a repeal.

Davis Papers, XII–B (1785), M.H.S.

An additional issue complicating the debate over trade regulation in Massachusetts concerned a proposal that all revenue from the impost duties be exclusively appropriated to the discharge of the state debt. This limitation was not enacted.

wick found many legislative activities with which to employ his boundless energy. He served on committees to obtain funds for Harvard College; to consider the right of individual senators to record their dissent in the journal; to draw bills punishing rape, larceny, and arson; and to grant the right of citizenship to the Marquis de Lafayette. Sedgwick's record of attendance was rather spotty during certain sessions and on occasion he would subordinate accuracy to anxiety, as in his approval of the Senate position that it, equally with the House, had the privilege to originate grants of money. On the whole, however, his work was of such amount and quality that he fast became what he so much desired, an influential figure of state-wide importance.

This growing importance was indicated by his appointment as Massachusetts' chief commissioner in negotiations concerning the long-disputed New York–Massachusetts boundary. On June 4, 1784, Sedgwick received word from Governor Hancock that the General Court had elected Joseph Hawley, Caleb Strong, Timothy Edwards, and himself as commissioners "on the part of this Commonwealth for the ascertaining a boundary line on the Eastern extremity of the late Province now State of New York, and extending from the Southern to the Northern boundary of the late Province now Commonwealth of Massachusetts." Together with the New York appointees they were to "ascertain, run, and mark" the boundary line and to agree upon the titles of individuals "to such lands as they may now respectively hold in virtue of any Grant." [8]

At first all went quite smoothly. Philip Schuyler and Gerard Barker, the New York commissioners, agreed that the line established by the 1773 Hartford Agreement had been invalidated by a magnetic variation of 20′ east, and that the line should be drawn at a northeast angle of 20° 50′ 30″. Negotiations soon ground to a halt, however. Massachusetts declared that she would not bind herself to confirm the title of every "Dutchman" that was found within her jurisdictional area, and the New York commissioners insisted upon such a pledge. More important, Sedgwick and his colleagues discovered, as they walked over the new boundary, that landmarks unmistakably those of Massachusetts kept appearing over on the left—the New York—side. The instruments of previous surveyors were proved most unsound; the magnetic variation was shown to have changed by at least 8′ 30″ more. Sedgwick and his fellow back-country Yankees soon declared that they could accept no

8. Copies of practically all the correspondence between Governor Hancock and the Massachusetts commissioners and between these men and their New York counterparts will be found in S.P., M.H.S.

line more easterly than 20° 42'. Jockeying continued on both sides, with tempers flaring and demands heightening with ever increasing rapidity. The net result of all this was the complete breakdown of negotiations late in November, 1784. Attempts were made during the following year to rehabilitate the survey commissions, but without much success. Massachusetts then tossed it into the lap of Congress, July 4, 1785. That body, aided by a more compromising attitude on the part of both states, finally succeeded—by means of another commission—in achieving a definitive agreement in 1787–1788. Massachusetts obtained the larger portion of the disputed area but ceded the western part of Hancock County to New York. As Sedgwick's 1784 report on magnetic variation was utilized during the final negotiations, his efforts in behalf of the territorial integrity of Massachusetts were finally vindicated.

There is little need to dwell at length on Sedgwick's second term as senator.[9] The issues facing the state were virtually unchanged from those of the previous year, and Sedgwick spent more time in 1785–1786 as a delegate to Congress than as a senator to the General Court. He was now ready to move beyond the confines of Massachusetts, at least physically. With the year 1785–1786 his political apprenticeship advances to the continental stage; his political commitment and concerns would only slowly follow.

Sedgwick was first chosen, by joint ballot of the General Court, as a delegate to the Continental Congress on June 16, 1785. He received 101 votes out of a total of 150 ballots cast, and was selected to join a distinguished delegation composed of Nathaniel Gorham, Rufus King, Nathan Dane, and John Hancock.

The body to which he was elected was in design as in practice the possessor of few inherent powers. The more radical elements had been preponderant in the Second Continental Congress at the time the Articles of Confederation were formulated. They had seen in decentralization the key to liberty and in centralization the tool of tyranny. Remembering their battles with the royal governors, they were suspicious of even native executive power, and made the legislative department, "the people's organ of expression," carry the entire tripartite burden of government. The union they had created was a confederative union of equal states in which the central organization was subordinated to its parts. The powers given the Confederation Congress were limited and, even

9. Sedgwick resigned from the Senate in February, 1786, after attending only the first of three sessions of the Sixth Court.

in purely Continental matters, largely advisory. Increasingly its authority appeared insufficient for the problems it faced.

The main issues of the 1785–1786 Congress were the Indian and western difficulties, the impost, the Jay-Gardoqui Treaty project, and the question of revising the Articles. Though Sedgwick was in Congress but four months during this term (December 12, 1785–January 13, 1786; June 1—August 22, 1786), he brushed against all of these long-discussed issues, and expressed strong opinions concerning every one. In many of these opinions there was evident a strong sectional bias. Sedgwick was at this time primarily eastern in his orientation, lacked an appreciation of the problems of the West and South, and was inclined to think of all issues from the standpoint of New England rather than that of the Continent as a whole. Protection of sectional interests, rather than considerations of centralized authority, provided his main preoccupation in these years. Shays' Rebellion and the increasing inability of the Articles Government to provide revenue and secure commerce would only subsequently, and erratically, broaden Sedgwick's horizon.

Though a citizen of a back-country area, Sedgwick had little appreciation of the frontier fear of the marauding Indian. If not unsympathetic with the pioneer's plight, he always thought of the necessity of national economy before the duty of national protection. This was true in varying degrees of the entire Massachusetts delegation, rooming together, in provincial seclusion, at Mrs. Osgood's New York boarding house, number 5 "hi board way." The prejudice of the Bay Staters towards the trouble-making frontiersmen was made very clear in the summer of 1786 in the debate over the Secretary of War's report calling for the recruitment of 1500 additional troops. This report led to a resolve that some of these troops be dispatched to the rapids of the Ohio to punish Indian depredations against settlers on the Virginia frontier. Sedgwick seconded a motion that this report be referred to a previously established committee for Indian matters, probably hoping to see the matter pigeonholed there for good.[10] This manoeuvre was voted down, however, and subsequent efforts to limit the number of government troops assisting the Virginia militia and to impose certain restrictions of economy on the operation were equally unsuccessful.

The final outcome of the western and Indian debates and troubles, the 1786 treaty with the Cherokees, was most pleasing to peace-loving, thrifty Theodore Sedgwick. The chief result of his own actions, though,

10. Among the *Papers of the Continental Congress* is a proposed ordinance for the licensing of all Indian traders under the supervision of the Superintendent of Indian Affairs, a portion of which seems to be in Sedgwick's handwriting.

and those of his colleagues had been to create a deepening suspicion of the motives and designs of the Northeast on the part of the West and South.[11]

The never-ending issue of Continental finance, of course, occupied much of the attention of Congress in these years. Chief hope was placed on the uniform acceptance by all the states of the fiscal system of April 18, 1783, whereby authority had been requested for a five per cent import tax, to be levied and collected by Congress. Worried by the delay of New York and other states in adopting the impost, Congress on February 14, 1786, again pressed the plan and forwarded with its request a statement of all the alarming facts concerning the acute pecuniary embarrassments of the Continent. Sedgwick, though not at that time attending Congress, was a proponent of the impost plan, and ever ready himself to paint an alarming picture. He wrote Nathan Dane:

> I am greatly pained at the stupid apathy of the united states, they seem incapable of being roused by objects of the greatest importance. Had the united states ever concerns of greater magnitude to manage than at the present moment? I think not. Had we been as indifferent to the concerns of the war as we now [are] to those of our union and independence, deserved destruction had been our portion. and can we now expect any thing less dreadful? especially when we reflect that jealousy & distrust have such a powerful effect on several of the united states and that the federal government is not posessed of any power sufficient to controul the baneful effects of those *cowardly passions*. No nation was ever more glorious than America was in 1783. the sad reverse is too painful to reflect on. under these circumstances I am pleased with the inteligence of the recommendation of congress to the states of the revenue system of apl. 1783. Should the worst now happen the blame will fall where it ought and congress stand excused to the whole world.[12]

11. Sedgwick's only contribution to a much larger western problem—the Northwest Ordinance—was a suggestion that the territory be divided into from three to five, rather than two to five, states.

12. Sedgwick to Nathan Dane, February 24, 1786. S.P., M.H.S.

It is, of course quite possible that Sedgwick overexaggerated the blackness of the scene. For a very different appraisal of the "Critical Period" see Merrill Jensen, *The New Nation: A History of the United States During the Confederation, 1781–1789* (New York, 1950), especially 342, 423.

By the end of March, 1786, Rufus King was telling Sedgwick that Rhode Island, Maryland, and Georgia had acceded to the system of a general impost, and it soon became apparent that it would succeed or fail on the actions of Clinton, Schuyler, and other leaders of the Empire State.[13] Sedgwick, coming to Congress in June, went about declaring that unless the impost was passed and the finances of the Continent taken in hand, accident alone would determine the state of the nation's future existence. Though not yet desirous of any basic reform that would establish the national government as clearly superior to the state governments, he was a strong believer in the sanctity of contract. He felt that the debts of the Continent must be paid to the last shilling and that an independent and secure source of revenue for Congress was essential to that end. He declared himself in hearty accord with the report of the King Committee, of July 27, 1786, in its insistence that not only should Congress have the power to levy certain duties upon goods imported into the United States, but that the collectors of these duties be "amenable to and removable by the United States in Congress assembled alone." This report declared that Congress should have the power of "declaring the money in which the said duties shall be received, of establishing the number of revenue officers, and . . . [of ascertaining] their duties."[14] The authorizing acts of Pennsylvania, Delaware, and then later New York were unacceptable as they refused to grant Congress these powers.

Sedgwick's sectional orientation was clearly evident in the debate over the Jay-Gardoqui negotiations of 1785–1786 concerning American rights to the navigation of the Mississippi. Sedgwick was very anxious to secure a Spanish-American commercial treaty, and spoke at length on the advantages such a treaty would afford eastern fishing, shipbuilding, and carrying interests. To obtain a commercial convention with the Spanish, he was seemingly quite willing to forego the free navigation of the Father of the Waters. He was, indeed, one of the guiding spirits in the attempt of the New England delegates to alter the Congressional instructions of the Secretary for Foreign Affairs and so permit such a renunciation.[15] This attempt to modify Jay's instructions came to noth-

13. Revenue collection by any other means than that of requisitioning the sovereign states was not countenanced by the Articles, and could be authorized only by *unanimous* amendment.

14. Ford, Hunt, Fitzpatrick, Hill, eds., *Journals of Congress*, XXX, 439–440.

15. Portions of the draft of the motion are in Sedgwick's handwriting. *Papers of Continental Congress*, No. 81, II, 246–248. Library of Congress.

ing; nor was Sedgwick any more successful in his fight for the commercial treaty itself. His appeal was purely sectional, as he was repeatedly told by such irate southerners as Grayson and Monroe of Virginia. Grayson warned that the South would never grant Congress more power if that body soiled itself by sacrificing the West, just so Massachusetts might sell cod a little more easily.[16]

Monroe insisted that the main object of King, Sedgwick, and other easterners was really the dismemberment of the Union and the erection of a northern confederation, and that their actions in the Mississippi debate were part and parcel of their evil purpose.[17] Actually Sedgwick had no such purpose. He was disgusted, it is true, by the fact that it seemed impossible to obtain sufficient fiscal and commercial powers for Congress, and he did speak once or twice of secession. A study of all his actions and words at this period, however, forbids a conclusion that he was either involved in any actual secessionist plot or wished—or even expected—to see a division of his country.

His most suspicious letter in this regard was one written August 6, 1786, to Caleb Strong, then a senator in the Massachusetts General Court. It should be taken, however, in the manner one takes the threat of a good, if disgruntled, soldier that he will damn soon up and desert this man's army. Sedgwick wrote:

> It well becomes the eastern and middle States, who are in interest one, seriously to consider what advantages result to them from their connection with the Southern States. They can give us nothing, as an equivalent for the protection which they derive from us but a participation in their commerce . . . an attempt to perpetuate our connection with them which at last too will be found ineffectual, will sacrifice everything to a mere chimera. Even the appearance of a union cannot in the way we now are long be preserved. It becomes us seriously to contemplate a substitute; for if we do not controul events we shall be miserably controuled by them. No other substitute can be devised than that of contracting the limits of the confederacy

16. If Sedgwick's native land was more likely the Commonwealth of Massachusetts than the Continent, he had succeeded in casting off any sense of colonial subordination. In debates concerning depredations by the Barbary pirates, commercial restrictions by the British, and other aspects of foreign affairs, he was inclined to attribute the most questionable motives to all foreign powers. Britain, he was sure, "would go great lengths in gratifying her malice and jealousy" towards America. Sedgwick to Caleb Strong, August 6, 1786. Edmund C. Burnett, *Letters of Members of the Continental Congress* (New York, 1921-1936), VIII, 415.

17. See letter from Monroe to Governor Patrick Henry, August 12, 1786. *Ibid.*, 415–416.

to such as are natural and reasonable, and within those limits instead of a nominal to institute a real, and an efficient government.[18]

The spirit of sectional suspicion was in evidence on all sides during the discussion on projects and proposals for the revision of the Articles of Confederation. Sedgwick, though in later years he forgot the fact, was at first opposed to subjecting the Articles to the "chance of alteration."

Governor Bowdoin had suggested to the Massachusetts legislature in May, 1785, that a convention should be held to consider revising the Articles so that Congress might possess certain general powers experience had shown to be essential. The General Court had endorsed the proposal and ordered the state's delegates in Congress to suggest the plan to that body. Tactfully, but firmly, the delegates refused to obey the instructions of their masters. Sedgwick and other delegates from Massachusetts were in favor of giving Congress the power to regulate trade and the power to raise an independent revenue by means of the impost system, but were at this time strongly opposed to any major or full-scale revision of the Confederation. Sedgwick explained the viewpoint of the Bay State delegates in an interesting letter to Caleb Davis, the Boston merchant, January 31, 1786:

> But can it be the wish of the general Court to submit whether the great outlines of the federal constitution founded in democratic principles shall be subjected to a *chance of alteration?* and may not laying the subject open to free discussion give birth to new hopes of an aristocratical faction which every community possesses? I am as clearly of opinion as any one can be that it is greatly to the interest of the northern States that, Congress should be empowered to regulate our commerce, without it I do not see indeed that we can possibly be protected at home or respected abroad. Probably it . . . [will also be] necessary that some more sure mode should be adopted to supply the Treasury.[19]

Sedgwick in 1786 wished cautious, piecemeal revision, at most. He feared that once a convention began to pull apart and examine the Confederation, it would have trouble gaining unanimous consent to any new reconstruction, whatever its form; and anarchy would be its sole reward. He even opposed the Annapolis Convention, which was to prove the initial step in the formation of the new Constitution. As a "sectionalist," Sedgwick doubted the motives of the southerners favoring the proposed "commercial convention." He wrote Caleb Strong that: "No reasonable

18. *Ibid.*, 657.
19. *Caleb Davis Papers*, XIII–A (1786), M.H.S.

expectation of advantage can be formed from the commercial convention. The first proposers designed none. The measure was originally
brought forward with an intention of defeating an enlargement of the
powers of Congress. Of this I have the most decisive evidence." [20]

Together with his friend Rufus King, Sedgwick soon began to see that
the Confederation was the wrong kind of government. Vague and rather
insincere talk of the "birth of aristocratical faction" soon gave way to
earnest discussion of the necessity for transforming the Articles into a
government of "energy." "Energy" was essential, if anarchy—the dread
specter of all Sedgwick's dreams—was to be avoided. A variety of factors
brought Sedgwick to the conclusion that the Articles should be
scrapped: the influence of new friends such as Alexander Hamilton; a
conviction that Congress as it was presently constituted could never pay
the debts it owed various private citizens of Massachusetts; a sense of
the ever-increasing lethargy which characterized public affairs; and a
temperamental disposition to favor a course of energetic action. All these
factors would be heavily reinforced by the lessons taught by Daniel
Shays. During the winter of 1786–1787 Sedgwick joined George Washington, Henry Knox, Alexander Hamilton, and the camp of the counterrevolutionaries—those men who felt that both their country and their
property were in great danger from the delusive idea that, even in
periods of transition and crisis, the less government there was the more
happy everyone would surely be.

It was at this time, incidentally, that the close friendship of Sedgwick and Hamilton began to develop. This friendship was to prove of
immense importance in Sedgwick's life. Sedgwick found in Hamilton
a highly articulate kindred spirit. Their political desires and philosophy
were almost identical. Both assumed that man was largely governed by
self-interest, and that the purpose of government was to direct this
self-interest into channels most conducive to national strength and well-
being. Sincere republicans, they would have nothing of monarchy or
democracy. Convinced of the inevitability of class divisions in society,
they both believed that the only men capable of appreciating what was
best for the nation were those men who had a stake in the nation; *i.e.*,
those possessed of property. If judged by the political philosophies then
current in the various European nations, they were liberals. If allowance
is made for the wide distribution of property in America in the late
eighteenth century, their emphasis on property rights must be considered indicative of a conservative rather than a reactionary tempera-

20. Burnett. *Letters*, VIII, 415.

ment.[21] However one classifies their philosophy, there can be no question as to the similarity of their respective intentions or the national importance of their close co-operation during the next decade.

Quite apart from the influence of Hamilton, events were transpiring in 1786 which furnished cause for one with Sedgwick's love of exaggeration and order to reshape his opinions concerning the necessity of risking political revision. By the late winter of 1787 Sedgwick was definitely in favor of a new constitution and government. He declared that a stronger government was absolutely necessary if justice was to be revived and properly regulated; if financial heresies were to be discouraged; and if the United States was ever to be treated with respect by other nations. Whether the Confederation was the victim of circumstances—postwar demobilization, economic transition, expansion—or the victim of inherent weakness was of little matter. The fact remained that it had lost the confidence of a majority of the propertied, the educated, the "best and most virtuous" parts of the community. It had to be radically transformed or, perhaps best, displaced altogether.

When Sedgwick had left Congress on August 22, 1786, however, he had been preoccupied less with the problem of governmental revision than with the ingratitude of the General Court. He had not been re-elected to Congress for the year November, 1786–November, 1787. Actually he had not wished to be, but his pride was wounded at being, alone of the delegation, dismissed from service.[22] In May he had told John Bacon and certain other members of the General Court that he would be unable to serve after the expiration of the current term. When he had seen, however, that the newly selected Massachusetts Senate contained many persons antagonistic to the "order of lawyers," he had withdrawn this informal resignation, lest he be accused of being "apprehensive of defeat." Not long afterwards, he was informed that a Mr. Holton, a man unafflicted with the stigma of bar membership, was elected in his stead. Deprived of the solace of resignation,[23] Sedgwick

21. See Richard Hofstadter, *The American Political Tradition and The Men Who Made It* (New York, 1948), 15–16.

22. The other members of the delegation seem to have entertained a high regard for Sedgwick and his efforts as a delegate. King called him a "virtuous, firm and sensible man." Nathaniel Gorham said he was a man of honor, well acquainted with the affairs of Congress. King to Elbridge Gerry, July 2, 1786, King, *King,* I, 186; Gorham to Caleb Davis, June 16, 1786, *Davis Papers,* XIII-A, M.H.S.

23. Nor was he soothed when the state proved slow in awarding him £275, 11s. for 167 days "going to attend. & returning from Congress." *Sedgwick Day Book #3,* S.P., M.H.S.

considered himself very badly treated and sought consolation in un-
burdening his woes to his devoted second wife Pamela Dwight
Sedgwick:

> On Saturday night I had a letter informing me that I was left out
> of the delegation of the next year. Whether because I am an old
> offending lawyer, or because I had previously declared my intention
> not to serve I am not informed. if the former, and I can get the
> information before the rising of the general court, I shall hold myself
> obliged in honor to resign, at all events I believe you may rely
> upon it that I shall have this information by the middle of August, &
> then return to the vale of private life for many years perhaps forever,
> when I do it I shall possess a consciousness that in the vanity of
> tumultuous scenes thro which I have passed, in no instance have I
> been induced to deviate from the strict line of my duty either thro
> motives of self interest or actuated by views of popularity—and I do
> not think it can hardly be considered as arising from vanity when I
> declare, that I think the public owe me more for my exertions,
> than a ballance for the pageants conferred on me. you know the
> pride of my heart, I hope it is not a dishonest pride, but such as it is
> it will always prevent on the one hand the meanness of sacrificing to
> popular vices or popular frenzy, and on the other . . . the adulation
> of any man or body of men in power. I will be myself, and actuated
> I hope by purity of intention, having performed my duty, the event
> with humble resignation I will leave where it ought to rest.[24]

The following year saw the General Court more sensible of Sedgwick's exertions, and on June 27, 1787, he was again elected to Congress.
Both this and the following Congress [25] were held under the shadow of
the new Constitution and the changes in government which that document forecast. Sedgwick consequently seems to have taken but little
interest in its doings. His main labors involved an unsuccessful effort
to utilize national militia to check any revival of rebellion in Massachusetts and more successful efforts to make provision for the commencement of the new government. In Sedgwick's eyes these efforts
were closely connected. For it had been Shays' Rebellion—more than
any other single factor—which had convinced him that the needs of
his beloved Massachusetts demanded a central government of greater
power. Shays' Rebellion had served to activate Sedgwick's slow-growing
discontent with the Articles Government.

There is, indeed, good reason to believe that Sedgwick's later career

24. July 4, 1786. *S.P.*, M.H.S.
25. Sedgwick was elected to, but never attended, the term from November, 1788
to March, 1789.

was tempered in the heat of the civil war which embroiled Massachusetts between September, 1786, and March, 1787. For if Shays' Rebellion strengthened his conservatism, it jarred his provincialism. Never again would Sedgwick be so positive that Massachusetts was sufficient unto herself.

EVOLUTION OF A NATIONALIST:

SHAYS' REBELLION AND THE NEW CONSTITUTION AND GOVERNMENT

IV

Smiting the Insurgents

*This ferment is not to me unaccountable, Massachu-
setts has lost every advantage, she as a state expected
in consequence of independence. In addition to this
she feels herself pressed with an almost intolerable
burden of taxes, under the circumstances how easily
are her passions agitated even to a degree of frenzy?
The people who are merely an instrument in these
cases are greatly to be pitied, while those who drive
them into excesses are the proper objects of gibbets,
& racks.*

Theodore Sedgwick [1]

Rᴇᴠᴏʟᴛ was brewing in Massachusetts long before the Hampshire
County and Worcester County disorders of September, 1786, and economic conditions provided its basic inspiration. Complaints were voiced
against the salaries of executive officers and the inequalities of political
representation, and against the arrogance of neo-aristocrats and the
clique-rule of town affairs, but beneath all else was the despairing sense
of poverty, indebtedness, and general economic depression. Even a
cursory comparison of the tax assessment records for the years 1774 and
1786 shows the very real decrease in property and property values experienced by most of rural Massachusetts.

The economic difficulties of Massachusetts were not caused by
radical modes of financing. They were the results of the unproductive
nature of war, the disruption of the vital fishing, shipbuilding, and commercial activities of maritime Massachusetts, and the national monetary
chaos of the time, and were aggravated by the too stringent financial
measures of Massachusetts *conservatives* of the Bowdoin-Sedgwick
school. In a time of great scarcity of cash,[2] these men had attempted too

1. Letter to his wife Pamela, June 24, 1786, S.P., M.H.S.
2. Notes of the newly created banks circulated only among the merchants, and
the various forms of public debt that still had some value were either being taxed out
of existence or concentrated in fewer and fewer hands.

rapid an amortization of the debt, by means of too heavy taxes, un-
equally apportioned both as to geographic section and economic class.[3]
For the frontier farmer of western Massachusetts, who in certain areas
labored under the hardships of the new settler, such taxes were especially
distasteful.

The size of the state debt,[4] the high tax delinquency rate, the overdue
Continental obligations should not obscure the fact that the financial
policies of the Commonwealth were, for the time, basically harsh and
distinctly conservative. With most forms of "cheap money" depreciated
beyond utility,[5] Massachusetts was entering into a period of unhealthy
deflation. Barter was once again the style in Berkshire.[6]

Though the basis of the discontent was economic, the complaints
against legal conditions and legislative policy were vociferously reiterated. Court dockets were submerged with suits for the recovery of debts,
and the state's lawyers became increasingly unpopular. Actually, it does
not seem that the accredited bar as a whole hounded the poor with any

3. Taxes averaged more than three pounds a year for each of the ninety thousand
adult males in Massachusetts. The farmer class paid a share of the taxes dispropor-
tionate to its share of the state's wealth. The property tax bore on this class very
onerously. Plows and other farm equipment were taxed, whereas certain of the
luxuries of the urban dwellers were not. See unpublished doctoral dissertation by
Joseph Parker Warren entitled, *The Shays Rebellion* (1902) in Harvard University
Archives. See, too, Robert J. Taylor, *Western Massachusetts in the Revolution*
(Providence, Rhode Island, 1954), 108–109, 138–139.

4. In addition to the state debt of nearly five million there was the liability to
holders of paper money emitted during the war. These state bills circulated and depreciated with the Continental money. Their depreciation—the lessening value of
savings—was in itself a heavy tax burden for citizens of Massachusetts.

5. Edward Bellamy in his historical novel, *The Duke of Stockbridge* (Boston,
1901) portrays most graphically the plight of the returned soldier faced with the un-
marketability of his "hero's reward." At one point he has one of the potential Shaysites advise and lament as follows (pp. 19, 23):

> "Every kind a' money runs daown, only it's the natur' a' bills to run daown
> a leetle quicker than other sorts. Naow I says—an' I ain't the only one that says
> it—that all gov'ment's got ter dew is ter keep on printin' new bills ez fastez the
> old ones gits run daown. . . . I fetched my knapsack full of gov'ment bills
> home from the war. I jedge them bills wuz all on 'em debts what gov'ment
> owed tew me fur fightin'; Ef gov'ment ain't a-goin' ter pay me them bills—
> an' 't ain't—it don't seem fair ter tax me so's it kin pay debts it owes ter other
> folks."

6. See letter of Sedgwick's mother-in-law Abigail Dwight to Mrs. Morton (January 10, 1785) in which she complained bitterly of the revival of bartering, declaring it left the country "without a Glimpse in Prospect for the Credrs. security and
welfare." S.P., M.H.S.

great amount of viciousness; it was a group of third-rate legal hacks, making a business of purchasing and prosecuting debtor suits in the inferior courts, who brought public odium upon the bar in Massachusetts.[7] Politically, the chief points of dissent concerned equality of representation and religious treatment, the size of official salaries, the number of appointed officers, and the existence of the Senate.

All these grievances worked on one another, and almost imperceptibly protest conventions were followed by demonstrations against the courts and these in turn by insurrection and treason. High misdemeanors became civil war as discontent once aired assumed a social content and an ever more violent expression. Though the original intention had been to reform, not overthrow, the government, the war-taught followers of Shays lacked the ability to articulate in any but physical terms.

Faced with the fact of rebellion, Governor James Bowdoin and the merchant financiers of Boston put a government force onto the field in commendably quick order. The actions of the legislators were less decisive. Obliged to compromise principles with actualities, they came forth with a series of mongrel measures which threatened and soothed in equal parts. Balancing the dangers of retroactive violation of contract against those of economic discouragement, the dangers of weakness against those of fraternal division, the majority in the General Court worked very hard and pleased nobody. Surely their modest proposals for tax reform did not appease the Insurgents of Berkshire County.

Berkshire, with its tradition of opposition to judicial process, its frontier characteristics, its heavy tax apportionment and postwar poverty, was quick to hear the trumpet call of revolt. Berkshire had, however, a hard core of loyal government men, and their chief was Theodore Sedgwick. Early in 1786 Sedgwick had moved from Sheffield to the near-by town of Stockbridge. There he rented "the Jonathan Edwards house" while supervising the completion of a large two-storied "mansion," and there he quickly took the lead in the fight against the disaffected.

The first test had come at a county convention in the last week of August, 1786, and Sedgwick, delegate from Stockbridge, had triumphed. He described the meeting later in a letter to his good friend, George Richard Minot, the historian of the insurrection:

> The towns where the well affected to Govermt. had a majority, conceived it their duty to endeavor to quiet the popular ferment,

7. See "Honestus" articles, *Independent Chronicle* (Boston), March 9–30, April 13–27, 1786.

by being represented by men of information & respectability. Though the majority when first assembled were actuated by the passion of jealousy, & rage for reformation which so generally prevailed, yet the result clearly demonstrated that want of information was the cause. they explicitly approved the appropriation of the revenue arising from impost, the grant of supplementary fund &c. and manifested a decent & respectful regard toward the administration of Government in general. they disapproved the paper money & tender law system & solemnly engaged to use their influence to support the courts of justice in the exercise of their legal powers & to endeavor to quiet the agitated spirits of the people.[8]

The general populace of Berkshire, however, proved less amenable to reason than their convention delegates. On the second Tuesday in September, in what was the first blow of the rebellion, eight hundred discontented farmers and ex-soldiers marched on Great Barrington's combined tavern and debtor's prison. They enjoyed free refreshments, liberated their unfortunate neighbors, and compelled the three judges of the Court of Common Pleas to agree to hold no session until all grievances had been redressed.

About a month later another Berkshire mob descended on Great Barrington and, after seeing that the General Sessions and Supreme Courts did not sit, began to harass certain of the better dressed citizens. One of the objects of their attention was Theodore Sedgwick, passing through that town on business. Sedgwick stormed his way through "the rabble," stared them down, and rode off only after pronouncing their actions and demands those of creatures in the pay of Britain.[9] A man in whose every gesture lay a sense of conscious superiority and power, his haughtiness seems to have cowed as well as angered the rebels on every occasion. In November "some violent desperadoes" pursued and captured him only to be shamed into granting his escape.

The rise and fall of Captain Daniel Shays occurred, of course, in

8. Undated letter. *S.P.*, M.H.S.
  This letter was in the form of a page correction of Minot's manuscript which had been sent to Sedgwick for his perusal and criticism.
  9. Sedgwick's outspoken enmity to the insurrectionists must be viewed in the light of the fear, current at that time, of political anarchy and government paralysis. This fear is well expressed in a letter to Sedgwick from his fellow congressional delegate Rufus King, September 29, 1786:

> I Pray God that moderation may soon succeed to the tumult, and Disorder, which has prevailed in Massachusetts. It will be humiliating indeed, if the Blood & Treasure expended so gloriously by our country should establish only Disgrace and furnish just grounds of exultation to the advocates of Tyranny and Despotism. *S.P.*, M.H.S.

Worcester and Hampshire counties, to the east of Berkshire. The clash at the Springfield arsenal and General Lincoln's march on Petersham essentially settled the rebellion by the end of January, 1787, with Shays having received little more than a few volunteers and an occasional sleigh load of supplies from Berkshire. For Sedgwick and Berkshire were reserved the post-climactic, guerrilla aspects of the revolt; for both man and county this proved sufficient.

Concerned for his property and even for his life, Sedgwick had early taken steps to thwart any rascals with designs on either. First he had taken the precaution to deposit his papers in the safekeeping of Dr. Stephen West, a man of God who firmly believed that the Caesars of this world should be permitted to retain their own. Sedgwick had then helped organize, during the last weeks of 1786, an independent county force of volunteers, with their headquarters at Stockbridge.[10] Sedgwick's previous political service, his increased professional prominence, and his new "mansion" had enabled him quickly to assume the position of leading citizen of that town. His promotion was signalized by his status as bête noire of the insurgents and leader of the local counterrevolutionaries.

Under Sedgwick's direction Stockbridge became an armed garrison for the protection of principles of law and order. Guard turns, passwords, counterspy reconnaissance, and armed forays became the life of this small village.

These defense measures had been precipitated by the pressure of events, the evident inability of either the militia or the "regulars" of Generals Lincoln and Shepard to give aid, and the requests and authorizations of the General Court. Previously each town had been at the mercy of stray bands of rebels or individuals eager to draw personal advantage from communal chaos. In Stockbridge Sedgwick's law clerk, a young boy named Hopkins, had been ridden on a rail up and down Plain Street until he consented to exchange the white paper cockade which decorated his hat for a sprig of hemlock—the symbol of the insurgents. Throughout the countryside the shrieks of boards being drawn across rosin-smeared sawhorses, fiddle fashion, shattered the air and the slumber of the "good people" so serenaded. These events and the fear that the defeated Shays would attempt a last stand in the highlands of eastern Berkshire had produced the Stockbridge-based volunteer organization. Its first test of battle came in near-by West Stockbridge, with Sedgwick the dramatic hero in what was essentially an opéra bouffe.

10. See Sedgwick to Governor Bowdoin, October 5, 1786. Massachusetts Archives, CXC, 277–278.

With rumors abroad that the pursued but unrepentant Shays was going to withdraw into Berkshire, and that parties of his sympathizers were gathering and preparing actions in support of the rebel king, Sedgwick and his group decided to take the initiative. Five hundred volunteers assembled at Stockbridge on January 20 and made plans to march on a propertied but disaffected gentleman, Paul Hubbard, and the force of almost two hundred he had collected at West Stockbridge. This force was serving as a rallying point, with the discontented flocking to it from every part of the county. Sedgwick believed it essential to stifle the monster in its infancy. The entire body of volunteers was formed into three groups which, converging on the hamlet of West Stockbridge by three different routes, were to surround the malcontents and force their surrender. Sedgwick led a vanguard of thirty-seven infantry and seven cavalry in advance of the center group. In their eagerness to reach the enemy, this reconnaissance party lost contact with the main force, and in this detached state stumbled across Hubbard's sentries. These worthies fired the alarm and the whole rebel force was at once drawn up in line and commanded by Hubbard to fire on the exposed salient of "government men." Taking advantage of a slight hesitation on the part of his opponents, Sedgwick rode into their midst. In stentorian tones he demanded they lay down their muskets at once. Awed by this exhibition of courage and authority on the part of a well-known if ill-liked neighbor, the line wavered and then broke. Only a few hardy souls are recorded as firing a random shot or two as they retreated. By this time the three "volunteer groups" were all upon the scene and they pursued what was now a disorganized rabble, capturing Hubbard and eighty-three of his cohorts.[11] These were incarcerated in Stockbridge for a time, but for the most part soon accepted the Governor's second offer of pardon, took the oath of allegiance, and were released.

For a while there was a lull in the contest. When, in February, 1787, General Benjamin Lincoln made his journey from Petersham to Pittsfield, in the northern portion of Berkshire County, all was fairly quiet.[12]

11. For a time General Paterson was given the credit for the victory of West Stockbridge. See *Journal kept with Gen'l Lincoln's Army*, S.P., M.H.S. and *Independent Chronicle*, February 22, 1787. At most, however, his contribution was that of rounding up an already defeated enemy.

12. Sedgwick entertained Lincoln at "Saturday dinner" while the latter was "occupying" northern Berkshire. See Sedgwick to Lincoln, February 15, 1787. MSS. Berkshire Athenaeum, Pittsfield, Massachusetts.

There seems, indeed, to have taken place in the winter of 1786–1787 a major defection within the Berkshire insurrectionists. The farmer-yeoman element, discouraged by defeat and disgusted with the plundering and violent actions of their colleagues, began to leave the rebel ranks; the final opposition would be composed of only the most bitter and impoverished.

Certain of these, loosely organized in guerrilla bands, still roamed the country. One such band, taking advantage of a temporary absence of any armed government men in Stockbridge, swept upon that town one night and began a series of escapades that led to the bloodiest encounter of the entire rebellion.

This group was led by Perez Hamlin, a former officer in the Revolutionary Army, who with about ninety followers had been lurking just across the New York border. Seizing an opportunity for one last slap at the "old order," they swept down on Stockbridge in the early hours of February 27 and began to pillage at pleasure. The first stop of one squad was the new house of the hated Mr. Sedgwick.[13] Sedgwick was in Boston on business, but there on guard was his faithful Negro servant Mumbet. Sedgwick had gained Mumbet's freedom from slavery in a famous court case of 1781, and she was now determined to prove her gratitude. Her service, beyond the loudest calls of duty, is described admiringly by one of the town historians, Miss Electa F. Jones:

> At the house of Judge Sedgwick . . . they found one who was prepared for them,—Elizabeth Freeman,—generally known as "Mum Bett." She allowed them to search the drawers, knowing that the valuable papers were on the hill, and the silver all in her own chest, and to run their bayonets under the beds and into the darkest corners to find Judge Sedgwick, for he, too, was absent. But she forbade all wanton destruction of property; and arming herself with the kitchen shovel, no light weapon in those days, she escorted them to the cellar, jeering them at her pleasure, and assuring them that they dare not strike a woman. When one of them, wishing for a

13. Typical probably of the conception of Sedgwick held by the rebels was an anecdote recounted years later by his son Harry. This was to the effect that Sedgwick, late in 1787, when riding from Great Barrington to Stockbridge, had fallen in company with two strangers who assured him that there was a person named Sedgwick in the town just ahead who "had stabbed a man in West Stockbridge through the heart and washed his hands in his victim's blood!" Papers of H. D. Sedgwick, S.P., M.H.S

Another family version was that the strangers had expressed a wish to stab this Sedgwick and refresh themselves with a cup of his blood.

share of the "gentleman's" cheer, broke off the neck of a demi-john, she offered to serve them like gentlemen, but declared that the next one who uselessly destroyed a vessel, should be instantly leveled by her shovel. They affected to scorn the bitter liquor, and left the remainder for "gentlemen who drank such stuff."

On searching the chambers and entering Betty's, one pointed to her chest, and asked what that was. "Oh, you had better search that," she replied, "an old nigger's chest! You are such gentlemen; you had better search that,—the old nigger's as you call me;" and thus she shamed them quite out of it, and saved the silver.[14]

This detachment of Hamlin's invaders had thus to be satisfied with only a horse, clothing, and some linen from Sedgwick's house, but a search of his law office proved more rewarding. There after throwing their "gentleman's underclothes," ruffled shirts, and "parlor costumes" out of the window, they seized young Elisha Williams and his fellow apprentice Henry Hopkins and added them to a growing group of "respectable inhabitants." With thought of the future, Hamlin decided that the possession of certain silk-stocking hostages might not be amiss. At dawn's break after a night of profitable revel and vandalism, Hamlin led his newly supplied men, with their thirty-two hostages, out onto the Great Barrington Road and began his march to the border of New York State, a sanctuary he was never to reach.[15]

Grown careless with success, Hamlin's men insisted on a halt at the public house in Great Barrington, a bit of excellent fortune for their pursuers. For pursued they were. News of the Stockbridge eruption had reached Sheffield by galloping messenger, and that town had immediately raised a force of eighty, who were marched from the center green by Colonel John Ashley. This group, reinforced by some Great Barrington men, began tracking Hamlin down and finally succeeded when both forces unexpectedly took the same deceptive detour. On a back road out-

14. Electa F. Jones, *Stockbridge, Past and Present: Memories of a Mission Station* (Boston, 1857), 193–194.

Another version of this famous encounter has Mumbet urging with immense sarcasm, "Now better take a look in the poore ole nigger's clo'se chest . . . seein' as you-all are such gen'lemans." And the foul rebel rejoins: "Aw, let the ole nigger alone . . . there ain't anything here except her tongue—and that ain't worth takin'." *Federal Writers Project of the U.S. Works Progress Administration for Massachusetts, The Berkshire Hills* (New York, 1939) 111.

15. See *Worcester Magazine*, II, #52, 648 for an interesting account of the Hamlin expedition as told by one of that gentleman's hostages. Also, *Independent Chronicle*, March 8, 1787; Sarah C. Sedgwick & Christina S. Marquand, *Stockbridge, 1739–1939: A Chronicle* (Great Barrington, 1939), 16c–164.

side the village of Egremont they came upon each other unawares, and
there began the one engagement of Shays' Rebellion where mock-heroics
were less noticeable than battle courage. Neither Hamlin nor his men
ran or retreated, and they suffered, in consequence, not only defeat but
over thirty casualties—Hamlin among them. The victorious "government party" suffered few wounded and but one dead. The latter was one
of the hostages, schoolteacher Solomon Glezen. General Lincoln's lieutenant General Paterson arrived just after the engagement and, perform-
ing his usual mopping up operation, took fifty of the rebels prisoner.

The action at Egremont completed the military actions of Shays'
Rebellion. There was still some fear of insurgent emigrés ensconced in
New York, Vermont, and Connecticut,[16] but these bands slowly dissolved, either secretly returning home or heading west into a land of
greater democratic opportunity.[17] The remaining contest concerned the
respective advantages afforded by policies of harshness and clemency.

In Berkshire County itself, six men were sentenced at the March term
of the Supreme Judicial Court "to be hanged by the neck until dead."
Of these six, all but one either escaped from jail or was pardoned by the
Governor. (The unlucky exception, Hamlin's lieutenant William Manning, had his sentence commuted to seven years at Castle Island at hard
labor.) Sedgwick, together with Caleb Strong, had been appointed as
attorney for the accused at this session of the Supreme Court. Despite his
previous belief that a stern course and harsh object lesson was in order,
Sedgwick seems to have served them to the very best of his ability and
secured for them a fair trial. After their conviction, furthermore, he wrote
several letters to Governor Bowdoin pleading special clemency for three
of the convicted, and generally proved both charitable and farsighted in
victory.[18] With a flash of his old Revolutionary liberalism, he declared
that "for the public good" the wounds of class division should not be
unnecessarily aggravated, and announced that he had no desire to see

16. See, especially, Abigail Dwight to Mrs. Morton, May 3, 1787, S.P. M.H.S.;
Uriah Tracy to Sedgwick, May 28, 1787, S.P., M.H.S.; and Sedgwick to General
Benjamin Lincoln, April 30, 1787, *Shays' Papers*, M.H.S.

17. Fifteen of the Insurgents escaped trial by "inlisting in the Federal Army."
Independent Chronicle, April 19, 1787.

18. See Sedgwick to Bowdoin, April 8, 1787, and May 10, 1787, as quoted by
D.M. Wilcox, "An Episode of Shays's Rebellion," *Magazine of History*, XX, 105–106
(March, 1916); Sedgwick to Governor and Council, January 28, 1787, Massachu-
setts Archives, CLXXXIX, 164–166.

For an excellent analysis of the dangers inherent in a general proscription, see
Henry Van Schaack to Sedgwick, February 16, 1787. S.P., M.H.S.

the little men receive the punishment due their insurgent masters, "the most proper objects of capital punishment." [19]

In the state as a whole, though fourteen of the rebels were sentenced to death, no one was executed and all eventually pardoned. Perhaps the most stringent penalties actually imposed concerned the disqualification of the insurgents and their sympathizers from certain privileges of citizenship (Acts of February 16 and 20; March 10, 1787)—and even this proved to be of a temporary nature.

The election in May, 1787, climaxed the whole problem of the proper treatment for the defeated enemy. Sympathizers of the rebellion wished to defeat Bowdoin, whose firmness of purpose and speed of action had so contributed to the suppression of the armed revolt, and to secure a governor and General Court that would pardon the convicted and generally forgive the past trespasses of all followers of Shays. Sedgwick, actively engaged in combatting insurgent influence in the highlands and valleys of Berkshire and in securing his own election as Stockbridge's representative, described the situation in a letter to Governor Bowdoin:

> The idea (as far as I have been able to learn) of success by arms is not now so prevalent, as heretofore. The manifest if not open and avowed object with the party at present seems to be to obtain their wishes by a change of administration, and by procuring a legislature who will be disposed to establish iniquity by Law. A paper money executive & legislative will give them everything they can desire excepting only a division of property. From such may the good Lord deliver us.[20]

Sedgwick and a few other conservatives were elected in Berkshire [21]

---

19. He remained obdurate in his belief that little mercy should be shown the leaders of the revolt, who had deluded "the lower sort" from good principles. See Sedgwick to Lincoln, April 30, 1787, *Shays' Papers*, M.H.S., and Lincoln to Sedgwick, May 3, 1787, S.P., M.H.S.

Samuel Adams, fiery radical in the War with England, shared this view.

20. Sedgwick to Bowdoin, April 8, 1787, cited in Wilcox, *An Episode of Shays's Rebellion,* 106.

21. Sedgwick was elected both to the Eighth and Ninth General Courts as the representative from Stockbridge to the lower house. Though now recognized as a major political figure, his legislative efforts were almost identical with those of earlier years.

His chief concerns in the Eighth Court (1787-1788) were to tidy up the remains of the quenched rebellion, promote certain minor financial reforms, and author a bill for the relief of imprisoned debtors. The Ninth Court saw Sedgwick elected Speaker of the House, much to his delight. Besides proving himself an able parliamentarian, he labored during its tenure (May, 1788–January, 1789) for a new tax bill and a major reform of the state's judicial system—the latter to no avail.

and elsewhere, but the results of this election generally favored those not stigmatized by service in the rebellion-reproving General Court. The old Revolutionary hero John Hancock was elected by a large majority over Bowdoin and began serving his sixth term as the state's supreme executive. His election, however, gave the malcontents relatively little of the radical reform of government which they had expected. Indeed, the most important result of the turnover of the 1787 election was possibly its cementing of the Bowdoinite party, Sedgwick among them, whose members were now joined by the adhesive of undeserved defeat. It would be this party—or better, faction—that would in 1788 be so instrumental in securing the ratification of the Federal Constitution in Massachusetts. The nationalism they would exhibit on that occasion had been fashioned in part on the anvil of Shays' Rebellion.

V

Sedgwick and the Ratification of the Federal Constitution in Massachusetts, 1787–1788

> [*The Anti-Federalists*] *are very industriously endeav-*
> *oring to keep their forces in the field . . . with the*
> *temper described by Milton of his Devils gener-*
> *al[ly]. . . . But on the other side the friends of order,*
> *of government and the constitution possess such a su-*
> *periority not only in their cause but in their talents*
> *as gives the most pleasing prospect of success.*
> Theodore Sedgwick [1]

DURING the summer of 1787 the Philadelphia Convention, after much struggle and compromise, brought forth a new frame of government for the thirteen states. Sedgwick was at the time busy with his law office in Stockbridge, but all of his hopes and certain of his ideas [2] resided with Rufus King and the other Massachusetts delegates in Philadelphia. He expressed deep concern for their success and looked to the Constitutional Convention to balance liberty with order and secure the protection of virtue and property. Increasing prosperity and social status, together with his experiences with the Confederation Congress and Captain Shays, had eroded the liberal and revolutionary sentiments Sedgwick had expressed when forming the Sheffield Resolves of 1773. His role as Revolutionist had been even then a cautious and self-limited one, and by 1787 the Revolutionary had become, in a not uncommon transition, the Conservative. Once strongly opposed to the Order of Cincinnati, he now looked favorably on its members as a source of strength in the battle at hand.[3] Sedgwick expressed his mingled hopes and fears in a letter to Rufus King:

1. Letter to Henry Van Schaack, January 10, 1788. S.P., M.H.S.
2. See letter from King to Sedgwick, June 10, 1787, in which King wrote: "I shall ask your opinion by an early post on some points of consequence." S.P., M.H.S.
3. See letter from David Humphreys to Washington (private), January 20, 1787. *Washington Papers*, Library of Congress.

I am happy to be informed that the characters composing the convention give us a prospect of deriving advantages from their deliberations. Much is to be done. Every man of observation is convinced that the end of government security cannot be attained by the exercise of principles founded on Democratic equality. A war is now actually levied on the virtue, property and distinctions in the community, and however there may be an appearance of temporary cessation of hositilities, yet the flame will again and again break out.[4]

On September 17, 1787, the Constitution was signed and shortly afterwards the Confederation Congress recommended its own extinction by submitting the document to each of the states for their ratification or rejection. The advocates of the Constitution were initially better prepared than its opponents, but the latter, the Anti-Federalists, were soon in evidence in Massachusetts and elsewhere. They seem to have felt that the Constitution was not only illegal—the Convention had been commissioned to modify, not replace, the Articles—but also designedly productive of a favored "aristocracy of wealth and property" and of a consequent loss of liberty. Appreciating that it was a document far less democratic than most of the state constitutions, they declared that it would tend to the creation of an extensive bureaucracy, and would eventuate in a near total loss of control by the people over their representatives. The Anti-Federalists complained of the lack of a bill of rights, of alleged unequal representation between state and state, and of the impossibility of reconciling in so glib a fashion the great economic and cultural differences between the states. The sovereignty of the individual states would be undermined, and undue influence granted the mercantile interests at the expense of the agrarian. Less articulate but undoubtedly present was a fear on the part of certain ex-Shaysites of a strong government, able to punish with effect, and a fear on the part of some Anti-Federalists that the Constitution, with its clauses forbidding violation of contract or state issue of bills of credit, would defeat any future efforts to alleviate or renounce their burden of debts. In short, political fears supported in the majority of cases by economic considerations stood in back of the protest of the Anti-Federalists of Massachusetts.

The Federalists, being composed chiefly of those of conservative proclivities, the educated, prosperous, and professional classes, supported the Constitution as favorable to the security of property, the encouragement of commerce, the salvage of public credit, and the protection of "liberty without license." The seaboard merchants, the clergy,

4. June 18, 1787, Box 1, *King Papers*, New-York Historical Society.

the bar, certain ranking officers of the Massachusetts line, and the sufferers at the hands of Shays generally [5] were disgusted by the collapse of credit and situations of partial debt repudiation, public and private, in both nation and state; by the growing discord between the states; and by the slow recovery of our trade, commerce, and agriculture from the ravages of war. Whatever their subdivisions of opinion previously, they now formed a solid front. They insisted that only through a more energetic, efficient continental government could internal peace, the ascendancy of law, and the development of commercial and industrial wealth be secured, and national honor and dignity upheld in foreign relations.[6] The vestigial remains of the native aristocracy of colonial times and the *nouveau* aristocracy of postwar Massachusetts, to which class Sedgwick had laboriously attained, girded themselves for battle with unwonted unity. In certain areas the battle was already virtually won, in others there was much fighting yet to do, and in still others their cause was hopeless.

The seaboard counties on the east and the Connecticut River valley towns in the southern portion of the western boundary were the natural Federalist strongholds. The interior counties and the northern half of the western frontier (uninfluenced by Connecticut River trade) were Anti-Federalist territory.[7] Back-country social conditions tended to favor radical economic remedies and consequent suspicion of strong, debt-

---

5. A rather extreme example of the still active fear of "Shaysism" of this class was a piece in the *Independent Chronicle* (October 4, 1787) describing the probable state of things should "the federal government be rejected (AWFUL WORDS)." Shays would become governor of Massachusetts and an epidemic of revengeful executions would sweep the country, under the theory that the only good conservative was a dead conservative.

6. They did not appreciate that the disease of political irresponsibility from which the nation suffered during the "Critical Period" was probably traceable more to state than national lethargy, radicalism, and inefficiency.

7. See Orin Grant Libby's monograph, *The Geographical Distribution of the Vote of the Thirteen States on the Federal Constitution, 1787–8* (Madison, Wisconsin, 1894). Also, J. T. Main, *The Anti-Federalists*, 201–209.

Sharp objection to Libby's tabulation will be found in Robert E. Brown's study, *Charles Beard and the Constitution.* . . . (Princeton, 1956), 172–173. See, too, Forrest McDonald, *We The People: The Economic Origins of the Constitution* (Chicago, 1958), 191–199.

8. Most of the literary efforts of the opposition, though, were of eastern origin. The only Anti-Federalist articles of length appearing in the western part of the state were "A Watchman" in the *Worcester Magazine*, IV, 242 and the letters by "Cornelius" in the *Hampshire Chronicle* (December 11, 18, 1787).

respecting government.[8] This area instructed many of its town delegates to the Ratification Convention to oppose the Constitution.[9]

On October 25, 1787, the General Court had agreed to call a Ratifying Convention by a vote of 129–32, and shortly afterward had instructed each town to hold a town meeting and select a delegate or delegates to the Convention which would meet in Boston the following January. The Stockbridge meeting was announced to take place at the end of November, and Sedgwick set about purifying home waters. There were many "disaffected" in Stockbridge, and they were ably led by John Bacon, a well-respected and propertied townsman. When the meeting opened there was to be seen a decided majority against the Constitution and in favor of instructing their delegates to reject it. Sedgwick had the Constitution read in full and then proceeded to speak throughout the afternoon and until nearly ten o'clock that evening, describing its merits and pardoning its offenses, and by his "honest, forcible, just and nervous reasoning . . . [bringing] tears into the eyes of a great number present." He proclaimed the genuine republican properties of the Constitution, the security it gave to life, liberty, and property, and the prospect it held out "if adopted, of promoting our national happiness, dignity and wealth." [10] Bacon was temporarily silenced and the opposition defeated. Stockbridge voted to approve the Constitution (60–30), and send as their delegate the silver-tongued Sedgwick.

With Stockbridge in hand, that gentleman enlarged his field of operations and began to organize the "friends of order" in the neighboring towns of Pittsfield, Great Barrington, Sheffield, Becket, Richmond, etc.[11] It was at this time that he began to erect an informal county organization of lieutenants, supporters, and propagandists that would become in the next decade a virtual "machine." Sedgwick in his correspondence with Federalists in other Berkshire towns laid down the propaganda line to be followed. He stressed that Massachusetts as a large creditor of the

9. The delegates from Sedgwick's Berkshire County would vote 15–7 against the Constitution.
   See Libby, *op. cit.*, for a correction of the total given by Elliot. John Elliot, *The Debate in the Several State Conventions on the Adoption of the Federal Constitution* (Washington, 1845), II, 105, 178.
   10. *Massachusetts Centinel* (Boston), December 15, 1787. See also *Worcester Magazine*, IV, 139, and Samuel A. Otis to Caleb Davis, December 14, 1787, *Davis Papers*, XIV–B, M.H.S.
   11. See as samples of this activity, Sedgwick to Henry Van Schaack, November 28, December 5, 1787. *S.P.*, M.H.S.

general government had everything to gain by the restoration of credit and a settlement of governmental debts and emphasized that the Constitution left many powers with the individual states and established a "mixed" not a "national" government.[12] These points he would make again and again during the Convention itself.

The Massachusetts Ratification Convention convened January 9, 1788, and, after establishing itself in the Representatives' Chamber, selected a committee to prepare the rules and regulations that should govern the Convention. Sedgwick was appointed to this committee, and from that moment seems to have been accepted as one of the major Federalist spokesmen and the leader of the cause in the westernmost portion of the state. Though the Constitution had to be accepted or rejected in its entirety, its advocates, appreciating that they were at the moment in a minority and needed further time to proselytize and convince, succeeded in having the document discussed paragraph by paragraph. The paragraphs which seem to have created the most discussion, and in the debate on which Sedgwick was most vocal, concerned the provision for the biennial election of United States representatives, the right of Congress to levy a direct tax, the authority of that body to raise and control an army, and the lack of a bill of rights.

Massachusetts was accustomed to electing both its state and Congressional delegates annually, and certain members sharply opposed the Constitution on the change it effected concerning the latter. Sedgwick gave perhaps the best answer to this objection. He explained that though annual elections might be quite satisfactory for state offices, the great affairs of the vast expanse that was the United States offered complicated problems which would require extensive deliberation. A man called into national public service could not be expected immediately to "divest himself of local concerns, and instantly initiate himself into a general knowledge of such extensive and weighty matters." [13] Not only should

12. See as a typical example his letter to Henry Van Schaack, December 13, 1787, in which he explained the absence of a bill of rights:

> The whole business of internal police is to be left in the hands of the State Government. Had the national Government undertaken to guaranty the several rights of citizenship contained in their declaratory Bills, it would have given a right of interference in every instance of a complaint of the infraction of those rights & hence, every reasonable mind will easily comprehend a plausible pretence would have been afforded for an interference which would naturally tend to check, circumscribe and finally to annihilate all state power.

S.P., M.H.S.

13. Elliot, *Debate on the Adoption of the Federal Constitution*, II, 4.

a representative be allowed a two year term but, in Sedgwick's opinion, he should also be allowed to determine his own salary. The new representatives would not and should not be creatures of the state legislatures as were the delegates to the Confederation Congress. They would have enough sense of their honor and reputations not to assess exorbitant wages. Members of the General Court of Massachusetts had this power and it had not proved harmful to the interests of the people; nor would the exercise of this necessary authority by representatives of the federal assembly.

Thwarted by this reasoning on the part of Sedgwick and others, one Anti-Federalist, with an inconsistency typical of political discussion, attacked the Constitution for not providing any property qualification for membership in Congress, solemnly warning that "when men have nothing to lose, they have nothing to fear." Sedgwick was quick with a ready-made retort. He was surprised, he said, "that gentlemen who appeared so strenuously to advocate the rights of the people, should wish to exclude from the federal government a *good* man, because he was not a *rich* one." Sedgwick, a strong opponent of democracy, in so far as that term refers to government by as well as for the people, spoke on this objection in shocked tones, declaring it to be "founded on anti-democratic principle" and unworthy of any serious consideration.[14]

Shortly after this exchange, the Anti's as a whole began in earnest to strike at what they felt was the most vulnerable aspect and the major fault of the Constitution, that it destroyed the independence and sovereignty of the individual states, the taxing power being the especial case in point. Parsons, King, Dana, Ames, and others were the chief orators for the Constitutional side here, but Sedgwick struck several telling blows. He insisted that if he believed that the adoption of the proposed Constitution would interfere with the state legislature, he would be the last to vote for it, and, hopping heavily on the semantic trapeze, declared that the proposed "consolidation of the union" was to be a consolidation of the strength and power of the confederacy not of the states, and that as the national government was *divided* into three branches it could not be considered a *consolidated* form of government. This definitely did not satisfy a Mr. Pierce who said he "could not conceive if the individual states are to retain their sovereignty, how a sovereign power could exist

---

14. *Ibid.*, 35. He also admitted—in less lofty tones—that it was doubtful if any man without property would ever be chosen, anyway, unless he displayed "outstanding talent and virtue."

within a sovereign power." [15] Sedgwick, unwilling to express fully his true conviction that the national government had to be definitely supreme in large areas of authority, concentrated on the specific matter at hand, national taxation.

He felt very strongly that it was absolutely necessary that the national government have the right to levy taxes directly on the individual citizen. The government whose duty it was to protect and secure the whole had to have the means necessary to effect this object and therefore various sources of revenue should be unquestionably available to it. Its powers in this field should be unlimited; Congress could well be trusted to raise money in the manner easiest to the people. Imposts and excises would surely be tried before direct taxes (a poll or land tax, for example), and the latter, as a "stand-by power," would be used most probably only in emergency situations, such as sudden invasions by an enemy. It must be in reserve, however, for just those situations.[16]

He expressed the same line of thought during the debate over the eighth section of the Constitution, which granted the national government power to raise a standing army. The people and their representatives were equally subject to the last and could have but one and the same interest. The nation would never be enslaved. "How is an army for that purpose to be obtained from the freemen of the United States?" [17] He asked whether "gentlemen could think it possible, that the legislature of the United States should raise an army unnecessarily, which, in a short time, would be under the control of other persons?" [18] He insisted that in the Constitution every possible precaution had been taken against an abuse of power, and that the likelihood that any would-be military dictator could use the power granted in Section 8 to destroy personal security and representative government was slight indeed. It was, similarly with the authorization to levy direct taxes, a case of trusting the government of their own creation.

Sedgwick perhaps best expressed his belief in the necessity of counterbalancing popular liberty with trust in properly elected authority during the debate over the power of Congress to determine the time and place of federal elections:

[The] objection supposes the power will be used to the worst pos-

15. *The Massachusetts Gazette*, February 8, 1788; *Debates and Proceedings in the Convention of the Commonwealth of Massachusetts Held In The Year 1788* (Boston, 1856), 177.
16. Elliot, *Debate on the Adoption of the Federal Constitution*, II, 60–61.
17. *Ibid.*, 96.
18. *Debates and Proceedings*, 198.

sible purposes; if we are to suppose that, we had better dissolve all government and live as the savages. But in forming a government, we must grant the necessary powers, and not contemplate only the possible abuse of power; otherwise there is the same objection to our own [state] government—they may call every man into the field, take away all our money, erect courts in every street, give judges £ 10,000 a year, unite all the counties into one, and make Penobscot a shire town. But to suppose this, is to suppose the legislature devils, or worse. A sufficient check against the wanton abuse of power is the spirit of the people, as in the encroachment of Great Britain, but where there is a common interest we are not to presume an abuse of power.

But the controlling power is necessary to preserve the general government. Those who wish this power alone existed in the several legislatures, are, influenced because it would [then] be safe from the common interest.[19]

As the Convention wore on, the sides came more evenly into balance. The Federalists, however, saw that they still might well be defeated unless they compromised on the matter of amendments, especially as respected the guarantee of certain individual rights and liberties. At first opposed to any "tampering" with the Constitution, and convinced that the guarantees of state constitutions made unnecessary a federal bill of rights, Sedgwick and his friends now agreed that certain *recommendatory* amendments would be in order.[20] In a masterful coup, they proceeded to secure the services of the popular hero John Hancock, president of the Convention, as their supposed propounder.

After Hancock had submitted these amendments to the House, a committee was appointed to consider them and any other modifications that might be proposed. This committee was formed on the principle of selecting from each county a friend and an opponent of the Constitution; thus Sedgwick was joined on the committee by John Lusk of West Stockbridge, an Anti-Federalist. The only two Convention delegates from Dukes County were Federalists, however, and this necessitated, perhaps

19. *Ibid.*, 292.
20. Sedgwick had early considered the possibility of nominal compromise and had declared on one occasion: "It has been given out . . . that I have said that the Constitution must go down, right or wrong; I beg leave to declare . . . the idea . . . has not even entered my mind." Elliot, *Debate on the Adoption of the Federal Constitution*, II, 4.

Sedgwick initially opposed the incorporation of a federal bill of rights in the Constitution on the ground that state constitutions were the proper instruments for the protection of individual liberties and other concerns of "internal police." See Sedgwick to Henry Van Schaack, December 13, 1787. S.P., M.H.S.

not solely by chance, the absence of an "Anti" on the amendment committee from that county. Furthermore, as discussion proceeded in this committee, three "Anti's" were won over to the "side of reason," and Sedgwick and his Federalist colleagues were able consequently to report out the amendments with but slight modification. The more important of these amendments provided: that all powers not expressly delegated remained with the states; that Congress should regulate the holding of elections only when a state ignored or refused to perform this duty; that direct taxes should not be levied unless revenue from customs and excise taxes proved insufficient; that grand jury indictment should precede criminal trials; that the prohibition against acceptance of foreign titles should be made absolute; and that no trading company should be granted any commercial monopoly or discriminatory advantage by the government.

The committee came back to the floor of the Convention and advised that the Constitution be ratified and that the now reported amendments be attached to the resolve of ratification as indicative of reforms which the Commonwealth wished and expected the new government to attend to once it was established. After a final wrangle, the committee report was accepted and the Constitution of the United States ratified by Massachusetts in the form advocated by a vote of 187–168. The "interior" and "far western" counties of Middlesex, Worcester, Hampshire, and Berkshire persisted in their opposition, and the isolated counties of Bristol and York (Maine) as well, but with nothing like the uniformity that was predicted when the Convention opened. Sufficient converts had been made to allow Sedgwick and his colleagues to squeeze out a narrow victory in their battle for the creation of a national government possessed of vigor, endurance, and needful power.

There were, of course, charges then and later that these converts had been bribed, but they seem to have been without foundation. Sedgwick would have insisted that the only corruption in evidence was that of their reason before the truths of Federalism pierced the shadows of their brain. Nor can any great case be made to the effect that it was *primarily* the presence or absence of federal securities in a delegate's possession that determined his vote. Economic considerations, generally, had much to do with the way a man thought on the issue of strong government, but there is no proof that the "converts" were swayed by thoughts of financial gain and profit.

It is interesting to note that very few of the delegates who voted in the negative enjoyed the appellation "esquire," and that a majority of the delegates who voted in the affirmative were so titled. But more important, perhaps, was the tendency of delegates living in or near news-conscious urban areas to favor the Constitution and of those in relatively isolated farm areas to oppose it. This is not to imply, however, that the contest was primarily a class struggle—the propertied versus the proper-tyless—for the farmer had property interests as well as the merchant, lawyer, and manufacturer; and the urban laborer as well as the urban merchant seems to have favored the Constitution.[21] The struggle was, indeed, of a complex political-economic nature, firmly based on geographical considerations.

However bitter the struggle during the Convention, however clearly it had at points foreshadowed the opposition that would later meet the Federalist party of the 1790's, it seems safe to say that with the declaration of the vote all organized opposition ceased in Massachusetts. Not all participated in the "loud huzzas" or the "ringing of the bells in every public building," [22] but all seemed to have agreed that the decision was an honest one, and that the new frame of government should be given a fair chance.

None hoped more anxiously for its success than did Sedgwick. He determined to promote that success by his person as well as his prayers. The offertory was made only with some difficulty.

21. Certain of the Old Patriots of 1775 were enrolled among the "Anti's" and not as Repudiationists or Social Equalitarians, but as opponents of Strong Government.

Professors McDonald, Nettels, Taylor, and Main have done much to clarify the controversy concerning the "class divisions" apparent in the ratification vote in Massachusetts: Forrest McDonald, *We The People,* 191–202; Curtis P. Nettels, *The Emergence of a National Economy 1775–1815* (New York, 1962), 89–103; Robert J. Taylor, *Western Massachusetts in the Revolution,* 172–175; Jackson T. Main, *The Antifederalists: Critics of the Constitution, 1781–88,* 206–209.

22. See *The Massachusetts Gazette,* February 8, 1788, for a description of the celebration in Boston.

Sedgwick sent an express to Van Rensselaer in Albany with the glad tidings, in an effort to aid the Federalist cause in New York. He willingly agreed with Benjamin Lincoln that Rhode Island, which had seen fit to reject the Constitution, was indeed no better than a "little trollop." Benjamin Lincoln to Sedgwick, September 7, 1788. S.P., M.H.S.

VI

Sedgwick Helps Launch the New Government, 1789

> *Shalle he [the Secretary of State] be continued . . .*
> *against the will of the President? If he is, where is*
> *the responsibility?*
>
> Theodore Sedgwick [1]

WHEN the First Congress of the new government convened in March, 1789, it contained no representative from the Hampshire and Berkshire counties district of western Massachusetts. Sedgwick was still engaged there in a bitter struggle with Samuel Lyman of Springfield. Only after five separate and exhausting elections would he be declared the winner, and then by a scant margin of eleven votes.

Sedgwick with somewhat feigned reluctance had allowed his neighbors to present him as a candidate for Congress. The style of the time—in emulation of Washington—demanded that one be surprised into office by the overwhelming insistence of friends. Sedgwick accordingly had felt obliged to electioneer under the most elaborate guises and to pretend he knew nothing of various plans of his own invention. Even when writing his wife Pamela, he assumed complete ignorance, declaring: "If the partiality of my friends consider me an object, on whom to devolve so important a trust, their delicacy is extreme, & nothing but their silence induce me to suppose this is the case." [2] He was sure, he said, that anyone as unwilling to toady to popular passions as he could not possibly be elected, but if he were elected, he promised to be absent from her side for no more than a single congressional term. His wife, a sufferer from chronic pregnancy and loneliness, timidly hinted that perhaps one owed duties to one's family as well as one's country, but then abdicated from the discussion with expected humility.

Sedgwick patently wished to unite all lovers of law, order, and

1. *Annals of The Congress of the United States* (Washington, 1834), I, 613 (June 29, 1789).
2. November 9, 1788. S.P., M.H.S.

the Constitution on himself, if possible; if not, then on some other sound and worthy Federalist. His task was not an easy one. He had to keep his mutually jealous Hampshire and Berkshire supporters in reasonable alignment, had to fight the county patriotism of the Hampshirites and their desire to give the palm to a native son, and had to counteract the foul rumor spread by a Deerfield minister that he was a Deist.

The initial election in the Berkshire-Hampshire district, December 18, 1788, proved inconclusive. Twenty-two hundred and one votes were cast; Sedgwick received eight hundred and one, three hundred short of a majority, and Samuel Lyman, William Whiting of Great Barrington, and Thompson J. Skinner of Williamstown trailed in order.[3] None of the last three favored the repeal or even the basic revision of the Constitution, but all were less ardently Federalist than Sedgwick. Of the four, only Sedgwick was considered a strong government man. Sedgwick was the major target of all the other candidates and, with the preparations for a second trial, target practice was conducted with little decorum. Slanderous articles on one candidate or another were not infrequently published, and one of these brought Sedgwick and Lyman into sharp dispute. Sedgwick's friends accused Lyman of instigating the insertion of an article highly unfavorable to Sedgwick; Lyman, in turn, outraged at the accusation, claimed that Sedgwick was trying to ruin his reputation by insinuating that he was a slanderer, an insurgent, or worse.[4]

The "Lyman Insult" affected Sedgwick's total adversely in the second election, and again no candidate received a majority. A near total impasse seemed to have been reached. Skinner's supporters touted him as a compromise candidate, and, though Sedgwick's friend Henry Van Schaack tried to put the damper on this "division of the Berkshire vote," Theodore mournfully exclaimed to Pamela: "My own opinion on the event of the election coincides with that of every other person who desires me to serve on this occasion. They are loth to give me up but yet they nearly dispair."[5]

Sedgwick was never at any time in his life, however, a quitter. He rallied the disheartened, damned Skinner as a near anarchist, and circulated the word in Berkshire County that he alone of Berkshirites was sufficiently well-known in Hampshire to gain support in the eastern and southern parts of the congressional district. The organization back in

3. See *Thomas's Massachusetts Spy: or The Worcester Gazette,* January 1, 1789, and *Vermont Gazette* (Bennington), January 19, 1789.

4. Sedgwick to Thomas Dwight, January 23, 1789. *MSS.,* Historical Society of Pennsylvania.

5. Sedgwick to Pamela, January 27, 1789. *S.P.,* M.H.S.

gear, he slowly forged nearer and nearer the needed majority. In the third election, March, 1789, he trailed Lyman by over 100 votes, but in the fourth, a month later, he again led the field (1564 out of 3328), having scotched the rival Berkshire candidacies of Whiting and Skinner. A certain amount of bitterness arose before and during the latter election over the brief notification given Berkshire of its advent by Governor Hancock, and Sedgwick's Hampshire chieftain Samuel Henshaw spluttered in rather modern parlance:

> Precepts for next election were issued sooner than I had thought, else I would have had Butler's paper putting a hot-foot to the Lymanites last week. . . . But Mr. Governor & his advisers will have their match—Our sheriff is as good a General as any of them—and he has taken care to send the Precepts *by very safe hands* to such Towns as will vote like rational Beings.[6]

Near victory Sedgwick considered quite unsatisfactory. He saw he would need to make additional converts if he was to be elected. In hopes of doing so he wrote Henshaw as follows:

> You observe that the primary objection is "that I have not publickly declared my sentiments in favor of amending the national constitution of government," and that therefore the people conclude I am "against any amendments at all." . . . My friends and acquaintance know . . . that I have been and am now a zealous advocate for many amendments. Before the constitution was ratified by this state, I did every thing in my power to forward its adoption; because I then thought and do now think that the happiness, the permanent happiness of the people would be established by it.—not the happiness of any professional order of men, or of the great and rich, but of the bulk of citizens—of the various citizens and innumerable yeomanry of the country. But I never once dreamed but what the constitution would be perfectly agreably [sic] to the provision in the 5th article—and those amendments which will render it more perfect—more congenial to the sentiments and feelings of the PEOPLE who are to live under it and to support it, can never meet with successful opposition from any quarter. But my friend we must guard against partial or local amendments. Should amendments of this kind which are proposed by some of the states be adopted, the most essential advantages of a commercial nature would be lost to this state.
> You mention that the people are groaning under the weight of public taxes, and that they imagine I do not feel for them. This my dear Sir, gives me pain. Is it possible that the people who have so often experienced the humanity of my heart, and who have often

6. Henshaw to Sedgwick, March 27, 1789. *S.P.*, M.H.S.

saw and heard me declare, my abhorrence of heavy land taxes, is it possible for that people to beleive that I do not feel exquisitely feel for them. To lesten land taxes and to enable government to raise a revenue from other sources has been the wish of my heart and the employment of my head for years past. To effect this desirable object the several *state debts*, should be assumed by the general government,—at least so far as they were contracted to effect our independence. . . . This more than any thing else would annihilate local prejudices, give liberality of sentiment and lead us to embrace with united affection, the whole Continent of america. . . .

Should congress take the whole of the debt upon themselves and should agriculture, arts, manufactures and commerce be duly encouraged by them, we must soon become a great and happy people. . . . The industrious husband man would then be stimulated to rural improvements—would make "the wilderness blossom and bud and fill the face of the world with fruit." and (commerce being duly regulated) he would find a ready market for all his surplusage produce and this above all things would encrease population and give life and viger to agriculture. Indeed . . . I hope to live to see the day when that class of virtuous citizens, who till the ground for the support and pleasure of animal life will be more encouraged, (because they are more beneficial,) than any other order of men in the community.

Thus, my dear friend I have given you some of my sentiments, in much haste on the subject of your letter. But it does not comport with your idea "of a public declaration." and pardon me, my dear sir, for telling you I never can do it. That would look like electioneering. a business I am not versed in. If the people should see fit to chuse me, I shall unceasingly exert every nerve to advance their happiness. If they permit me to retire to the private walks of life, after having served them faithfully for many years they will add to my personal ease & domestic felicity.[7]

If not versed in electioneering, Sedgwick in this revealing epistle was hardly the complete novice. In none of its expressed sentiments was he untruthful, but the emphasis laid on the wishes of the PEOPLE, on the superiority of the agrarian way of life, and on the importance of *immediate* constitutional amendment betokened more the skill of the politician than the heart's mind of the individual. Henshaw was undoubtedly expected to make judicious use of its contents.

As the fifth—and, as it would prove, final—election came closer, partisanship intensified. Henshaw warned that steps should be taken

7. Sedgwick to Henshaw, April 6, 1789. MSS., Houghton Library, Harvard University.

to see that the votes of "Reasonable towns" be guarded on their way to the state secretary's office, so that no mishap or instance of "damnation manourvering" befall them, and further insisted: "Let your Friends be very cautious to whom they write, & even by whom they send," and let the carrier be charged not to disclose "the design of his riding; but let him deliver his Letter as tho He knew nothing of their contents." [8]

On May 14 [?] the fifth trial was held, and on May 26 Theodore Sedgwick was officially declared elected, receiving 1,984 votes out of a total of 3,946. The "Shaysites" had been defeated; their expresses into every town, their "vile and wicked arts," generally, had been expended to no avail. Mr. Lyman took his seat on the Governor's Council, and Mr. Sedgwick, June 9, 1789, left Stockbridge for New York, via Spencetown and Poughkeepsie. He was accompanied for a short ways and in high style by some dozen of his supporters who sent the new representative off in a burst of local glory. Sedgwick's self-appointed adviser Henshaw, now a representative in the Massachusetts General Court, felt obliged, indeed, to dampen the general elation by a word of caution: "Be cool. . . . Say nothing about Lyman—the victory is yours—that is enough for the present. You know some people think you are rather sudden. . . . I would therefore advise you . . . not to speak much in Congress— and never but on great questions;—let the little folks do the little Business." [9]

When Sedgwick took his seat in Congress, June 15, 1789, New York, though giving evidence of its future greatness, was not particularly im- posing in appearance. Its 3,300 inhabitants did not enjoy the architec- tural beauty of Charleston, the topographical symmetry of Philadelphia, or the quaint charm of Boston. Sedgwick, as he took up residence at Mrs. Dunscomb's on Dock Street, with Ames, Partridge, and Leonard of the Massachusetts delegation, seems to have been more aghast at the inflationary prices charged by the "villains" who served him than im- pressed by the area which spawned them. Among the city's architectural features, only the remodeled City Hall, where the Continental Congress had sat, now christened Federal Hall and serving as the Capitol, seems to have elicited much admiration. He had not come to sight-see, how- ever, in any case, but rather to help lay a firm foundation for the Great

8. Henshaw to Sedgwick, April 15, 1789. S.P., M.H.S.
9. Henshaw to Sedgwick, June 2, 1789. S.P., M.H.S.

Experiment in republican government. Dressed in black satin small-clothes, white silk stockings, and broadloom coat he presented his credentials, and, speaking to the matter at hand, began a twelve-year battle against "legislative encroachment" on the executive branch.

The matter under discussion was the creation of a Department for Foreign Affairs, more especially, the removability of the secretary for that department. There were three main views in evidence during the debate: 1) the secretary was appointed with the advice and consent of the Senate, so could never be removed but with the approval of that body; 2) the Constitution vested control of the executive departments with the President, and Congress consequently had no power to participate in the removal of his advisers; 3) Congress had a *right* to put any stipulations it desired on any office it created—the secretary and like officers were absolutely the creatures of the law—but in the present instance they *should* not in any way bar the President from removing the secretary at will, due to considerations of expediency and practicality. Sedgwick was a leading exponent of the third interpretation. It was a much less tenable stand than the second, or Madison, position which he would shortly assume. Sedgwick's prime concern on this occasion, however, lay not in the pursuit of legal logic but, rather, in fighting those representatives who would hamstring the executive. He argued strenuously for the retention, in the act establishing a foreign affairs department, of the paragraph specifically authorizing the President to remove the departmental secretary at will, but was defeated by a coalition of those who did not wish the President to have this unassisted authority and those who felt the President had the authority without congressional grant. His chief effort was to describe to his colleagues the stupid inefficiency that would result were Washington unable to remove members of his official family, speedily, promptly, and unaided:

It requires but a small share of abilities to point out certain cases for which a person ought to be removed from office without being guilty of treason, bribery, or malfeasance; and the nature of things demands that it should be so. . . . is there [to be] no way suddenly to seize the worthless wretch, and hurl him from the pinacle of power? . . .

It has been said that there is a danger of this power being abused if exercised by one man. Certainly the danger is as great with respect to the Senate who are assembled from various parts of the continent, with different impressions and opinions. It appears to me that such a body is more likely to misuse this power than the man

whom the united voice of America calls to the Presidential chair.
. . . the power of removal . . . [should] be exercised . . . by a
hand capable of exerting itself with effect.[10]

Sedgwick helped defeat a motion that the department be established
on a temporary basis, and the upshot of the whole debate was the permanent establishment of the foreign affairs department, and a phrasing
of the section concerning the removal of the secretary which implied the
constitutional right of the President to dismiss him unaided. Sedgwick
voted for the final passage of the bill, and was, on the whole, well satisfied with the result. He now came quite prominently into the notice of
"the good Washington," who was highly pleased with his advocacy of
sufficient responsibility and independence for the executive branch. An
important, precedent-setting decision had been made; the division of
power between the executive and the legislature established by the
Constitution remained intact.

The first year of the new government was largely devoted to the
erection of the machinery necessary to its operation. The Constitution
was but an overlay, the vital detail work had still to be sketched in. The
duties and administrative practices of the new departments had to be
established and methods of communication between the different
branches of the government arranged. Sedgwick expressed a keen interest in all these matters, determined that no false precedents should
be established that would endanger the success of the new national
government. Especially was he concerned that the department of his
friend Hamilton be quickly established and its relations with Congress
made smooth. In this connection Sedgwick supported a provision re-
quiring the Secretary of the Treasury Department to digest and prepare
for Congress plans for the improvement and management of the revenue.
Though a strong advocate of the separation of powers, he took the position that a certain degree of reliance by Congress upon the information
and initiative of the executive was right and proper. The representatives
would not have the time or facilities to acquire and assess the complicated data involved in financial affairs. Its task was to decide the cor-
rectness of the fiscal plans presented by the Treasury, to modify these
plans, and to devise, if necessary, alternatives. Congress should concen-

10. *Annals*, I, 460–461 (June 16, 1789), 523 (June 18).

trate on matters of general policy and not get bogged down amidst administrative details. On a later occasion, he declared:

> It was impossible precisely to define a boundary line between the business of Legislative and Executive; but from his own experience, as a public man, and from reflection, he was induced to believe, that as a general rule, the establishment of principles was the peculiar province of the former, and the execution of them, that of the latter. He would, therefore, at least, generally, as much as possible, avoid going into detail.[11]

He maintained this position in the debate over the powers and chores of the Post Office Department. Here he ran up against the "pork barrel" desires of his fellow congressmen. Sedgwick, and a majority of the Senate, wished to grant the Postmaster General, with the approval of the President, the authority to designate post roads. He considered such to be an administrative not a legislative task. Having received several "advisory" letters on postal roads and arrangements himself, he appreciated the probable inability of many congressmen to act with sufficient detachment. His colleagues in the House seem to have felt few such qualms, however, and he was defeated by a large majority.[12]

More successful was an earlier attempt to establish the duties of the Foreign Affairs, or State, Department. Sedgwick had headed a committee which reported a bill placing in the hands of the Secretary of State, as the Secretary for Foreign Affairs now began to be called, the tasks of keeping the acts, records, and great seal of the United States, of publishing, preserving, and authenticating the acts of Congress, and of prescribing the forms of the various commissions that would issue from the national government. After a brief struggle with some "extravagant" individuals who wished to see these duties become the concern of a new department—the Home Department—Sedgwick had the pleasure of seeing his report passed, and precedent established for the conglomeration of tasks that were to fall to the lot of the unhappy Secretary of State well into the present century.

If, in co-operation with most of his colleagues, Sedgwick was not at all times perfectly certain about the exact state of relations between the presidential and congressional sovereignties, he always felt quite sure of the position and responsibilities of the individual representative. He was shocked when Mr. Livermore of New Hampshire implied that the state legislatures had the power of instructing members of the national

11. *Annals*, III, 239–240 (January 7, 1791).
12. *Annals*, II, 1641 (June 16, 1790), 1686 (July 22, 1790).

House. Sedgwick thought it would be disrespectful to the rights of the people to admit such an authority, and a retreat to the evil days of the Articles of Confederation. He was not, he declared, a representative from the General Court of Massachusetts but, rather, the representative of the people *as a whole*. The Senate had been provided to represent the states as states. Sedgwick, in this instance, not only showed his growing "nationalism" but also his occasional addiction to British forms and theories. A member of Parliament represented the British nation; a member of Congress, his district.

Sedgwick was additionally prominent during the erection of the new political scaffolding as the chief spokesman of economy, especially in the matter of official salaries. Not unappreciative of the mood of his particular constituents, the thrifty, penny-wise farmers of western Massachusetts, and recalling the commotion in the Massachusetts Ratification Convention over the danger of allowing Congressmen to establish their own salaries, he tried zealously and almost fruitlessly to pare the governmental salary scale. Again and again he attempted to have the wages of the representatives reduced from six to five dollars a day. He argued that the Constitution itself had made a distinction between the two branches of Congress. The Senators were required to be of "advanced age" and would most probably be too old to "return to their former occupations when the period for retirement from the Senate arrived." Therefore six dollars a day might well be lavished upon them, but "as economy ought to be particularly studied by the Legislature," five dollars was quite enough for a congressman. He hoped that the yeas and nays would not be called as there was "a principle in mankind which revolted at the idea of inferiority," but for himself he did not feel that such discrimination in pay would be in any manner insulting. "There are grades in society which are necessary to their very existence. This is a self-evident proposition." [13] His motion, reasoning, and motives were furiously denounced by Elbridge Gerry and others, and, as he mournfully related to Pamela, his "self-evident proposition" quickly dismissed by the wastrel majority:

> The ideas of the Southern gentlemen as to allowances to officers of the government and as to their own wages are so very different from our own. . . . Indeed were the wishes of some to be gratifyed I much doubt whether the whole resources of this government would not be exhausted by the civil list. . . .
>
> You, my love, know my disposition, that having done what I think to be right, I am not very anxious about the consequences. But such

13. *Annals*, I, 651, 656 (July 16, 1789).

appears to me to be the thoughtless profusion of the majority of the house that I dread the effects our measures in that regard may have on the public mind. . . . I have been left to struggle almost alone . . . an attempt to give evidence of economy, and self denial is endeavored to be represented as arising from poverty of spirit and a man of disposition to acquire popular applause.[14]

More promising and pacific than his economy drive was his effort to establish promptly the federal judicial system. Sedgwick insisted that not only the Supreme Court but also federal district courts must be established at once. The country had already had opportunity to discover "how dangerous . . . [it was] to make the State Legislature[s] the sole guardians of the national faith and honor." Federal courts were needed to see that the *bona fide* debts due from the citizens of America to the subjects of Britain were paid and the Treaty of Peace secured. The execution of national laws could not be left to the determination of an authority independent of the national legislature, such as the state courts. Very great difficulties "would arise from giving the state courts cognizance of federal questions." The national government must have its own judicial tribunals if it was to have "any degree of reputation and dignity." [15] Advocating four judges for the Supreme Court, "as in Great Britain," Sedgwick supported a broad interpretation of the areas of "original jurisdiction" granted the Supreme Court by the Constitution.[16]

Sedgwick's attitude respecting the establishment of a federal judicial system reflected his burgeoning nationalism; his attitude toward various western problems reflected the lingering sectional bias that would periodically restrict and mar that nationalism. The Nationalist was still the New Englander. Surely Sedgwick took a purely eastern approach on the questions of western land sales and Indian negotiation. He wanted the land office to be in New York under the control of the Secretary of the Treasury, rather than under the supervision of the Governor of the Western Territory, for he wished close supervision of land sales and a

14. July 23; August 8, 1789. S.P., M.H.S. Sedgwick concisely stated his position on government "charity" in a speech opposing additional compensation for officers of the Revolutionary Navy: "It was a principle from which he professed himself determined never to depart, not to dissipate [government] property in idle or visionary projects of generosity." *Annals*, II, 1651 (June 24, 1790).

15. *Annals*, I, 805–806 (August 29, 1789).

16. Sedgwick also took a leading part in the drafting of bills establishing the penalties to be applied to "federal crimes." He opposed promises of leniency as a means of persuading a criminal to confess, favored giving "science" the bodies of murderers, and fought strenuously to enable a judge passing sentence on a counterfeiter to prescribe the death penalty.

policy productive of the greatest amount of revenue possible. "He was moreover decidedly opposed to selling unless the whole of the purchase money was paid down." [17]

The same lack of appreciation of the problems and importance of the West was evident during the debate in August, 1789, over the appropriations for the forthcoming treaty with the Creek Indians. Sedgwick was for slashing the appropriation in half. More justifiably, he sought to strike out the clause restricting the President to the use of three commissioners. Foreshadowing his fight in behalf of the Jay Treaty six years later, he declared that he thought it "a dangerous doctrine to be established that the House had any authority to interfere in management of treaties." [18] This constitutional issue seems to have been quickly smoothed over, however, Sedgwick winning his point; for soon thereafter he was giving the majority of his time to the matter of constitutional amendments.

Sedgwick's initial reluctance to take up the task of amending the Constitution was the result not of prejudice but of priorities. He was anxious that first attention be given to measures which established the machinery of the new government or set matters to right financially. James Madison, with a better feel of the popular pulse, appreciated that the people would judge the good faith of the new government largely by its actions concerning the recommendations which had accompanied ratification in the various state conventions. Sedgwick succeeded in postponing consideration of these recommendations for a time, by having them referred to a committee of eleven, but was unable to delay matters further once the report of this select committee was introduced, August 13, 1789. Initially, Sedgwick's criticism of this report was of a rather captious variety. He complained, for example, about the redundancy of the amendment granting the people the right to assemble as well as the right to speak, snappishly observing that "if people freely converse together, they must assemble for that purpose." [19] Soon, however, he took a more constructive attitude. Agreeing to those amendments which guaranteed certain personal liberties, Sedgwick (and Madison, as well) fought vigorously any amendments which would seriously limit the powers of the national government, as those powers were expressed, *or*

17. *Annals*, I, 1069 (January 20, 1790).
18. *Annals*, I, 690 (August 11, 1789).
Washington was arranging to treat with Chief McGillivray and the southern Indians, so he might concentrate on the irreconcilable Indians of the Northwest Territory.
19. *Annals*, I, 731 (August 15, 1789).

implied, by the Constitution. Sedgwick assisted the rejection of a proposition which would have forbidden Congress to impose direct taxes until it had made an attempt to lay a requisition on every state for its share of the needed sum, and until moneys from duties, excises, and impost were shown to be insufficient to the needs of the government. He helped defeat a proposal that Congress should not alter or interfere in the times, places, or manner of holding elections except where a state had neglected to act.[20] And he helped quash a motion by Elbridge Gerry which would have restricted the national government to the powers *expressly* listed in the Constitution. Sedgwick declared on this occasion that he did not believe any government had ever existed which was not obliged to exercise some of its powers by implication.

To the amendments finally passed Sedgwick had little or no objection. He was, in fact, one of a committee of three who rearranged and polished them for their passage by the House, and the deleting and redrafting done by the Senate, Sedgwick thought all to the good. The defeat there of Madison's pet amendment to compel *the states* to respect the more basic of individual civil liberties did not disturb Sedgwick, as he considered that the state bills of rights made such an amendment more or less superfluous. The twelve articles which were finally submitted to the states he considered proper and sufficient.

Sedgwick's lot in the capital was not, of course, exclusively one of toil and business during this his first year in Congress. Always a highly sociable creature, he seems to have attended during these months a number of functions organized by the self-conscious hostesses of New York's *haut monde.*[21] Despite one attack of "the ague" and several of "the headake," Sedgwick, on the whole, enjoyed a busy and a pleasurable year. The next would be even busier, but rather less pleasurable. He would be fighting for "the national honor" and the funding plan, for the welfare of Massachusetts and assumption. He would become, in the House of Representatives, "Mr. Hamilton's lieutenant."

20. The Massachusetts Convention had favored just such an amendment, but Sedgwick did not feel he was bound by its recommendations. Fisher Ames, a fellow congressman, wrote Sedgwick: "by concealing facts, we shall frequently prove each other friends—especially with regard to voting against the instructions of the Convention." Ames to Sedgwick, October 6, 1789. *S.P.,* M.H.S.

21. The more vulgar social occasions, such as the mob celebration of the Fourth of July, Sedgwick avoided. Instead, he and ten other gentlemen took "a ramble on long island." Sedgwick to Pamela, July 5, 1789. *S.P.,* M.H.S.

IN SUPPORT OF MR. HAMILTON: SEDGWICK IN CONGRESS, 1790–1793

VII

Securing the Public Credit

On the wise and prudent measures of the present session will depend the future respectability and welfare of this country, and indeed principally on the measures which may be adopted relative to funding the national debts. . . . In my opinion the real security and efficiency of the Government will depend more on a . . . punctual performance of its engagement than on every other circumstance combined.

Theodore Sedgwick [1]

I_F any one cause had proved the downfall of the Confederation it was its inability to establish the national credit, to put the finances of the general government on a firm and stable basis. Alexander Hamilton and his admiring friend Theodore Sedgwick agreed that the likelihood of active support of the new government by the moneyed classes was slight unless fiscal order and confidence were restored. The new government would succeed or fail as it was able or unable to fund the domestic and foreign debt, raise sufficient revenue to meet its charges, and gain the gratitude of the influential debt-holding class.

The debt was rather complicated and, for the time, very large. The foreign debt, including arrears of interest, totalled $11,710,378, the great bulk of which was owed France for her invaluable services during the Revolution. It was agreed by all that it must be paid in full in the exact manner contracted. The domestic indebtedness was of two types: 1) the obligations incurred directly by the government—loan office certificates, commissary certificates, indents, soldier claim certificates, Registry of Treasury certificates; 2) the indirect obligations incurred when the states had advanced and paid for services and supplies during the Revolution. The initial concern of Mr. Hamilton was with the directly incurred domestic debt of the Continent. It totalled roughly $40,500,000

1. Letter of Henry Van Schaack, January 31, 1790. S.P., M.H.S.

plus $2,000,000 of unliquidated claims and currency. Hamilton sent to the House a plan to fund the entire sum at full value.

As subsequently slightly modified, the plan was as follows: A loan was to be opened by Treasury commissioners, appointed for that purpose, in each state. Only government security holders were to be allowed to subscribe to the loan, and they were to pay therefore in the evidences of the old debt which they held, such evidences to be receivable at their *face value*. For the *principal* due them, the subscribers were to receive stock in the new debt, two-thirds to bear six per cent interest at once, one-third to be non-interest bearing until 1801, when six per cent would accrue. The government was to have the right, but not the duty, of redeeming eight per cent of these new bonds every year. The *interest* due the holders of the old debt was to be similarly funded. Certificates in the new debt bearing three per cent interest would be given for arrears of interest payment prior to January 1, 1791. Holders of indents received as payment for interest due on loan office certificates, or other portions of the liquidated debt, would be treated in the same way. The government would have the right to redeem at will any or all of the three per cent stock.

Sedgwick was in complete accord with this report, but realized it was sure to cause considerable controversy. As he wrote his friend Van Schaack, four very material questions would be raised: should there be no differentiation made between the original holders and the secondary purchasers of governmental securities? should the securities be funded at full face value or merely at their current market value? should arrears of interest on the old debt be converted into additional capital in the new? should the rate of interest for arrears of interest be but three per cent? He optimistically expected "small divisions" on the first three considerations; on the last, great difficulty. Three per cent interest was less than that nominally given by the Confederation, and Sedgwick was afraid there would be some criticism from the *debt-holders* at this "repudiation." Perhaps they would not understand that matters must be conditioned on the ability of the government to pay. Sedgwick does not seem to have begun to appreciate the extent of the opposition that would arise from the people who held no government securities and from their spokesmen. Rather, his initial worry was over the lethargy evinced by Congress in putting this vital issue to a speedy decision. The limited views if "pure motives" of the majority discouraged him, as did the lack of any "union of councils." [2] In hopes of bringing matters to a head, he

2. Sedgwick to Pamela, January 30, 1790. S.P., M.H.S.

several times rose in debate to analyze the dangers of delay and to urge more legislative speed, lest "the ardent expectations of the people" be disappointed:

> And while the public expectation is kept thus alive and in suspense gentlemen cannot but suppose designs will be framed and prosecuted that may be injurious to the community. For, altho I do not believe that speculation, to a certain degree, is baneful in its effects upon society, yet . . . if the capital employed in merchandise is taken from that branch of the public interest, and employed in speculations no way useful in increasing the labor of the community, such speculations would be pernicious. . . .
>
> There are a variety of opinions prevailing. . . . This diversity of opinion may probably irritate, and produce heats and animosities, which may terminate in forming factions among the people. The State debts may produce a difference between the General and particular Governments. If the matter is taken up as the business of a party, one may be pitted against the other, until, in the end, they . . . sacrifice the general welfare to opposition and party spirit. . . . [The public] expect that justice and equity will be administered, as far as the abilities of our country extend. . . . If congress pursue the present enquiry, and come to a determination without delay, the public sentiment will be brought to a point, and a general acquiescence may be expected, but, if it is postponed to a future session, such may be the effect of faction and disappointment during the recess, that the probability is, that no one party will comprise a sufficient number to comprehend the majority of the whole.[3]

Before Madison broached his project of discrimination between the original holders and the secondary purchasers, there had been considerable feeling among certain congressmen that, as all security holders had received their evidences of the national debt in return for inflation-priced goods and services, *all* of the domestic debt should be scaled down to either its present market value or the highest hard-money value it had ever enjoyed.

At first Sedgwick had not been greatly shocked by such a suggestion; in fact, had rather favored a *slight* amount of devaluation, if this partial repudiation would facilitate the assumption of state debts and could be done with the voluntary consent of the creditors. He was soon convinced by Hamilton, however, that prospective government revenue could take the strain of funding at par, and thereafter he was an ardent opponent

---

3. *Annals*, I, 1097 (January 28, 1790), 1163 (February 9, 1790); *Congressional Register*, III, 296; *Annals*, I, 1169–1170; II, 1171 (February 10, 1790).

of any type of retroactive governmental interference with the sanctity of private contracts, except in the direst of emergencies.[4]

He was from the first strongly opposed to James Madison's proposal for a "more just discharge" of the debt. Madison wished to discriminate among debt-holders between the original and secondary holder, allowing the latter only the highest market price of the security. The difference between this market price and the face value of the security was the rightful due of the original holder, the alienator. Sedgwick felt this proposal was positively anarchistic in its destruction of the public faith and the agreed word of gentlemen. Neither alienator nor alienee had imposed on one another, he insisted; the latter had simply had more faith in the government and in its prospective financial ability. Mr. Madison's plan would surely cost the government every penny as much as Mr. Hamilton's prima facie arrangement. It was completely impractical; endless litigation would be its only result. Why this distasteful suspicion of the present holders? Were not "a great and respectable body of our citizens" creditors of the United States? Perhaps certain of the "present possessors" would make a large profit from their transaction, but that could not be helped; it was impossible to draw a line between just and unjust profit in this way. It was admitted that a depreciation of eighty per cent would not authorize the proposed interference. Would someone kindly indicate the point of depreciation which would authorize it? Would not such retroactive interference "lay a foundation for infinite frauds and perjuries"? Here were certificates, described for a definite face value, which the Continental Congress unequivocally promised to make good; to that promise this Congress was the legitimate successor. Once violate the national honor in this fashion, and it would be impossible to re-establish the general confidence or to borrow on anything like favorable terms ever again:

A contract receives an additional value from its capacity of being transferred, if the circumstances of the possessor should render a sale of it necessary or convenient to him. To render the transferable quality of such evidences of contract in any degree advantageous to the possessor, it is necessary to consider, in case of sale, the alienee possessed of all the property of the original holder. . . .

To deprive the citizen of the power of binding himself by his own voluntary contract, or to prevent a disposition of property in its nature alienable, would be a violent and unjustifiable invasion of one of those rights of which man, as a citizen, is the most tenacious and

4. See *Annals*, I, 1169 (February 10, 1790).

would indeed break one of the strongest bonds by which society is holden together. . . .

I have to observe . . . that of course the original holders have sustained a loss; that if the loss resulted from the fault, and not the misfortune of the Government, the creditors have, undeniably, a demand against the Government for compensation; that this demand, however well founded, can never authorize the Government to invade the honestly acquired property of the present possessors. . . .

Little dependence will be placed on the plighted faith of a Government which, under the pretence of doing equity, has exercised a power of dispensing with its contracts, and has thereby formed for itself a precedent of future violations. . . . With regard to discovering who was the original holder, except so far as respects the army debt, I am certain there are no documents by which the necessary facts can be discovered.

[The Madison Proposal] will lay a foundation for infinite frauds and perjuries, and . . . will, beyond all powers of calculation, multiply the evils of speculation.[5]

Sedgwick's views were representative of the entire range of arguments which the supporters of the Secretary of the Treasury directed against the now "falling angel" Mr. Madison. The essence of these arguments against discrimination in the payment of the public debt can perhaps be summed up with the homely proverb: "Two wrongs don't make a right." It was too bad if certain original holders got less than their due, but the government must not destroy sanctity of contract in an impractical attempt to correct matters.[6] The impracticality and questionable legality of the Madison proposal, the obvious fact that it was as expensive as the Treasury plan, and perhaps the personal interest of certain congressmen in speculation and speculators insured its defeat. In similar fashion these motives defeated a later attempt by the "Father of the Constitution" to require that original holders should have the *exclusive* right of subscribing to the new debt certificates for a space of six months.[7]

The motive of "personal interest" requires perhaps some further con-

5. *Annals*, II, 1205–1208 (February 15, 1790).

6. One legal contract, the sanctity of which was virtually ignored by all parties, was that represented by the "Continentals" or bills of credit. This form of paper money had depreciated to such an extent that it was virtually worthless; to have attempted to fund it at anything like face value would have been hopelessly difficult and costly. Sedgwick, however, did work to have it funded at a specified ratio of depreciation. By degrees he was forced to consent to a higher and higher ratio, finally agreeing that one hundred "Continentals" should be considered the equivalent of one dollar in specie. *Annals*, II, 1585–1586 (May 20, 1790).

7. *Ibid.*, 1711 (July 24, 1790).

sideration. Professor Charles Beard declares that of the sixty-four members of the House, twenty-nine were holders of government securities. Six (Ames, Leonard, Partridge, Sedgwick, Gerry, and Grout) of the eight members of the Massachusetts delegation, which voted solidly on all occasions for the funding bill, were personally "interested." [8] To be a security holder was not, however, as Beard explains, necessarily to be a speculator, a pipeline to speculating friends, or a man more interested in personal profit than the national welfare. Certain congressmen would perhaps qualify for reproach on all three scores, but not many. Sectional economic environment, and sincere political conviction, convinced many more representatives than did considerations of personal dollar-and-cents gain.

Sedgwick is a case in point. Though it is impossible to secure complete information on the extent of his bond holdings, so complex was the settlement of accounts of the five army departments, he did have, *as an original holder*, a fair number of loan office, quartermaster, and commissary certificates, which, when his accounts were finally settled, June, 1790, were eligible for funding at full value under the Hamilton plan. He would thereby definitely profit from congressional acceptance of that plan. He does not seem, however, to have been a *speculator* in Continental securities, or, except on one unimportant and confused occasion involving Andrew Craigie of Boston, to have allowed his friends "inside" information on the probable future of the domestic debt.[9] He was most irritated with the public creditors when, after the funding system was passed, they clamored for additional provision for the debt. An objective view of his conduct and correspondence throughout the debate on the funding bill demonstrates that, though he was by no means loath to have his securities bear such fine fruit, Sedgwick's vote was determined chiefly by the general economic predilections of his friends and himself, by a sincere belief that the nation could not long survive unless it protected the public faith, and by an honest conviction that the support of the propertied classes was essential to a strong, stable government.[10]

8. Charles A. Beard, *Economic Origins of Jeffersonian Democracy* (New York, 1915), 146. Benjamin Goodhue, also of Massachusetts, should probably be added to the Beard list, though he does not seem to appear as a security holder on the Loan Office Books of Massachusetts.

9. Sedgwick fought for assumption and for a national bank just as vigorously as he did for the funding bill. He was definitely not a stockholder in the national bank, and as he believed state paper a bad risk, most probably held very few if any Massachusetts certificates. A few of his clients did, of course, hold state paper.

10. Certain of his contemporaries—and some recent historians have followed suit—classified Sedgwick as an "interested speculator," with the understood as-

The influence Sedgwick exerted in support of the funding plan was on balance beneficial to the nation. The funding system can be criticized on many grounds; it was extravagant, overpaid even the original holders, and gave speculators excessive margins of profit. The times, however, required drastic measures. Some great and sweeping reorganization of the public financial structure was needed if the public credit was to be restored, private credit encouraged, and the faith of foreign and domestic capital in the word of the new and untried government established. The coldly pragmatic approach of Hamilton, however slanted in favor of the propertied classes, was more to the long-run, general interest than the tenderhearted, equity-seeking approach of Madison. There are occasions when the public interest may coincide with the interest of the few rather than with that of the many.[11]

Besides its importance to the credit and financial structure of the country, the funding debate was also important as the first occasion on which Madison definitely, if unsuccessfully, opposed the administration forces. There was at this time no Federalist *party*, in so far as that word implies an organized political body with definite supporters, leaders, motives, and ends, but there was a fluctuating majority group of administration supporters. It was from this group that Madison seceded when he undertook to fight the funding system. By doing so he ended the initial honeymoon period of the Washington administration; split, to some ex-

---

10. (cont.)

sumption that the pull of his purse determined the direction of his vote. Of his contemporaries none hated him more violently nor indiscriminately than that experienced hater James Thomson Callender. Callender spoke bitterly of "Mr. Sedgwick and others of the favourite detachment of speculators," and in one tract virtually dedicated to Sedgwick, rhetorically asked:

> Suppose that a bankrupt has an hundred creditors and that by a dexterity of manoeuvring, he forces ninety-nine of them to pay out of their own funds the whole sum due to the odd one. This is exactly what the new government has done, and what Theodore Sedgwick pretends to call *the preservation of public faith.*

James T. Callender, *Sedgwick & Co., or A Key to the Six Per Cent Cabinet* (Philadelphia, 1798), 16, 29. See also: Anon., *An Examination of the Late Proceedings of Congress Respecting the Official Conduct of the Secretary of the Treasury* (n.p., n.d.), 26fn.; John Wood, *History of the Administration of John Adams, esq.* . . . (New York, 1802), 182; and Claude G. Bowers, *Jefferson and Hamilton: The Struggle for Democracy in America* (Boston, 1925), 50.

11. For a rather different appraisal, see the incisive if harsh analysis of Hamilton's Financial System by Joseph Charles in "The Origins of the American Party System," *William and Mary Quarterly*, 3d Series, XII (1955), 241–244.

tent, the "original" Federalists; combined a part of them with certain of the vanishing Anti-Federalists, 1787–1788 variety; and began the congressional and national cleavage which would eventuate in the years 1795–1798 in the creation of the Republican-Democratic party and the two party system.

Sedgwick was most intolerant of Madison's behavior. Madison had turned traitor to the forces of reason and virtue. It was "the more astonishing that Mr. M. who was the author of the address of 1783 . . . in which the doctrine of discrimination is reprobated in pointed and unequivocal language, should now take ground so entirely different." [12] Nor were even the social amenities kept up in anything like a wholehearted spirit, as Sedgwick sorrowfully informed his wife:

> When I made my appearance in the house every member with an appearance of cordiality bid me welcome excepting only my once friend Mr. M—— He did not deign to come nigh me, and it was not untill friday . . . when I met him in a narrow passage where he could not avoid it without indecency that he condescended to take me by the hand.[13]

This latter description, however, was written after the debate over federal assumption of state debts. Compared with the ferocity of this debate the discussion on the funding bill was but a teapot tempest.

The federal assumption of all unpaid debts incurred by the individual states in prosecution of the war was, if debated separately, an integral part of Hamilton's funding plan. The state creditors in question were to look to the national government for payment, bringing additional reinforcement from the propertied classes to the support of that government, and, consequently, strengthening its prestige and authority. By Hamilton's estimate, $25,000,000 worth of unpaid, war-incurred state debts were to be assumed—a sum later arbitrarily reduced to $21,500,-000. A loan would be issued to which individual state creditors might subscribe, giving in payment certificates and notes which they held against their state governments. The states would cease to be debtors to their individual citizens, but would have the amount assumed listed as a debit in their account with the national government. Four-ninths of the new stock issue was to draw interest at six per cent, as of January 1, 1792; one-third at three per cent, also as of January 1, 1792; and two-ninths at six per cent, as of January 1, 1801.

Sedgwick had favored assumption since at least as early as the winter

12. Sedgwick to Peter Van Schaack, February 13, 1790. *S.P.*, M.H.S.
13. December 26, 1790. *S.P.*, M.H.S.

of 1789. He had written his good friend Caleb Davis a letter in August of that year which clearly foreshadowed the line of argument which he would utilize six months later:

Eventually all the state debts *which were contracted for national purposes,* must be assumed by the general government. Otherwise I cannot conceive how we shall ever become truly and in fact a nation. What more just, equal and liberal than all the expence incurred for the attainment of a general purpose should become a general charge. . . . What more wise than in this instance to consider the state legislatures as the agents and factors for the joint concern? and what more candid than to suppose that in their respective negotiations they conducted fairly and honorably? [14]

Sedgwick was an *aide-de-camp* to Hamilton in this business, but his was an obedience which was the result of profound conviction and a strong appreciation that his beloved Massachusetts was suffering greatly from her burden of debt.

Never conspicuous as one who could view both sides of a question, Sedgwick quite failed to comprehend the disapproval of assumption by many congressmen.[15] Quite understandably, states such as Virginia, Maryland, and Georgia which had paid much of their debt were not eager to be taxed to pay that of Massachusetts, Connecticut, South Carolina, or others similarly situated. It would be another chance for the speculators to make huge profit and gain an undue influence over the government. The North, which had the free capital with which to engage in speculation, would grab up all the certificates of all the states and wax ever more prosperous and influential at the expense of the other sections.

Sedgwick, one of the more eloquent and certainly the most loquacious of administration supporters, would have none of these arguments. Appealing to the hearts as well as the minds of the devil-tainted faction, he asked them to remember the glories and troubles that were Massachusetts'. Shays' Rebellion, he declared, was directly caused by the heavy taxation necessary to satisfy creditors of a debt incurred by Massachu-

14. August 9, 1789. *Caleb Davis Papers,* XVI (1789), M.H.S.

15. Madison wavered between outright opposition to assumption and advocacy of a plan whereby the federal government would assume the debts of the states as they had stood in 1783—prior to the successful efforts of such states as Virginia to liquidate a large part of their debt. *Annals,* II, 1407. Madison's speech of April 22, 1790, perhaps the most able of the anti-assumption pronouncements, Sedgwick declared "composed of unfounded facts, monstrous premises, and inconclusive deductions." *Lloyd's Debates* (May 25, 1790), as quoted by Rives, *Madison,* III, 108 fn.

setts for national purposes. That debt had been created with the utmost economy and was held by its original holders, men by whose exertion in the hour of danger the liberties of the nation had been preserved. The creditors of the states had a claim on the honor and justice of Congress.

He ridiculed the argument that the assumption of state debts would undermine the independence and importance of the state sovereignties. A heavy debt and the resulting tax burden were not engines necessary to the energy or popularity of a government. Federal assumption was certainly constitutional. Was not Congress authorized to levy money in all instances where the expenditure should be for "the general welfare"? "If prudence, policy, and justice dictated the assumption" of state debts, and it did, then "it must be for the general welfare that they should be assumed." It would be of general advantage to the nation to set the various states once more upon their feet.

Cutting short a possible move to delay action until the complex accounts between each state and the federal government had been settled, Sedgwick insisted that it was most important that private and public claims for justice be not confused. The equalization and balancing of cross-claims between the nation and the states would be a long and difficult affair and would not serve the individual creditor. Assumption *would* directly benefit the needy private citizen, and would, moreover, actually facilitate the eventual settlement of federal-state accounts by removing one of the main obstacles in the execution of that business.

He asked his colleagues to pause and reflect on the causes which had produced a variation in the size of the debts of the thirteen states. The variation was chiefly the result of differences in exertion and differences in the profits derived from confiscation of Tory property and acquisition of western territory. Against whom, he demanded, did active Loyalists offend? Against the united colonies, surely. Why then should the forfeit of their property accrue solely to the benefit of the state in which it happened to lay? For example, New York, which neither "commenced, prosecuted, nor concluded" the war, became heir to large amounts of property with which to cancel much of her debt, thanks largely to the exertions of noble Massachusetts. Similarly, Virginia came into the possession of much western land with which to expunge most of her debt because of national efforts expended under national direction. Everyone knew this, and if the unfortunate states who did not happen to fall heir to large quantities of confiscated property or western lands were left to support their burdens of debt unaided, they would consider themselves invidiously discriminated against. Many of the citizens of these states would emigrate to escape the necessarily high tax levies, leaving an ever larger load to be borne by those who remained behind. A spirit of hostility between states so situated and the national government must be the result. They would naturally be unwilling to see the national government lay impost and excise taxes, and they would demand the right to levy such taxes themselves as their only means of making payment on their debt. In such an event, interstate commerce would be in as chaotic a condition at it was under the Confederation, and the Union would soon be splintered beyond repair.

On the other hand, the advantages of assumption were obvious. It would make the national government the center of the affections of the people. The encouragement it would afford to every useful improvement and occupation would so increase the wealth of the country that its cost would be easily absorbed. By relieving the states of much of their heavy burden of debt, assumption would give state securities a fixed value, and they could serve as an approved medium of exchange. The stability and reputation of all American securities would be enhanced, in consequence. Relieved of their onerous burdens, the states would be able to attend to the improvement of their internal police and to other true concerns of state sovereignty. We would be, in short, a great, a flourishing, a happy people.[16]

Sedgwick's entire attitude with regard to assumption was that of a man with a cause, an attitude of virtual dedication. As is often the case, this led him to confuse honest opposition with malignant enmity,[17] and to excesses, generally. Perhaps the least excusable of these was his statement that he would rather see the debt completely ignored than have only that part of it funded which was "denominated as national." The plan to fund the national debt had been accepted in principle before the

16. *Annals,* II, 1333–1338 (February 24, 1790).

17. Sedgwick wrote of Madison:
   He is an apostate from all his former principles. Whether he is really a convert to anti-federalism—whether he is actuated by the mean and base motives of acquiring popularity in his own state that he may fill the place of Senator . . . or whether he means to put himself at the head of the discontented in America time will discover. The last, however, I do not suspect, because I have ever considered him as a very timid man. Deprived of his aid the party will be weak and inefficient. Sedgwick to Pamela, March 4, 1790. *S.P., M.H.S.*

   Sedgwick had to admit that his own opponents were somewhat more charitable. He wrote his wife that the papers in Virginia were paying much attention to his conduct in the House, and went on to say: "I am told however that the writers have invariably treated me with respect and that their strictures have been conveyed in decent language." Sedgwick to Pamela, May 17, 1790. *S.P., M.H.S.*

topic of assumption came before the House, and Sedgwick had surely worked ardently in its behalf. So strongly did he feel about the plight of Massachusetts, however, that in certain rash moments he swore to vote against the whole program if it failed to include assumption.[18] Similarly he threatened to oppose any excise on distilled spirits if assumption were defeated, warning that if the citizens of Massachusetts were not relieved of their present burden the least Congress could do was not add to the load.

These blustering threats were probably but a means of emotional re-release and intimidation. More important were his efforts to keep the majority united and bring the all-necessary Pennsylvania delegation in line. Without the support of the Pennsylvanians, assumption could not pass. These gentlemen outraged Sedgwick as they wavered from side to side. He declared that they agreed to the policy and justice of the measure but were miserably influenced by its possible effect on their popularity back home. Very discouraging to Sedgwick was the disagreement in Massachusetts itself over the desirabillty of allowing the federal government to relieve the General Court of the worry of a large debt and a dreaded land tax which that debt might well entail. A few holders of state paper were afraid they would be disowned by the state only to be ignored by their new debtor, the national government. Others feared a loss of state independence and a final and irrevocable loss of authority to levy any impositions on imported articles.[19]

The great majority of Bay Staters favored assumption, however, and Sedgwick's friends in the General Court, working hard and successfully to postpone the laying of any new taxes that might conflict with concurrent federal taxing powers, kept the Berkshire congressman in close touch with the situation in Boston. They advised that Massachusetts would be most intractable in its demands for unhindered revenue collection and in its reluctance to support Hamilton's expensive national militia project if there was no federal "accumulation of the debt." Samuel Henshaw, Thomas Dwight, and others finally succeeded in having the General Court pass, by a large majority, a resolution instructing the national representatives from Massachusetts strongly to support federal assumption of state debts. This resolution was sent to Ames, Goodhue, Sedgwick and Company by Governor Hancock on June 4, 1790. The Massachusetts delegation gracefully acknowledged this letter and ex-

18. Sedgwick to Henry Van Schaack, January 31, 1790, Sedgwick to Pamela, March 4, 1790, S.P., M.H.S.

19. See *Lycurgus'* running debate with anti-assumptionist *Cornelius* in *The Western Star*, during the month of April, 1790.

pressed great satisfaction that their conduct was supported by the declared sentiments of the state legislature. They assured Governor Hancock that they would continue their unremitting exertions while there was any prospect of success whatsoever. They explained that though the House had passed a bill for the funding of the national debt without assumption, they were informed that an attempt would be made in the Senate to attach a rider specifying the assumption of state debts. They would bide their time until the success of that effort was ascertained.[20]

Sedgwick was not entirely pleased with the resolution of the General Court, as he deprecated any attempt by home forces to control a national congressman. He feared that if the Massachusetts representatives appeared to need instructions from their state legislature, the anti-assumption delegations might ask to postpone all further consideration of the measure until they, too, had received word from home. Still, he appreciated that his friends had meant well and so forgave their impetuosity.

By the time Sedgwick had received the "sentiments" of the Massachusetts legislature, he had sounded the depths of depression and was only then beginning to regain his faith in the honor and humanity of a majority of the House of Representatives. On April 12, 1790, the assumption bill had come up for a vote in the House of Representatives and had been defeated, 31–29. Pennsylvania's Senator Maclay, who had gone over to the House to witness the event, described Sedgwick's reaction to the vote: "Sedgwick . . . pronounced a funeral oration over it. He was called to order . . . he took his hat and went out. When he returned, his visage bore the visable marks of weeping." [21] This "funeral oration" was unquestionably one of Sedgwick's more histrionic performances during his twelve years in Congress:

> I now consider the question of assumption as ultimately negatived. . . . We [the people of Massachusetts] have demanded justice; we have implored the compassion of the Representatives of the people of America, to relieve us from the pressure of intolerable burdens; burdens incurred in support of your freedom and independence. . . . Exertions and services which were then acknowledged; and however they may be now forgotten, or disregarded here, believe me they will long be remembered within [Massachusetts].

20. Massachusetts Congressmen to Governor Hancock, June 8, 1790. *MSS.* Collection, Boston Athenaeum.

21. William Maclay, *Sketches of Debate in the First Senate of the United States 1789–90–91,* George W. Harris, ed. (Harrisburg, 1880), 194 (April 12, 1790).

. . . was she less frugal? It is not pretended. Does it not then follow, irresistably, that the excess of her debt must have been contracted for national purposes? Is there any one who supposes what they denominate the national debt, can be securely funded, without invading those objects of revenue, which are now appropriated for the support of public credit in that State? Can it be believed that the Government or the people there will voluntarily submit to sacrifice the interests of twenty thousand men, who adventured their lives and estates in the common cause? . . . The offer of justice . . . [is] little more than the pretence on the one side, and I can assure gentlemen is felt to be a little less than a mockery on the other. . . . I express directly the purpose for which I rose, which was to warn, solemnly warn, gentlemen of the dangerous consequences in the progress of this business of invading those funds which are preoccupied by that State. Let them . . . see whether without . . . [some] violent and unjust invasion it will be practicable to procure the necessary objects of revenue.[22]

While Sedgwick was declaiming in the above manner he was interrupted at one point by southern congressmen Page and Jackson, who demanded that he be called to order and reminded him of the great impropriety of these "passionate remonstrances" against the actions and motives of Congress. Sedgwick's allies countered with cries of "Let him speak!", and Sedgwick was allowed to intone his oration to its end. This speech offered perhaps little that was new or valuable to the discussion, but his outright threat that Massachusetts would now insist at all costs on uninhibited taxing power created something of a sensation.[23] Sedgwick, indeed, seems to have been accepted by the anti-Hamiltonians as a virtual symbol of all the "speculating and self-interested" assumptionists. A contributor to the *New York Journal*, describing the birth of the "brat" assumption, had sneered:

Mr. Sedgwick, who is gifted with canting talents, officiated as priest, baptized the infant, and his name stands on the parish books as Al-ex-der Assumption. The Methodists have reason to regret, that politics engross the talents, and that forensic eloquence employs the sing-song voice of the priest, who [would] have been as [a] *shining candlestick* on the altar and a leader of the canting tribe, and the champion of *Moorfields*. He finished this joyous ceremony by a long

22. *Annals*, II, 1525–1526.
23. Albert J. Beveridge in his study of John Marshall indicates that Sedgwick threatened secession at this time. If he did, it was but the hasty outburst of a defeated politician; for there never was any secessionist plot to which Sedgwick was a party. *Life of John Marshall* (Boston, 1919), III, 97.

Presbyterian prayer.—He invited all the blessings of heaven on this unfortunate illegitimate.—He solemnly invoked all his vengeance against any one who should hurt the hair of its head.[24]

Another humorist of sorts, writing to a friend, and metaphorizing assumption as a young lady, now described what was thought to be her demise with an equal emphasis on the prominence of Sedgwick:

> Last Monday Mr. Sedgwick delivered a funeral oration on the death of Miss Assumption. . . . Her death was much lamented by her parents who were from New England. Mr. Sedgwick being the most celebrated preacher was requested to deliver her funeral eulogium. It was done with puritanic gravity. . . . Mrs. Speculator was the chief mourner, and acted her part to admiration. She being the mother of Miss Assumption who was the hope of her family. . . . Mrs. Excise may have cause to rejoice, because she will be screened from much drudgery—as she must have been the principal support for Miss Assumption, as well as of her mother and all her relations.[25]

However typical and important Sedgwick might have been in the battle for assumption, the disillusioning fact remains that the measure chiefly succeeded not through the persuasiveness of its supporters' arguments but through the bargaining skill of Alexander Hamilton. There still remains some doubt as to the exact agreement, motives, and position of all concerned, but the net result was that certain southerners, friends of Secretary of State Jefferson, changed their votes on assumption in return for the acquisition of the necessary votes to locate the "permanent" capital on the Potomac River, after a ten-year stay in Philadelphia.

The "residency question" had dogged the assumption debate since its start. Sedgwick, personally, saw no reason to move from New York, but, though "shocked" at times by the base intrigues of the Pennsylvanians and the "Potomach men," never for a moment confused the relative magnitude of the residency and assumption issues. The latter was the major consideration that must be kept in mind at all times. It was not Sedgwick's way, however, to neglect the dissemination of his opinion, whatever the relative importance of an issue. Back in the autumn of the previous year he had expressed sharp disapproval of any scheme which would give the nation a southern capital, either tempo-

24. Quoted by the *Columbian Centinel* of June 19, 1790.
Fisher Ames wrote Timothy Dwight that Sedgwick had become a "perfect slave to the business." Seth Ames, ed., *Works of Fisher Ames.* . . . (Boston, 1854), I, 80.
25. *Gazette of the United States* (New York), June 2, 1790, published this letter of April 14, 1790 date, but without naming its writer or Virginian recipient.

rarily or permanently. In a speech that goes far to explain why Sedgwick was a favorite object of dislike for many southern congressmen, he had lashed out at those favoring a southern, even a Philadelphia, location:

> I believe that the true interest of the country will be best answered by taking a position eastward and northward of the Susquehanna. . . . the centre and influence of the government ought to incline to that part where [are] the sources of that energy which is the best security of the Government.
>
> The Susquehanna is, in my opinion, south-west of the centre of wealth, population, and resources of every kind. I would beg leave, gentlemen, to suggest another idea. In my view, on the principles of population, the Susquehanna is far beyond the centre; for I do not think it just, on this subject to take the constitutional computation. Will any gentleman pretend, that men, who are merely the subject of property or wealth, should be taken into the estimate; that the slaves of the country, men who have no rights to protect (being deprived of them all,) should be taken into view, in determining the centre of government? If they were considered, gentlemen might as well estimate the black cattle of New England.[26]

Sedgwick at no time wished to adventure further south than the eastern bank of the Susquehanna in search of a permanent residence and until suitable buildings could be erected in a permanent capital desired to remain in New York. He was gradually forced to the realization, though, that compromise, however distasteful, was sometimes necessary. Sedgwick apprised his wife-confidante of necessity's progress and gave an amusing description of a political cartoon of the day:

> For some time the citizens [of New York] have been in violent agitation on account of the proposed removal of Congress from this place to Philadelphia. the event has become probable from a coalition between the Pennsylvanians and the southern members. [There] is a caricature print designed . . . which is to present Mr. Morris [Senator Robert Morris, the Philadelphia financier] with the federal building on his shoulders. . . . The senators it should seem roused by the motion of the building are looking out of the windows and perceiving the cause they exclaim, "where are you going to carry us Robert?" He answers by a label "where ever I please." —In the back ground are represented the members of the house of Representatives with myself in front. These words are put into my mouth. "Stop Robert you rascal and take my assumption with you." To which he answers, "I'll be d—nd if I do." [27]

26. *Annals*, I, 847 (September 3, 1789).
27. July 4, 1790. *S.P.*, M.H.S.

Assumption was, however, given the necessary transportation. Sedgwick was undoubtedly conversant with the Hamilton-Jefferson bargain, and definitely considered the southern victory on capital residence a relatively small price to pay for the blessed resurrection of Miss Assumption. Supporting this judgment is a brief note to Pamela, July 13, 1790, in which he wrote:

> I was against the introduction of it [the question of "residence"], never retarded its progress, and indeed believed and do still believe that any determination is preferable to the state the government was in. Indeed I am not greatly dissatisfied with the result. . . .
> Today the question was put in the senate on the assumption and carried 14 against 12.[28]

The assumption measure returned to the House after its success in the Senate and edged its way past that body by a vote of 32–29, despite a last-ditch stand by Georgia's Representative Jackson.

The primary credit for this feat goes to Chief of Staff Hamilton,[29] but Sedgwick and other tireless field officers contributed a definite service.[30] Sedgwick, in particular, received much honor in his own country for the part he had played and was at this time, perhaps, as popular with his constituents as he would be until the XYZ Affair of 1798. *The Western Star* of Stockbridge declared that the "unwearied and persevering attention and patriotic exertions" of Sedgwick were positively instrumental in the "grateful passage" of assumption.[31] Nor were his political colleagues less generous in their praise. George Benson, an administration supporter from Rhode Island, declared that by their part in the assumption debate Sedgwick and Fisher Ames had the most "Distinguished Claim to the exalted Character of Enlightened, and Eloquent Statesmen." Sedgwick's sentiments and language had been such that they "should be recorded in 'Letters of Gold'—tho' they are more indelibly engraven on the grateful hearts of the numerous State Creditors, where they will erect a Monument to your Fame" that would be

28. July 13, 1790. *S.P.*, M.H.S. See, too, Sedgwick to Pamela, July 1, 1790, *Ibid.*

29. Irving Brant in the third volume of his brilliant biography of James Madison states that Madison saved the Hamiltonian financial system from destruction at the hands of its supposed friends by accepting assumption "as the extorted price of national safety." This picture of Madison as the true hero in the rehabilitation of American finance is possibly more provocative than convincing. *James Madison Father of the Constitution 1787–1800* (New York, 1950), 318.

30. Sedgwick wrote Pamela, June 24, 1790: "The whole business to be transacted out of doors . . . [has] been in my management." *S.P.*, M.H.S.

31. August 24, 1790. See also a letter from a Hampshire gentleman in the issue of September 28, 1790.

standing long after "Statues and Triumphal Arches, shall moulder in the Dust." [32]

The general approval that met Sedgwick and his Bay State colleagues on their return home is suggestive of the motivation of their actions. Theirs was not a personally selfish position—though they undoubtedly gladly saw their own individual state tax load lightened—rather they were moved in the assumption as well as in the funding debate by sectional economic considerations, and by a sincere conviction that what was best for the public creditors and taxpayers of Massachusetts was best for the country as a whole.

By September of 1790 the fiscal program submitted by Hamilton to Congress some eight months earlier had been, with slight modification, completely accepted. Its main features were the funding of the national domestic debt; the assumption of the unpaid, war-incurred state debts; and the authorization of a loan of $12,000,000 to be applied to the foreign debt. By these measures, largely encompassed by the omnibus fiscal act of August, 1790, the national credit was restored, James Madison was separated from the Federalists of 1787, and Alexander Hamilton achieved the position of near-premier in the government of the new nation.

All of these effects were furthered by the passage of the national bank act and the excise bill. Sedgwick was happy to promote this result. The debate over these acts made additionally clear his role and significance as the opponent of Madison, as the lieutenant of Hamilton.

Sedgwick, like Hamilton, considered the project of a national bank as necessary to the completion of the Hamiltonian fiscal structure and to the collection of the revenue. Madison considered it an unconstitutional project that was primarily designed to give further aid and comfort to the speculator.[33] Sedgwick as a "broad constructionist" was most impatient with Madison's narrow interpretation of the Constitution. If we go one way, he complained, "our ears are assailed with the exclamation of 'the Constitution is in danger!' if we attempt to obtain our objects by a different course, we are told the pass is guarded by the stern spirit of

32. Benson to Sedgwick, May 21, 1790. *S.P.*, M.H.S.

33. Sedgwick was personally never a stockholder in the Bank of the United States as best as can be discovered. Jefferson, however, believed him to be such. See list of "paper men" sent Jefferson by John Beckley, *Jefferson Papers*, LXXXII, #14, 232, Library of Congress. This is included in Jefferson's notes of 2–31 March, 1793, in which he analyzes the motives of the congressmen who opposed Giles' Resolutions and virtually admits sponsorship of those resolutions.

democracy." Construction and implication were necessary exercises in the operation of any governmental system. "The whole business of legislation was a practical construction of the powers of the Legislature." It was universally agreed that "wherever a power is delegated for express purposes, all the known and usual means for the attainment of the objects expressed are conceded also." Why didn't the gentleman from Virginia see the danger of "implied powers" when the matter of allowing the President to remove officeholders at will was under discussion? Mr. Madison had favored "construction" on that occasion; for surely the President was not *expressly* granted that power.

The Constitution gave Congress certain express powers and also the right to employ all the known and usual means "necessary and proper" to effectuate their stated ends. What did the words "necessary and proper" mean? They did not mean that the legislature was restricted to enacting such laws only as were absolutely *indispensable* to the execution of the expressed powers. Rather they meant that the legislature should employ those means which would effect the ends expressed in the Constitution with the greatest possible degree of public utility. The matter under discussion was a case in point. Banks were among the known and usual means to effect and facilitate the power to tax, the power to borrow money, the power to raise an army, etc.

Banks were especially important to a young nation like our own. The disparity between the commercial enterprise of our merchants and the size of their capital required that all steps possible be taken to utilize what metallic currency we had to the fullest extent, and to limit any large-scale exportation of it. A bank was needed whose paper could circulate throughout the entire country, and that bank should be one in which the national government had an interest. Did anyone really want the financial health of the federal government to depend on an institution over which it had no control?

He had heard it said that the provision to accept government securities in payment of bank stock would give unfair advantage to fundholders and that certain terms gave prospect of unduly large benefits for the bank stockholders. "He would leave this part of the subject to gentlemen who better understood it; only observing, that as the Government must rely principally on merchants to obtain the proposed stock, it would be necessary to afford to them sufficient motives to withdraw from their commercial pursuits a part of their capitals." [34]

Sedgwick seems not to have sensed the historic importance of the

34. *Annals*, II, 1910–1912 (February 4, 1791).

bank debate, but he offered a concise and compelling argument for the
necessity of construing broadly a brief and generally worded frame of
government, if one was not to stunt the growth and damage the spirit of
that document.[35] When the incorporation bill passed, February 8, 1791,
by a vote of 39–20, he declared that all "right thinking" men were to be
congratulated.

The Hamiltonian program, it was agreed by its opponents and supporters, required additional revenue for its operation. How was it to be
obtained? Declaring that most of the customs receipts would be de-
voured by the ordinary expenses of government, Theodore Sedgwick,
from a committee appointed for that purpose, reported a bill proposing
heavy duties (averaging seven per cent of total value) on distilled and
other spirits. Previously duties had been imposed on imported distilled
spirits, which duties were now increased, but the tax here proposed
was to be a revenue-raising duty on all liquor distilled within the
country. Madison, though favoring the bill as a matter of fiscal necessity,
sharply opposed it "on principle." Sedgwick favored it wholeheartedly
but as a revenue, not a temperance, measure. He was not influenced, he
declared, by "considerations of morality." He insisted that there was no
discrimination in the measure against the poor man, as had been
alleged; nor was it really an excise. It was but the tapping of excess
income, and excess income—that "amount which was left after a man
had paid the cost of living expected of him in his state in his community"
—not property, capital, or income *per se,* was the proper target for
internal taxation. Liquor purchases most always derived from excess
income. There was no thought of using military force in the collection
of these duties, nor would there be any need to; for it would not be

35. One of the least tasteful aspects of the bank bill fight was the way in which
certain of Sedgwick's friends turned against Washington when it appeared he would
veto the measure. Sedgwick did not participate in their pettish behavior, but neither
does he seem to have criticized it. Sedgwick declared he hoped Washington would
"be more discreet" than to veto such a vital measure. Sedgwick to Ephraim Williams,
February 23, 1791. S.P., M.H.S.

Aaron Burr, recently elected senator from New York, questioned the actual
necessity of the bank bill, but agreed with Sedgwick's analysis of the temperamental
differences between northern and southern congressmen: "The Pacific and Compliant
temper of the northern States, contrasted with the turbulence and Discontent of
the Southern had struck me as a fact, but till invited by your hint, I had not attempted to trace the Causes or Conjecture the remote Consequences." Burr to
Sedgwick, February 3, 1791. S.P., M.H.S. Sedgwick was inclined to believe that
anyone foolish enough to oppose the bank bill must suffer from temperamental instability at least.

attended "with any sensible inconvenience" for any consumer-citizen. A direct tax or a stamp tax might irritate, but not a patently necessary measure such as this.[36] Mr. Madison's worries were quite without cause. It was really shocking the way the South was "constantly hanging on our shirts and embarrassing every important measure," while all the time half the expenses of government were for the protection of the southern frontier.[37]

The manner in which certain of the southern states expressed their opposition to the excise bill especially irritated the Berkshire representative. North Carolina and Maryland had adopted "some angry resolves" and Virginia had had the temerity to send a circular address to all the states "instructing them in their political duties." Though Sedgwick was sure such unwarranted interference would "make no impression on my nerves," it was distracting to the Union, and he hoped Washington's prospective southern tour would restore good humor to citizens below the Potomac. He doubted it, however, for he felt economic troubles—the debts they owed foreign merchants, the smallness of their holding in public securities, their extravagance—lay at the bottom of their vagaries in the excise discussion as elsewhere.[38]

As Sedgwick's nationalism was often marred by regional bias, so, too, was it often supplemented by a sincere concern for constitutional rights and due process. He had a profound respect for the law and for legality. This was exhibited during his second year in Congress by his seemingly contradictory efforts to protect the Quakers' right of petition and the constitutional guarantees of their enemies, the slaveholders.

The Quaker societies of the Middle States petitioned in February, 1790, for the taxation and strict regulation of the African slave trade by Congress. Many southerners, though not Madison, insisted that this "insulting" paper should not even be received. Sedgwick and the ma-

36. *Annals*, II, 1849–1850 (January 6, 1791). The Whisky Rebellion would disprove this bit of optimistic prophecy.

Sedgwick helped defeat a proposal which would have prevented excise inspectors from participating in elections. This would degrade the office, he insisted; there was absolutely no need "to translate" the corrupt maxims of Britain here.

37. Sedgwick to Ephraim Williams, January 9, 1791. *S.P.*, M.H.S.

38. *Ibid.*

jority insisted that the House follow a course of respect for decent petitions. If he privately thought the commotion created over this matter rather foolish, he appreciated that a threat to the historic right of petition was in no sense ridiculous.[39]

The Quakers, he suggested, were good, respectable people who had come forward and properly suggested that Congress might effect two objects by the exercise of a constitutional authority which would give great satisfaction. On the one hand revenue would be gained and on the other a practice productive of great evil restrained. Didn't the Quakers have a right as citizens to give their opinion of public measures? No state need be alarmed, surely, from a mere commitment of the petition. Their representatives in Congress would never violate their rights by an exercise of unconstitutional authority.[40]

Savior of Mumbet and a member of Franklin's Abolition Society of Pennsylvania from October, 1792, until his death, Sedgwick was no friend of Slavery, but if he did not sympathize with the guarantees afforded that institution by the Constitution, he was prepared to respect and obey them. It was Sedgwick, as chairman of the committee appointed for the purpose, who virtually authored the first Fugitive Slave Law (November, 1791).

Sedgwick was during the First Congress a good "administration man." There were no parties then, but certain men were known as probable supporters and others as probable opponents of the administration. More than seventy-five per cent of the votes cast by Sedgwick were in support of administration policy, and on virtually every major item of legislative business he was to be found in firm agreement with Washington and Hamilton.

This "steadiness" entitled Sedgwick to Washington's friendship and gracious regard. Sedgwick saw "the Great Man" quite regularly, tactfully suggesting possible appointments to office,[41] enthusiastically agreeing that the national happiness was inextricably associated with the national virtue,[42] and solicitously inquiring for the President's state of

39. Sedgwick to Ephraim Williams, January 16, 1791, Sedgwick to Pamela, February 20, 1791, S.P., M.H.S.

40. *Annals*, II, 1187–1188 (February 11, 1790).

41. A herd of candidates for government office converged on New York at this time. Sedgwick was cautious in aiding their respective claims, but did recommend several, such as John Fenno as "printer to the Executive." Sedgwick did not entirely approve of Washington's policy of retaining Confederation officeholders whenever possible, feeling that many were "dead wood."

42. See Sedgwick to Pamela, July 21; August 8, 1789. S.P., M.H.S.

health.[43] May, 1790, was an especially trying time on the latter score. The President was "amasiated" from the disorder of pleurisy, and at five o'clock on the afternoon of May 15 "the physician declared that they had no hopes of his recovery. But about six he began to sweat most peacefully." [44] It was a relieved and grateful Sedgwick who, tired of the heat of the city and the "numerous company" at his tavern residence, took a short journey with friends to the Passaic Falls in New Jersey. He found the "exchange of the poluted air of the city for the sweet fragrance of the country . . . the enchanting music of the birds, the prospect of well cultivated fields and the good humour of the company" most salutary.[45]

If New York had proven both hot and costly, Sedgwick did not at first find Philadelphia any great improvement when Congress established itself there in December, 1790. He was, however, delighted to find that the move had not resulted in any increase of southern influence,[46] and soon, what with the receipt of "many kind attentions" from the ladies of the Quaker metropolis, he became more than reconciled to the new capital. There was Mr. Peale's American Museum to entertain him, highly interesting with its exhibits of a shark's jawbone and the "skins of beasts, & birds, minerals, fossils, coins, shells, insects, moss & dirt," even if its owner, "one of those virtuosi," was a rather poor creature. He could witness a fine showing of *The Taming of the Shrew*, browse about a library of over ten thousand books, or simply enjoy the neat charm of the city. Sedgwick sent Pamela his "considered impression" of Philadelphia and its citizens:

This place is large, handsomely laid out, the streets every where

43. When Sedgwick had first arrived in New York in 1789, Washington had been seriously ill with "the anthrax." He had recovered quickly, however, and Sedgwick had had the pleasure of attending the President's first levee, where he was most graciously and particularly noticed:

He did me the honor particularly to distinguish me, with great cordiality took me by the hand, and expressed much satisfaction to see me here. He is very peculiarly qualifyed to shine in his exalted station [;] he has a personal dignity I have not seen in any other man, while the unaffected simplicity of his manners makes one easy in his presence. A recollection of his meritorious virtues, and the obligations they have laid one under, excite a pleasing sensation of gratitude difficult to describe.

Sedgwick to Pamela, July 10, 1789, *S.P.*, M.H.S.
44. Sedgwick to Pamela, May 16, 1790. *S.P.*, M.H.S.
45. Sedgwick to Pamela, June 14, 1790. *S.P.*, M.H.S.
46. This, he said, much irritated Mr. Jefferson. Sedgwick to Pamela, February [?], 1791. *S.P.*, M.H.S.

intersecting each other at right angles. There is a universal appearance of richness, the streets excellently paved, and on each side with bricks for foot passengers. . . . The citizens seem very plain and simple in their manners, and affect a stately distance in their intercourse with strangers. In their Economy they are . . . frugal, and in their business industrious. They believe themselves to be the first people in America. . . .

As to the relative improvements in the arts [between Philadelphia and New England] my knowledge is incompetent to form an opinion, but in point of polished manners, they are certainly in a grade vastly below the inhabitants of Boston. Since I have got into lodgings I have been treated by the citizens with great and studied attention.[47]

Sedgwick's first lodgings in Philadelphia were with five other congressmen in a rooming house near Federal Hall, but as three of these fellow lodgers were enemies of the fiscal measures of Hamilton and two, Gilman of New Hampshire and Williamson of North Carolina, not "even gentlemen," Sedgwick found the situation impossible. He left to board in the private home of Dr. and Mrs. Jackson, friends of Pamela's. There he spent many agreeable evenings, playing with the young children of the household and occasionally interrupting the preparation of his speeches to enjoy a glass of the Doctor's "splendid Madeira."

His days were usually full and his schedule crowded. Congress met at ten and seldom adjourned until four. There were Vermont's commissioners to see or committee meetings of one sort or another to attend. There were gay balls and formal routs, and there were the levees of President Washington where Sedgwick pridefully paid court. At the time of the residency debate, Sedgwick had briefly fallen from favor by his opposition to the Potomac location,[48] but by the time Martha Washington was settled in Philadelphia, Sedgwick was once again *persona grata*. Washington signalled full restoration of confidence by drinking his health in a significant and "perticular manner." Sedgwick was on several occasions given the honor post at the head of Washington's table, where the President never placed himself, and at least once was privileged to stay and hear Nelly Custis, Mrs. Washington's grandchild, play several selections on the pianoforte.[49]

47. January 9, 1791. *S.P.*, M.H.S.

48. Washington greatly favored a southern capital; Sedgwick suggested that Washington wished to have the government located in Alexandria, "contiguous to which is his estate." Sedgwick to Ephraim Williams, January 24, 1791. *S.P.*, M.H.S.

49. Certain aspects of the President's Birthday Ball, however, he did find a bit strange:

Sedgwick was on excellent terms, too, with the second executive of the nation, Vice-President John Adams—a man with whom he would quarrel fiercely seven years later. They had at this time a very cordial regard for one another, and Sedgwick would sometimes ride out to Richmond Hill and have breakfast with Adams and his wife Abigail, "one of the most excellent of women."

Social engagements with Alexander Hamilton were relatively infrequent. It was Hamilton, however, whom Sedgwick viewed and admired as the most brilliant figure of the Administration and it was Hamilton whom he would gladly defend against all opponents of that Administration.

---

49. (cont.)

In the evening was a very crowded and brilliant assembly at which I was present. . . . When the president entered the assembly, the tune called his march struck up, and he was saluted with three Huzzas. A ceremony more proper in my opinion for savages than the first citizens of the first city in America. . . . The picture of the President, in which he is represented trampling under his feet a british standard . . . was procured for the occasion. . . . There were present several british officers, and I could not but notice there [*sic*] frequently directing their view that way.

Sedgwick to Pamela, February 23, 1791. *S.P.*, M.H.S.

VIII

A Charter Federalist: Congressman
Sedgwick, 1791–1793

*The Opposition has been as busy as the Devil in a gale
of wind.*   Theodore Sedgwick [1]

THEODORE SEDGWICK was elected to the Second Congress by a large
and satisfying majority. The forty-four year old congressman made little
attempt to hide his pleasure. He would return to Philadelphia as a figure
respected by some and familiar to all. His haughty and commanding
manner, his periodic eloquence and acknowledged skill in debate assured his prominence if not his popularity. Though not, in fact, either a
major political leader or a policy maker, he was recognized as a confidant
of the great and a hard-working and influential component of the Federal régime. He was typical in motives and opinions of the majority of
both houses who supported that régime.

He was typical, too, in yet another way. As an organizer of a political
machine in western Massachusetts that operated to gain support for
"Federal men and measures," he was one with other supporters of
the Washington Administration who sought to secure their local pre-
eminence as they sought to insure the energy and success of the national government. Sedgwick, with many of his colleagues in the House,
was a Federalist politician before the formal birth of the Federalist
party. By the time that party would take concrete shape, many of the
local organizations that would furnish its membership had already
formed under the careful tutelage of such charter Federalists as Theodore Sedgwick.

Sedgwick's prominence in the Second Congress as a supporter of the
Federal régime saw him assume the role of administration "work-horse."

1. Sedgwick to unnamed correspondent, January [?], 1793. *S.P.*, M.H.S.

Whether he was laboring to improve the administrative procedures of the federal courts and modify the Judiciary Act of 1789 [2] or working to temper the congressional censure of Washington's unfortunate general Arthur St. Clair, Sedgwick was to be counted on the side of the administration. Convinced of the virtue of that administration, he was determined to stand forth as the champion of its programs and officials.

In the matter of military operations against the Indian, Sedgwick wished the executive to have wide discretionary powers. Washington, as Commander in Chief, and the War and Treasury departments, which illogically shared the tasks of army procurement, should be given full responsibility in the determination of policy. Madison, Elbridge Gerry, and other congressmen criticized Sedgwick's position sharply. They insisted that he wished to render the House unconstitutionally dependent on the heads of departments and give the President authority to legislate by proclamation. Sedgwick was pleased to report to his business colleague at home that he had retorted in a speech "as severe in sentiment and in language" as invention aided by resentment could manage. Although his motion carried the House, he was for months solemnly to mourn the "factious spirit" that had been displayed.[3]

Sedgwick continued an advocate of economy in military and frontier measures and an opponent of both aggression and extravagance. He was not oblivious to the demands of national honor and the just claims of the pioneer settler and gave significant support to the passage of the Frontier Bill in the spring of 1792, but he cast a cold eye on the claims of wounded military pensioners and voted against an act authorizing the army to

2. Sedgwick as chairman of the House Judiciary Committee studied the possibility of a constitutional amendment that would specify more exactly the superiority of the federal judiciary and its exclusive jurisdiction in certain legal areas, but came to the reluctant decision that such would have to wait until "anti-federal passions" were more dead than dormant. Sedgwick to Peter Van Schaack, November 20, 1791, as quoted by Henry C. Van Schaack, *Life and Letters of Peter Van Schaack* (New York, 1842), 436.

Ironically, when Sedgwick did propose an amendment to the consideration of Congress, February 19, 1793, it was that which became the Eleventh Amendment: only with its express consent could a state be made a defendant in a suit in any of the federal courts at the initiation of a citizen of another state. The result of the Supreme Court's markedly unpopular decision in Chisholm *v.* Georgia, this amendment was, in Sedgwick's opinion, a necessary concession to political practicality.

3. Sedgwick to Ephraim Williams, December 11, 1791. *Loose Letters* of Theodore Sedgwick, S.P., M.H.S. See, too, Sedgwick's speech in behalf of a motion "that the Secretary of the Treasury be directed to report to this House his opinion of the best mode for raising the additional supplies requisite for the ensuing year." *Annals,* III, 437–438 (March 8, 1792).

carry out "an offensive action" against the Chickamaugas. His attitude was conditioned not only by his eastern orientation and constant concern for the strength of the Federal Treasury, but also, it would appear, by a rather unique appreciation for the position of the Indians themselves. The sympathy which Sedgwick would withhold from the debt-burdened frontiersmen he often gave to those who were legally his acknowledged inferiors. Almost alone among his contemporaries, Sedgwick made an honest effort to understand the dilemma of the Indian. "They have everything to apprehend from the gradual encroachment of the whites," he wrote, "many injuries to resent & revenge and a certain prospect if events proceed as they have done of utter extermination." [4]

Sedgwick's chief task as he saw it was not, however, to succour the Indian but to provide support for the Secretary of the Treasury. Hamilton and Sedgwick worked almost in tandem at this time. Hamilton provided Sedgwick with support and advice in the latter's strenuous effort to obtain additional assumption of state debts,[5] and Sedgwick tried earnestly, though finally unsuccessfully, to allow executive departments continued freedom in the application of public revenue.

The Appropriation Bill for 1792 was to an amount and in a form most satisfactory to both Hamilton and Sedgwick. That of the winter of 1793, however, reflected the insistence of Madison that the House must not abdicate its power to initiate all money bills and generally control the strings of the national purse. The House during the previous sessions had applied to the Secretary of the Treasury for suggestions concerning the raising of initial and supplementary supplies. Madison now sought to persuade the House that such dependence ill befitted Congress and demanded that the House henceforth make specific appropriations. Sedgwick believed that narrowly itemized appropriations unduly restricted the executive departments and decreased their efficiency, but Madison's arguments proved the more persuasive. The bill for the annual appropriation for the War Department included an itemization of the goods and services expected from each authorized sum.

Madison and his friend Jefferson now felt the time had come when it was essential to restrict the dimensions of executive discretion and

4. Sedgwick to Ephraim Williams, December 11, 1791. *Ibid.*

5. A limit of $21,500,000 had been placed on the amount to be assumed and Sedgwick inspired a motion advocating that the Secretary of the Treasury consider "a compleat assumption of the state debts." Hamilton privately informed Sedgwick that a report would be forthcoming "favorable" to his wishes. See Sedgwick to Ephraim Williams, November 13, 1791, *S.P.*, M.H.S.

wage a full-scale attack on the dominating fortress of the Treasury Department. In the month of February, 1793, Jefferson wrote and Representative William Branch Giles presented a series of eight resolutions, the object of which was to limit the personal authority of Hamilton by revealing the illegal liberties he had taken with the legislative directives of Congress. In summary the most important portions of these resolutions accused Hamilton of the following misdemeanors: 1) violating the law of August 4, 1790, by applying some of the principal he was authorized to borrow to the payment of the interest falling due on that principal; 2) drawing certain moneys into the United States without the authorization of the President; 3) failing to give Congress prompt information on the moneys drawn by him from Europe and of the reasons for such drafts; 4) drawing greater sums from Holland than Congress had authorized to be borrowed by the Act of August 12, 1790— this without the knowledge of the President; 5) undertaking to judge the motives of the House of Representatives in calling for information demandable of him, and failing to give all applicable information within his knowledge in response to the congressional references of January 19 and November 22, 1792.

The charges were admittedly technical and on the whole rather captious. Their object was to prove that Hamilton had exercised his pro-English prejudices in depriving our Revolutionary savior France of prompt and generous payment of the debt owed her, his pro-speculator proclivities in neglecting to redeem portions of the national debt, and his monarchical bias in disregarding legislative instruction.

The Virginians and their supporters had undoubtedly chosen the end of the session as a time which would afford them the chance of damning Hamilton in the public eye without fear of immediate rebuttal. Hamilton, however, worked virtually around the clock in an attempt to answer all allegations, and his supporters, Sedwick possibly chief among them, forced the resolutions to a vote and to oblivion before the Second Congress was declared terminated.

The rebuttal of the administration supporters proceeded along two lines: proving the charge false, or the conduct of Hamilton necessitated by circumstances of administrative convenience or economy. Rather than ship sums of money to and fro across the Atlantic, money that was loaned abroad and intended to be drawn here for the redemption of the domestic debt had been utilized to pay interest on foreign loans, and money here originally intended for the latter purpose had been used as a sinking fund for the redemption of the domestic debt. Complicated perhaps but surely not illegal. There had been no provision in the act of

August 4, 1790, which forbade the removal here of money borrowed abroad, and authorizations under that act and that of August 12, in any case, had not been intended to be self-exclusive but, rather, supplementary. Moneys borrowed were borrowed under the joint authority of both acts. Perhaps certain drafts had at one time or another been made without the prior knowledge of the legislature, but the Secretary or the President had always respectfully notified Congress as soon as the press of business allowed. If there had been unimportant deviations in trifles, was this "sufficient to warrant the alarm's being sounded from St. Croix to St. Mary's," and the entire time of Congress being consumed with such a frivolous investigation? [6]

It was the duty of Congress to make laws, not execute them. Similarly it was the province of the President, not Congress, to oversee the executive departments. Only by impeachment could Congress remove an executive officer, Sedgwick declared, and that was admittedly not the object of the present persecution.

The net result of the debate was the decisive defeat of every one of Giles' Resolutions by majorities of from eighteen to twenty-eight. By projecting both too broad and too petty an attack the Virginians were unable even to achieve a mild censure of certain of Hamilton's methods. In retrospect the defeat seems well deserved. Hamilton was undoubtedly too highhanded on occasion, and he violated the spirit of certain legislation by allowing a part of some foreign loans earmarked for France to be transported to and remain idle in this country, but that he had disobeyed Washington, damaged the nation's honor and credit, or decreased its revenue was never even partially proven. [7]

Sedgwick was as much the practicing politician as the fledging statesman, and during the Second Congress, as in others, his thoughts were as often on candidates and offices as on measures and principles. Especially was this true in the election year of 1792. He and Aaron Burr no longer sent one another coded messages on the probable success of certain candidates, thanks to the coolness which had arisen from their conflicting views on the late and hotly disputed New York gubernatorial election, [8] but Sedgwick was in active correspondence with various political leaders of "the Eastern states." He worried over the character of

6. *Annals,* III, 924–925 (March 1, 1793).

7. For an attempt to prove that he had done all of these things, see the anonymous pamphlet, *An Examination of the . . . Conduct of the Secretary of the Treasury* (Philadelphia, 1793).

8. See Sedgwick to Burr, September 9, 1791. MSS. Collection, Historical Society of Pennsylvania.

the initial congressman from Vermont, expressed concern for the purity of the Massachusetts delegation, and strongly advocated the re-election to the Vice-Presidency of that firm and honest Bay Stater John Adams. Reports of a combination seeking to displace Adams and other staunch patriots incited stern anger. It was the effort of a criminal and seditious junto who wanted to destroy the funding system, overthrow the national bank, void the excise law, and generally render a nullity all the important measures which had been accomplished for the public weal. It was the need to combat such efforts, Sedgwick declared, that had persuaded him to run again, to the sacrifice of his ease, comfort, and family.

Troubled by his wife's extreme loneliness, ill health, and periodic "fits of melancholy," [9] Sedgwick for a time had pondered a withdrawal from political life. Wavering between duty to nation and family, he had allowed himself to be persuaded by his colleagues that—at least for two more years—the call of country superseded all other obligations. Determining "against my own happiness," Sedgwick, victim of political fever, worshipper of public acclaim, and true lover of country, entered the lists once more, running against Thompson J. Skinner for the office of United States Representative from Berkshire County. At the end of a bitter campaign it appeared for a brief time that the overconfidence of his friends and a clever manoeuvre by the Skinnerites had combined to defeat Theodore Sedgwick.

The "manoeuvre" centered about the post of "representative at large." Under the new representative ratio, which had raised the Massachusetts quota of congressmen from eight to fourteen, there were to be four representatives elected from western Massachusetts: one each from Worcester, Hampshire, and Berkshire counties and one from the three counties at large. Skinner's friends passed about the suggestion that it would be degrading for a man as important as Sedgwick to be the representative from Berkshire alone; he should represent all three counties. Sedgwick's friends were infuriated with such a bald piece of trickery. Skinner and his cohorts, they cried, were just trying to split Sedgwick's vote, so he would not be elected to Congress under any designation. The other counties, being larger than Berkshire, would surely not agree to allow Berkshire the honor of giving two of the four Western District congressmen.

9. Sedgwick took an authorized month's leave of absence from Congress, December 22, 1791, to visit his ill wife, who had given birth to another son three days earlier. He did not return to Congress until February 8, 1792, and had felt obliged meanwhile—despite his "independent" principles—to explain his absence to Governor Hancock. They were at the time in one of their fleeting moods of quasi-friendship.

"Right" did in the end win out; rumors of Sedgwick's defeat titillating the ears of "opposition" congressmen proved false.[10] A necessary number of Sedgwick's Berkshire admirers were apprised of the foul plot in time to secure a sufficient concentration of votes on the Berkshire post on the first trial. Sedgwick was immensely delighted when defeat became victory. His wife, gentle, unassuming Pamela, knowing how smitten he was with the color and clamor of public life, sympathized and abdicated:

> I doubt not my dearest love your tender attachment to your family. you must permit me to say that you have been so long in the habit of Public Cares—and theay appear from experience to be exceedingly fascinating theay seem to be a kind of agreable Drudgery—the mind gets innured to active scenes grows fond of them and grasps the country as its world whare all that is dear is centered—A Man who has faithfully served it as I know you my Love have feals that its Interests require his constant attention from which he cannot be saparated without fearing a Distressing and painful Void—as a fond Mother does when she is by some misfortune Detached from the care of her Family.[11]

The ability of Sedgwick's friends in Berkshire to defeat in time the plot of Mr. Skinner bore witness to Sedgwick's success in the years 1788–1793 in creating an effective political machine in western Massachusetts. Much of Sedgwick's "agreable Drudgery" was devoted to the task of assuring that this organization would express the aims and ideals of its creator, a charter Federalist.

Sedgwick's task was not an easy one. Western Massachusetts had been the hotbed of Shaysism in 1785–1786 and had cast a good majority against the ratification of the Constitution in 1787–1788. Sedgwick's particular concern, Berkshire County was an agrarian region, but recently incorporated and still bearing certain marks of its former frontier character. Massachusetts politics, moreover, was confused in these years by the personal popularity of John Hancock and Samuel Adams, and national politics awaited the Jay Treaty, and even the Alien and

10. When it appeared that Sedgwick had been defeated in his bid for reelection, that gentleman had kept his head determinedly high. He declared that though others could possibly serve the country more ably, he was sure it was not possible for them to serve it more faithfully. He was wounded, he admitted, not for his own sake but for the chagrin his friends would suffer. "He was a little hurt too by the smile of satisfaction" that the rumor of his defeat had produced among his adversaries in the House. Sedgwick to Pamela, November 26, 1792. Papers of H. D. Sedgwick, S.P., M.H.S.

11. December 11, 1792. S.P., M.H.S.

Sedition Acts, to solidify unorganized factions into well-staffed and disciplined national parties. Despite these difficulties, Sedwick fashioned a political organization of Berkshire Federals that would so dominate local politics in Berkshire in the 1790's that such opponents as John Bacon and Thompson J. Skinner would be driven to transform the once-numerous Berkshire "Radicals" and the even more numerous group of Berkshire Anti-Federalists of 1787 into a rather unstable association of Jeffersonian Republicans.

County-wide or district-wide party "conventions" would not take hold in western Massachusetts as early as they would in its eastern section, but informal gatherings of prominent "friends of government" from various towns of Berkshire and Hampshire counties were held, under Sedgwick's painstaking direction. They proved very "salutary" in their ability to unite "the good men" on the proper candidates for county senator, district elector (until 1796), district congressman, etc. These meetings, at least during the 1790's, were not in fact true "conventions," called by general invitation and attended by the party rank-and-file. Rather they were policy committee meetings called privately and attended solely by "the instrumental."

Unlike their counterparts of a later date, Sedgwick and his Berkshire friends persistently refused to tone down their political views in order to conciliate their neighbors. They believed that the people should aspire to their plane of understanding; any popularization was sheer appeasement. They endeavored to bludgeon the people into holding "respectable" opinions, and to frighten their fellow voters into believing that "the popular demagogues," once in power, would bring war, atheism, and poverty into the pleasant, peaceful valleys and God-fearing homes of Berkshire.

Sedgwick was early in appreciating the importance of the press in an area where primitive conditions of travel largely precluded mass meetings or electioneering devices based on constant intimate contact between candidate and voter. Equally alive to its value were his lieutenants: intellectual, aging Henry Van Schaack; [12] various members of the well-established and influential Dwight and Williams clans; store-

12. Van Schaack, a courtly and learned gentleman whom Sedgwick held in great esteem, moved to Pittsfield at the close of the Revolution. He was solely responsible for introducing the Lombardy poplar into Berkshire and largely instrumental in the introduction of fine wines and Episcopalianism into that region. Fast overcoming the incubus of a Tory past, he proved a stalwart champion of the Constitution, a firm Federalist, and an ardent advocate of religious equality. Joseph E. A. Smith, *The History of Pittsfield* . . . (Pittsfield, 1869–1876), II, 7, 11, 71, 450, 508.

keepers Timothy Edwards and Brigadier Silas Pepoon; printers Loring Andrews and Benjamin Rosseter; Samuel Henshaw, Edward Edwards, Elisha Lee, and others. Sedgwick, with his free franking privilege as a member of Congress, wrote prolifically to these various lieutenants and often enclosed pieces from Federal papers in Philadelphia and New York which he thought might be printed to advantage in Springfield, Stockbridge, Pittsfield, and Northampton journals. Henry Van Schaack received through the agency of Mr. Sedgwick the *Complete Works of Peter Porcupine*. He, with several others, was given permission to publish parts of Sedgwick's letters, as "from a Philadelphia correspondent," and virtually ordered to secure the reprinting of all of Sedgwick's more important efforts at congressional debate.

Such newspapers as *The Western Star*, costing as little as $1.00 a year in cash and $1.50 in certain preferred types of produce, could be afforded by many remote farmhouses, and served as one of the few means of maintaining contact with events on the national scene. Their importance as makers of opinion was much respected by Sedgwick. He was constantly "suggesting" proper press policies to his friends. They should support the Executive, Mr. Hamilton, and "the administration men" on all occasions. They should support the aims and *code* of the Federalists.

Only with the rise of Jefferson's "Democratic-Republican party" in the years 1795-1798 would the Federalists assume the form and structure of an organized party,[13] but the major principles and programs of that party were already in evidence by that date. The significance of

13. Certain of the tenets of the Federalist party of 1798 can, of course, be traced to the original Federalists of 1787. The present author does not believe that the Federalist and Anti-Federalist parties of 1787 and the Federalist and Jeffersonian parties of the late 1790's were respectively one and the same, but they were related. Not lineal descendants, they were equally products of the same general socio-economic division in American society.

The Federalists, of course, much sooner formed their followers, chose their planks, and selected their principles than did the Jeffersonians. Conceivably all the Federalists needed in 1791 to be an organized party in the modern sense was an opposition party. The Federalists distrusted formal party organization, however, for that implied emphasis on organizing the rank and file, which might lead to majority control. Appeals to the people for support were, they felt, highly dangerous.

The whole problem of the formation of the parties in the early years of the Republic is highly controversial. Some historians, such as Charles Beard, see the party division created during the ratification struggle as forming the basis for the Federalist-Republican division; others, such as Professor Orin Grant Libby and John Spencer Bassett, insist that this conception of a continuous two party system is quite

Sedgwick's efforts as a model Hamiltonian in the Second Congress and his labors to create in Berkshire an organization of "strong Federal men" becomes clear only when viewed in the context of the evolving membership and code of the Federalists.

The Federalists drew much of their strength and personnel from the educated, the wellborn, and the propertied; though obviously not all persons so blessed were Federalists. Geographically, the Federalists were nurtured chiefly in the northern and eastern sections, where their emphasis on commercial and financial interests was best appreciated. Federalism's aristocratic, rather urban viewpoint generally alienated the West. In the South, commercial centers such as Charleston and Baltimore were staunchly Federalist; the sparsely settled agrarian areas, not. The neo-aristocracy of the *noveau riche*, which had arisen in America since 1775 with the aid of the profits of war, trade, speculation, and land sales, tended to favor the Federalists, as did the professional classes generally, the remnants of the old pre-Revolution gentry, the trading and shipping interests, and in certain sections a majority of the clergy.

On the broadest terms, the Federalists were characterized by a refusal to rely for guidance on the majority will and by a sense of trusteeship in handling the affairs of their country. They were men with a discernible, taxable stake-in-society; men who believed that no society could exist without an orderly appreciation of the superior qualifications enjoyed by certain of God's children. There had always been distinctions. There had always been a class of respected "betters" to lead the way, and that pleasant burden was now theirs. Government was *for* all the people, surely, but *by* only the favored few. Property rule was an understood basis for society; the basis of politics was itself economic.

They were, however, practical men and were chiefly concerned with the specific. They had perhaps six major designs: 1) to create a strong sentiment of nationality; 2) to employ men's ambitions and interests to make the new government secure; 3) to put the public credit on a firm

---

13. (cont.)

erroneous. See Beard, *Economic Origins of Jeffersonian Democracy*, 10–32, 75; Orin Grant Libby, "A Sketch of The Early Political Parties In the United States," *The Quarterly Journal of the University of North Dakota*, II, 216–217; John Spencer Bassett, *The Federalist System* (Albert Bushnell Hart, ed., *The American Nation*, XI), (New York, 1906), 42.

For a recent and brilliant exposition on the slow, evolutionary growth of our two party system, see Joseph Charles, "The Origins of the American Party System," *William and Mary Quarterly*, Third Series, XII (1955) 217–267, 410–446, 581–630. See, too, Noble E. Cunningham Jr., *The Jeffersonian Republicans: The Formation of Party Organization, 1789–1801* (Chapel Hill, 1957), 77–85, 89–115.

basis and establish ample revenues; 4) to encourage a mixed economy by aiding manufactures, shipbuilding, the fisheries, and ocean-borne commerce; 5) to keep the nation at peace; 6) to protect its citizens from the "discontented," be they Redskins or Rebels. To accomplish these ends they appreciated that the national government had to be indisputably sovereign in certain areas of political power; the national administration, centralized, efficient, and energetic; the regular army and the militia, up to strength and well-regulated; and the Constitution, broadly construed and interpreted. There was to be no irresponsible exertion of power on anyone's part, but never again should America witness the governmental impotence of the Confederation era, or be victimized by the financial laxity and dishonesty and the exaggerated notions of freedom typical of that period.

Believers in a republican, representative form of government, the Federalists were determined that the republic should not be a democratic republic. The public good not the popular passions of the moment should mould the laws of America. Guiding this republic would be an aristocracy of virtue; for truth, justice, patriotism, and sound principles were the exclusive possessions of the educated classes. The public will should be filtered, should be channeled, by a system of checks and balances. Liberty there must be for all citizens, but liberty was not license.

Sedgwick was a composite of all the strength and frailty, patriotism and prejudice, vision and myopia that marked the Federalists. Hamilton, Adams, King, Pickering were all more important but none so typical. Hamilton was a genius, Adams an Adams; King was more tolerant, Pickering more fanatical than the average. Sedgwick, not they, represented the norm of the Federalist party.

Like the Federalists as a whole, he was neither a disinterested hero nor a selfish villain. Victim of a hunger to take a great part in great events, he was also sincerely devoted to the welfare of the new nation. Risen to prominence and a place in the sun by dint of hard work, two advantageous marriages, intelligence, and an endless store of ambition, Sedgwick had had perhaps more contact with "the lower orders" than many Federalists, but his view of these persons *en masse* was identical with that of his colleagues and friends. They were "miscreants," "sans-culottes," "Jacobins," if they attempted to override the accepted social and political order. Individually he liked them, condescendingly perhaps but sincerely. Collectively he considered them very inclined to be troublesome. Certainly, he would have said, all white males with the requisite small amount of property should have the right to vote for their congressional representative, but their votes of course should go to the educated and propertied, who were the only fit custodians of the larger interests and true traditions of the nation.

As a man who brought to politics the fervor that he denied religion, and as a man whose optic range was limited to black and white, Sedgwick was inclined to confuse opposition to his views with immorality of conduct and Federalism with godliness. Any talk of the "rights of man," "democratic opportunity," "the liberties of the citizen," or "the cherishment of the people" he viewed as camouflage for the evil designs of self-seeking demagogues. A self-assessed "realist," he felt it infantile not to accept the fact that self-interest was one of the chief—though not the only—ruling passion of mankind. This should be accepted and enlisted on the side of government. To do so was not only essential but beneficial; for as government became secure and stable, as the well-to-do prospered, so would the lower orders benefit as prosperity seeped down through the layers of society.

Brilliant, but curiously insensitive to the temper of the people or the current of the times, sternly setting themselves against the coming deluge of democracy, the Federalists were destined to end as officers without any army. They laid a magnificent concrete foundation for the edifice of America but lacked the vision to imagine its intended, complete design. As Henry Adams has written, the Federalists served as "a halfway house between the European past and the American future." [14]

Neither the beliefs of Sedgwick nor the Federalist party remained static or unmodified during the years of their power, of course. With the beheading of Louis XVI of France and the rise of the "democratic societies" in America, both Sedgwick and his party became more admiring of England and more scornful of democracy and democrats; with their sudden popularity during the XYZ Affair they became more truculent and martial; and with the prospect of defeat facing them in 1799–1800 they became spiteful and bitter, and increasingly shortsighted. But at all times they moved together, the man and the party.

14. Henry Adams, *History of the United States of America* (New York, 1889–1891), II, 76.

THE JACOBINS, THE JAY TREATY, AND WAR

IX

Sedgwick Labors for Peace and Wages War on the "Democratic Societies," 1793–1795

Their conduct differed as far from a fair and honorable investigation as Christ and Belial. They were men prowling in the dark.

Theodore Sedgwick [1]

THE second administration of George Washington was concerned as much with foreign as with domestic affairs. Indeed, in this period as in the period after World War II, the problems of foreign relations became important domestic issues. This new emphasis was not attributable to the conversion of the Jeffersonians to Hamiltonian finance; it was, rather, due to their conversion to the cause of French freedom. The French Revolution not only presented different problems to the makers of American foreign policy but also presented issues on which the American people were bitterly divided. The course of the French Revolution was followed by Americans with passionate interest, an interest which suggests that American isolationism was a development, if not an invention, of the nineteenth century.[2]

If Jefferson heralded the French Revolution as a new chapter in man's eternal quest for freedom, Theodore Sedgwick came to view it as another round in the long battle of liberty versus tyranny, of the forces of law and order against those of license and anarchy. In his views on the French Revolution as well as in his opposition to its domestic manifestations in America, Sedgwick remained representative of New England Federalism. Nowhere was this more true than in his efforts in the Third Congress to defeat the anti-British resolutions of

1. *Annals*, IV, 911 (November 25, 1794).
2. Not only did national papers such as the *Gazette of the United States* and *The National Gazette* feature foreign news, but a small-town paper such as *The Western Star* of Stockbridge would often fill half its space with "intelligence lately received from Europe."

James Madison and to denounce the American Jacobins who would form "democratic societies" and incite Pennsylvanians to rebellion.

It was only with the fall of 1792 that conservative opinion in America turned sharply against the revolutionaries of France. Initially, there had been general approval of the efforts of the French Estates-General to follow the example of America and check monarchical despotism. The reforms of Lafayette and Mirabeau and the French constitution of September, 1791, elicited general praise. Loring Andrews, publisher of the Stockbridge newspaper and virtual echo of Theodore Sedgwick, expressed warm admiration for the French nation. By the fall of 1792, however, a perceptible change had taken place within American conservative opinion. Loring Andrews began to warn the French against the mad extremists of the Paris Commune. When, in January, 1793, Louis XVI was beheaded, the transformation was complete. The French Revolution was now to be both damned and feared; it was but Shays' Rebellion writ large. Such violence, such anarchy revealed a people not ready for the republican experiment.

In similar fashion, American conservatives came to view France not as a nation besieged by an ever enlarging coalition of European monarchies, but as a subversive threat to the independence of all nations. The execution of Louis, and the revelation that France was able not only to escape annihilation but to commence a great crusade for continental liberty as well, soon brought Sedgwick and other Hamiltonians to the view that in English victory lay the hopes of all nations who respected law, order, and decency.

The growing conservative distrust of France and fear of French victory was intensified by the experiment of Hébert and the Mountain to replace Christianity with Deism, the Christ Child with the Goddess of Reason. But Sedgwick, like other "Federalists," could never have been sympathetic with the followers of Rousseau, whatever their religious predilections. Sedgwick certainly believed that man was equal before the law, but he was equally convinced that only an idiot would judge the besotted village drunk and the brilliant Alexander Hamilton to be equals. He did not agree that all human natures were potentially excellent, or that all humans were capable of infinite development if only the environment was right. Sedgwick believed in Locke's theory of inalienable natural rights, but he felt this was a constitutional, rather abstract, matter and should not be perverted into supporting nonsensical democratic notions. The individual was important, but one must also consider individuals en masse—society. The French, by their attack on all the governmental machinery of the Old Régime, had demonstrated that they would reduce government to a state of anarchy and chaos, and no individual, even "natural man," would be the beneficiary.

By the time, then, that the war between Britain and France had reached sufficient intensity to cause each combatant to take strong measures against neutral trade with the enemy, Sedgwick was definitely anti-French. If a man was a fool, so was he a Jacobin, a French-sympathizing Democrat, and vice versa.[3] That Sedgwick was anti-French does not imply that he was a sycophantic Anglophile. His distrust of France was always much greater than his sympathy with Britain. When France had declared war on that country, he had strongly approved Washington's decision to declare America neutral, though he had privately thought the Neutrality Proclamation should have received overt congressional approval.[4] Sedgwick wished America to involve herself with neither side but, rather, to serve profitably as a neutral carrier and thereby swell the national treasury and bulwark the national credit. When, in 1793-1794, both sides issued a series of orders restricting and restraining neutral trade with the other, and large numbers of

3. Sedgwick seems at times to have dealt more harshly with Francophiles than Frenchmen. Though he was horrified at Genêt's attempts to drag America into the war by outfitting privateers in this country and appealing over the head of the President to the people, he had, quite without protest, met the gentleman socially at a party given by his friends, Dr. and Mr. Jackson, February 14, 1794. He found the French minister polite, attentive, and easy in his manner, and, though they had a sharp discussion during the evening over the state of parties in America, personally fairly agreeable.

With Genêt's successor, Fauchet—"if you mean to pronounce in the french stile say Fosha"—Sedgwick was on even better terms. They paid each other courtesy visits in late February, 1794, and when the Frenchman was recalled a year later, Sedgwick declared him to be "very inoffensive," and doubted whether the mad French would send anyone half so sensible in his stead.

With those Frenchmen on the losing side Sedgwick was most sympathetic, lavishing many a compassionate sigh on the emigrés "condemned to cruel exile."

4. This was rather in opposition to Sedgwick's usual insistence on the discretionary authority that must be allowed the President in military matters and foreign relations. Sedgwick, however, seems to have had some uncertainty as to the exact strength of the French alliance and wished to draw Congress into the responsibility for a limited construction of its provisions. Sedgwick to Hamilton, August 26, 1793. Hamilton *MSS.*, Library of Congress.

American merchantmen were consequently seized and their cargoes ruthlessly confiscated, Sedgwick had angry words for both Britain and France. We should not, he said, "tamely submit to repeated and unmerited insult." [5] War against Britain, however, was unthinkable. It would lead to an alliance with Jacobinical France and the prostration of American liberty.

Possessor of the world's greatest navy, Britain had committed a majority of the depredations on American commerce, and it was against Britain—the old enemy—that an aroused America cried out in the winter of 1794. "Retaliation" was the demand, and Sedgwick's chief opponent James Madison took the floor of Congress (January 3, 1794) and trotted out his old discrimination resolve, refurbished and considerably strengthened.[6] The seven resolutions of economic retaliation which he proposed demanded complete reciprocity of trade limitations; discriminatory import and tonnage duties and port restrictions for goods and ships of nations not in treaty with the United States (i.e., Great Britain); and the reimbursement of United States citizens, victims of the illegal actions of Britain, from the proceeds of these additional duties.[7] Consideration of these commercial resolutions was twice postponed and on March 10, 1794, the day when they were to be brought up for discussion, Sedgwick gave notice of his intention soon to submit certain resolutions of his own with the design of putting the country in a better posture of defense in the present emergency.

He had written his friends that he was completely disgusted with Madison's proposals. They formed an insidious "water gruel system" that would do no earthly good, would assuredly bring on a commercial war, and might very possibly irritate Britain into a shooting war. They

5. Sedgwick to Dwight Foster, January 12, 1794. *MISC. Papers*, XVII (1784–1796), M.H.S.

6. In debates of 1789 and 1790 Madison had proposed that additionally heavy tonnage rates and port duties be levied against nations with whom the United States did not have a commercial treaty. Sedgwick had successfully opposed such "additional discrimination" either in port duties or imposts. He had supported discrimination in support of American bottoms, but wished American mercantilism to be unblemished by favoritism. *Annals*, I, 588, 616 (June 23, July 1, 1789); II, 1573–1574 (March 14, 1790).

7. Joseph Charles lays great stress on these resolves. He believes they marked a milestone in the evolution of the Republican Party and that they marked a conscious attempt to give the Republican Party a national basis. (Charles, *Origins of the American Party System*, 585, 589.) The present writer believes they were neither epochal nor new.

were, in short, actuated by "an infernal spirit." On March 12 Sedgwick would request the attention of the House and, in a long and much-discussed speech, expound his views on the present Anglo-American crisis and offer a "proper" plan of action. His plan was undoubtedly in broad outline as much Hamilton's as his own. Hamilton had suggested to Washington, and undoubtedly to Sedgwick, the necessity of pushing certain concrete measures of military defense through Congress.[8] Sedgwick, however, had been thinking along the same lines in February, 1794, while home at Stockbridge, and, as was so often the case, Hamilton's suggestions but pointed up and articulated his own more amorphous thoughts on the subject.[9]

Sedgwick began by offering a string of resolves. The first suggested that fifteen regiments of auxiliary troops, to consist of one thousand men each, should be raised, armed, and equipped at once; the second, that these men be enlisted for two years if the country should remain at peace and for three years after the commencement of war if that unwanted event should occur. Others proposed that revenue sufficient to defray the expense of these troops be provided; that these "auxiliaries" be disbanded when the emergency was conclusively past; and that, except in time of war, they should be entitled to pay only for attendance on training and exercise days. The last of this series of resolutions suggested that the President be authorized, whenever in his judgment the situation warranted, to lay an embargo upon certain or all ships in the harbors of the United States for a term not exceeding forty days, and also to prohibit for a like term the exportation of any goods or commodities from this country.

Sedgwick then explained these resolutions and their probable effect. The troops were, of course, primarily for the salvation of the nation if it were attacked, but they also had a retaliatory function. Britain

8. See Hamilton, *Works*, IV, 506–508; V, 509.

9. Madison and Monroe both wrote Jefferson that they believed Sedgwick was merely a puppet, mouthing the words and thoughts of Hamilton. See Rives, *Madison*, III, 408; Stanislaus Murray Hamilton, *The Writings of James Monroe* (New York, 1898–1903), V, 286–287.

Sedgwick was in fact not a puppet but rather the successor of William Loughton Smith as Hamilton's chief lieutenant in the House, especially where financial legislation was concerned. His growing importance was recognized when in February, 1794, upon Hamilton's first indication that he intended to resign the secretaryship of the Treasury in the near future, Washington approached Sedgwick concerning his possible acceptance of this post. Sedgwick gratefully declined the opportunity and a year later heartily approved the choice of Oliver Wolcott of Connecticut as Hamilton's successor. See Sedgwick to Ephraim Williams, February 20, 1794. *S.P., M.H.S.*

would be slow to antagonize the United States if she thought there was a readied force here capable of sweeping down upon the rich colony of Canada. The militia of the United States, even if it were to be strengthened and improved, would serve neither of these purposes. The terms of militiamen were too short; by the time they were effective, they had to be disbanded. They required too high wages, and their want of discipline occasioned great waste of private and public property. The presence of militia would not deter any aggressor; a force of "auxiliary regulars" was our only recourse. Nor should there be any fear that the latter would endanger the liberties of the people. They would be scattered throughout the country, "in the bosom of society," unless war necessitated their unification, and they were, in any case, fellow Americans.

The embargo authorization was equally necessary and unobjectionable. The British West Indies were very dependent on continental America for foodstuffs, and the mere threat that they might be cut off would do much to bring England to terms. If an embargo was necessary, its success would hinge largely on the promptness with which it was put into effect. The legislature was unable to keep secrets or act with sufficient rapidity; it must be the President who should decide. They could be sure he would use the power sparingly and only in situations of unquestioned national emergency.

His whole object, Sedgwick declared, was not to antagonize or irritate but to speak bluntly and, by repairing America's defenses, secure her peace and so her prosperity and credit. America should present to the belligerent powers motives of policy and interest to bolster considerations of justice. These defense measures would give us needed time to try and arrange matters by political negotiation. By clear words and calm actions we would dispel the false belief that America was a helpless pawn on the international scene. The European belligerents should know that we could make allowance but would not be imposed upon. A nation that received injuries with impunity would suffer them without end. "We should mark a line, and boldly declare that we will not permit it to be transgressed. —Such firm and manly language, backed by the means of enforcing respect and retaliatory injuries . . . must be heard; and he trusted, would produce the desired effect." [10]

10. *Annals*, IV, 500–503 (March 12, 1794). Sedgwick was very pleased with this speech and, though irate that John Fenno's sketch of the debate in his *Gazette of the United States* was both abridged and inaccurate, highly anxious that it be widely reprinted in Massachusetts. See Sedgwick to Ephraim Williams, March 13, March 18, 1794. *S.P.*, M.H.S

Sedgwick's advocacy of defense measures—the troops and the embargo authorization, together with the fortification of harbors and ports already agreed to—was judicious as well as sincere. There was a certain inconsistency in his mention of an attack on Canada so soon after his denunciation of Madison as a John Bull-baiter and the leader of the "War Party," but his general thesis was sound. Madison's measures would have antagonized the British and decreased the revenue to little compensating advantage. Retaliation might well wait on the completion of a defense program. It would surely be idle to deny that Sedgwick's disgust at the thought of finding himself an ally of France did much to explain his opposition to "discrimination," but of greater importance was his realization that infant America needed peace. It was not primarily as a party man that he counseled America to avoid war by preparing for it. He was not motivated by any diabolic urge to raise a great standing army that would help "the aristocrats" make America a centralized monarchy.

James Madison's resolutions were not set aside as easily, however, as Sedgwick had hoped. A motion on March 14 to consider Sedgwick's embargo resolve lost and consideration of Madison's resolutions resumed. Sedgwick, alternately thundering and pleading, continued his opposition to any program of commercial discrimination. He had always supposed that to establish manufactures our active capital must be increased, and to encourage navigation our trade must be extended. How Mr. Madison's proposals, which would lessen our capital and limit our trade, would aid the establishment of manufactures and the building of ships—as the Virginian claimed—he was at a loss to see. Britain would certainly not put her intercourse with this country on a more favorable footing as a result of calculatedly irritating measures and the rasping threats of an unarmed people. If Madison's resolutions did not effectively embarrass and harm Britain in her struggle with France they would be useless; if they did, they would be a provocation to a war for which we were unprepared. One thing was certain, the risk involved was greater than any possible attendant benefit.[11]

Madison's proposals—seemingly with his permission—were never brought up for actual vote, and were gradually pushed into the background by the more drastic proposals of New Jersey representatives, Dayton and Clark, and by the growing appreciation that an attempt at negotiation with Britain was perhaps in order. Sedgwick's resolutions, however, were brought to a vote and achieved, in mutilated fashion, a small quantity of success.

11. *Annals*, IV, 512–519 (March 14, 1794).

His first resolution, that raising 15,000 auxiliaries, was lost without debate, but when he asked for a vote to determine whether it was the sense of the House that any extra provision for the protection of the country was necessary, he neatly boxed his opponents into agreeing that steps should be taken to this end. To detail such steps a committee of nine was appointed, Sedgwick chairman. It eventually made three proposals: a select corps of 80,000 militia should be organized on a temporary basis; a force of 800 coastal artillerymen and engineers should be raised; a regular force of 25,000 men should be enlisted. The militiamen and artillerists received the approval of the House after a certain amount of modification had taken place; the "regulars," after scraping through in the Committee of the Whole, were defeated in the House proper (May 19) by a vote of 50–30.

Sedgwick's embargo resolution had somewhat better fortune. Though first defeated on roll call, 48–46—thanks largely to votes from northern commercial centers—news of additional British captures in the West Indies secured its passage by March 26. In the form passed it gave Congress, not the President, the authority to lay the embargo for a maximum of thirty, not forty, days. Such an embargo was actually authorized and in effect in April, 1794, but was dropped late the next month, as *both* France and Great Britain proved to dislike it cordially.

Sedgwick, despite his protestations against "popular frenzy," was uneasy about the popularity of his stand. His constituents, he believed, should appreciate that only Theodore Sedgwick and others of the "Eastern Phalanx" were working for the true political security of the nation. As the commercial center of the country, Massachusetts, however, was naturally incensed by British spoliations, and Sedgwick and the other New England Federalists in Congress had to tread warily. Though a majority of Massachusetts merchants opposed an English war at all costs, Anglophobia was rising, and to work for pacific negotiation took a certain amount of political courage.[12]

Sedgwick, representing an agrarian district, was most anxious to

12. Sedgwick's unpopularity with the Madisonians increased by geometric proportions at this time and there were many innuendoes that he was influenced by an inordinate love of Britain. James Carey's *Philadelphia Advertiser* (February 1, 1794) epitomized this view in a bit of verse:

From the speechification of Sedgwick and Ames
Some might think that they both had drunk deep of the Thames,
For "our dear Mother Country," the former stands forth
In strains that were worthy a pupil of North.

set the record straight for his constituents. Writing to all his friends in western Massachusetts, he laid down the policy they and the newspapers they influenced should follow. Agricultural prosperity should be revealed as dependent on peace; the Madisonians should be exposed as enemies of the credit structure and all programs which sought to give efficiency to the energies of the nation. The people must be made to see that the Jacobin demagogues were using the present troubles with England as a means by which they could grasp the reins of government in their hands and substitute personal power for federal law, justice, and honor. If the good citizens of Massachusetts wanted further proof let them study the senseless rebellion of the farmers of western Pennsylvania. Was not that rebellion the natural offspring of "the democratic societies"—bodies that sought to impose the will of France upon America?

Theodore Sedgwick played but a minor role in the Whisky Rebellion of 1794 and its suppression, which was largely an executive undertaking. He had voted for a tax on stills and an excise on the distilling of whisky in March, 1791, and seems to have thought, as did Hamilton, that subsequent amendments cancelling the levy on smaller stills would avert any possible trouble on the Pennsylvania frontier. When time and open rebellion proved him wrong, he was incensed. Not only did he heartily agree with Washington's and Hamilton's summary suppression of the uprising but moved in the House that a portion of the militia of the United States be stationed in the western counties of Pennsylvania until the last shreds of opposition to law and order were dissolved.

Sedgwick also wished to see the government compensate all loyal Pennsylvanian citizens for the property losses they had incurred in opposing these frontier Jacobins. This together with the cost of the victorious militia army would bring the bill to over $1,500,000. But who would promote economy at the cost of justice? Certainly when a private person came forward to support the execution of the laws it demonstrated a much greater degree of patriotism than when it was done by a revenue officer operating in the line of paid duty. "When a wild, unprincipled, mad attempt had been made to destroy this noble Constitution, were the Representatives . . . to make it a doubt whether those who saved it from, perhaps destruction, were to be indemnified?"

Was a reduction to beggary and misery to be the reward of these noble citizens? [13]

The exhortations of Sedgwick and other congressmen had the desired effect, and Pennsylvania Loyalists received subsequent compensation. This, however, was to Sedgwick a minor matter when compared with a projected public censure of the rebellion-inciting "democratic societies."

These societies, imitative of the new Parisian political clubs, began sprouting in America in 1793. Their background was, of course, by no means purely French. The Correspondence Societies of the American Revolution and the English Constitutional and Revolutionary Societies were both drawn on for experience and techniques. But whatever their true origin, Sedgwick thought they were the offspring of the devil. The complicated problems facing the United States were the task of its duly elected representatives; scatterbrained, troublemaking amateurs had no business offering suggestions or influencing decisions. At first he had tried to ignore them, but after the Whisky Rebellion he began to urge a frontal attack on these societies, with their "fulsome language of fraternization" and their evil designs to throw into disrepute all good men and true. Sedgwick was indeed ready to use these societies as "whipping boys" and as symbols of the domestic difficulties occasioned by the French Revolution.

The first real opportunity for a frontal attack on the societies came in conjunction with the Presidential message of November, 1794. In this communication to Congress, Washington had denounced the societies as seditious and as partly responsible for the recent rebellion on the Pennsylvanian frontier. Sedgwick was appointed to the House committee which was to prepare the answering address, and he eagerly seized the opportunity offered to imitate the Senate and publicly damn "the Jacobins." He was thwarted, however, by his fellow members, Chairman Madison, ever solicitous of the rights of free speech, and Representative Thomas Scott of Pittsburgh, "a timid man." The draft which was reported to the House made no mention whatever of the societies. Sedgwick had tried to "reecho the President's denunciation" and to state

13. *Annals*, IV, 985, 998–1000 (December 16, 1794).
Sedgwick was highly pleased with this speech and wrote Van Schaack, "[I] acquitted myself with more satisfaction to *myself* than I recollect ever to have done in my life." But he lamented: "There was no *note taker* in the house but that poor creature employed by Brown, and whether he will attempt to give any thing to the public I know not." Sedgwick to Van Schaack, December 20, 1794. S.P., M.H.S.

in addition that "the seeds of these disorders were sown by the factious & seditious speeches of members of the legislature," [14] but had been unable to shake Madison's firm resolve not to have Congress become a board of censors, judging the conduct of every individual citizen by an arbitrary set of standards. Sedgwick was not easily diverted, however. He helped secure the services of his friend Fitzsimons, of Pennsylvania, to introduce from the floor of the House an amendment to the address which reprobated "these self-created societies" in the strongest terms.

The debate on this amendment was sharp and violent. Madison, Giles, and Nicholas hotly opposed it as false and unconstitutional. They pointed out that most of the societies had denounced the insurrection and were composed of God-fearing, liberty-loving Americans. Ames, William Smith, Tracy, and Sedgwick were the chief performers on the "Federal side." The most denunciatory speech delivered by that side was that made by Sedgwick on November 24.

Sedgwick first established the propriety of the President's inclusion of a comment on the societies in his review of the present state of the Union. The President was not confined to the mention of suggested legislation alone; it was also his right to speak generally to the moral condition of the nation. He would have been derelict in his duty if he had omitted to mention that the insurrection was "fomented by certain combinations of men, under the general denomination of 'self-created societies.'"

That decided, only two questions faced the House, Sedgwick dogmatically declared: was the President's allegation concerning the societies true; was it the duty of the House to give voice in support of the President's declaration? An unqualified affirmative was the only answer to both questions.

Every allegation against the societies was all too true. These "illicit combinations" had purposely misrepresented every honest and beneficial measure promulgated by the government. They had displayed the public debt, not as it was in fact, "the purchase of our freedom and independence," but as wantonly and wickedly created by the legislature to destroy the true principles of our republican government, and "to substitute in its stead a vile aristocracy." They had, without doubt, purposely stirred up the people with this and similar baseless assertions.[15]

14. Sedgwick to Ephraim Williams, November 20, 1794. *S.P.*, M.H.S.
15. Sedgwick later declared, in rather contradictory fashion, that the people had already acquiesced in the funding system when Genêt came over and roused the

The House should certainly give a hearty and distinct approbation to the Presidential judgment. Mr. Fitzsimons' amendment, quite rightly, "would have a tendency to plunge these societies into contempt, and to sink them still farther into abhorrence and detestation." Not to denounce them would give them a new lease on life. There was no one, Sedgwick declared, less desirous of checking a fair discussion on public issues than himself, but these clubs which made so much talk of equality had assumed a fanaticism and an intolerance of the opinions of others completely antagonistic to true republicanism. These societies, "without delegation or control, not emanating from the people, not responsible to them, not open in their deliberations nor admitting to them any but those of their own political opinions, and of endless duration, have modestly assumed the character of popular instructors, guardians of the people's guardians, and governors of their government." They were conspirators against the Constitution and the peace and safety of these United States. They were the authors of all evils felt or to be feared.[16]

Fitzsimons' amendment passed the Committee of the Whole but was defeated in the House proper by a clever ruse of the opposition. A Mr. Christie suggested that Mr. Fitzsimons' motion approving the Presidential denunciation of "self-created societies" be amended to refer only to those societies located in the four western counties of Pennsylvania. To Sedgwick's rage, this was agreed to by the tie-breaking vote of Speaker Muhlenberg. As planned by Christie and his friends, the Fitzsimons' amendment was now palpably absurd. It applauded the President for a specific set of words which he had never written; it joined him in regretting what he had never regretted. Only nineteen members, Sedgwick not among them, were to be counted for the amendment on the final vote (November 27, 1794). The House finally adopted a much milder form of reference to the societies, and the incident was closed.

Sedgwick, angry and hurt at the turn events had taken, did derive some satisfaction in noting that the Philadelphia "mob" had quite turned against "the disorganizing party," and that at the theatre there

---

15. (cont.)

disaffected once again, incited the founding of the "democratic societies," and kindled the dying embers of sedition into a blaze that threatened the peace and the liberties of the nation. *Annals*, IV, 912 (November 25, 1794).

16. *Annals*, IV, 897, 911–912 (November 24, 25, 1794); James T. Callender, *The Political Register* (Philadelphia, 1795), I, 108–112.

See Anthony Pasquin [John Williams], *The Hamiltoniad: or An Extinguisher for the Royal Faction of New England* (Boston, 1804), 47 ff. for an amusing caricature of the Federalists' fear of political-minded members of the "lower orders."

had been a long ringing burst of applause from the pit at the entry of the President. He trusted the "vile miscreants" who had attempted to destroy Washington's fame and good name would feel properly rebuked. As a further affirmation of his abhorrence of these "miscreants," Sedgwick subscribed for a dozen copies of Reverend Osgood's soon famous sermon denouncing the odious societies.

Shortly after the debate on the reply to the President's address was completed, another matter came up for congressional attention that also concerned—if indirectly—the "democratic societies." This was the revision of the Naturalization Law. Sedgwick and his political colleagues, incensed over the misuse of citizenship by certain newly arrived Frenchmen and Irishmen—highly liable to join the societies and the "incindiary" opposition, wished to stiffen the standards of admittance into the United States.

Ironically, however, it was James Madison, desiring to make its provisions more clear and efficacious, who first obtained leave to bring in a bill to amend the Naturalization Law.[17] Sedgwick and nearly "all the able federalists" immediately seized the opportunity to further their aim of rendering American citizenship "less cheap." [18] They secretly conferred, and it was agreed that Samuel Dexter should bring forward a motion to raise the naturalization requirements. That gentleman proposed, December 22, 1794, that "no alien should be admitted to the rights of citizenship, but on the oath of two credible witnesses, that in their opinion he was of good moral character and attached to the welfare of this country." Sedgwick seconded this motion and offered a few observations.

America, Sedgwick declared, had chosen for herself a form of government which left to its citizens as great a portion of freedom as was consistent with a social compact. Her government rested on public virtue and the general intelligence of the people. The damaging effect of

17. Madison wished to require an oath of allegiance, three years' notice of intention, and only five years' residence. Sedgwick considered this apprenticeship too short, and, for some not readily understandable reason, seems to have thought Madison was mainly motivated by a desire to exclude the further entrance of British commercial capital into this country.

18. Sedgwick to Ephraim Williams, December 12, 1794. *Loose Letters* of Theodore Sedgwick, S.P., M.H.S. Sedgwick was happy to note in this connection: "My policy on this subject which was formerly without support, is now considered as authordox [sic] by every intelligent man with whom I converse." Noah Webster wrote Sedgwick that recent emigrants "seem to make no just distinction between arbitrary govt & a govt of Laws" and that many of them were "warm Democrats." Noah Webster to Sedgwick, January 2, 1795. S.P., M.H.S.

irresponsibility in the individual citizen was correspondingly greater than in a non-republican government. Here, citizens early acquired the habits of "temperate discussion, patient reasoning, and a capacity of enduring contradictions" in the training ground of local community government. In our schools, community activities, and libraries were planted and fostered "the seeds of Republicanism." Should we "alone adopt the rash theory that the subjects of all Governments, Despotic, Monarchical, and Aristocratical, are, as soon as they set foot on American ground, qualified to participate in administering the sovereignty of our country?" Should we hold the benefits of membership in our nation so cheap "as to invite, nay, almost bribe, the discontented, the ambitious, and the avaricious of every country to accept them?" Did we wish a duplication of the troubles inflicted on the English by the Saxon, Danish, and Norman invaders?

The need for peopling the western lands was not so great as to excuse an indiscriminate acceptance of foreigners. A sparsely settled West did service to the nation's future. The vacant lands he considered "as the best capital stock of the future enjoyment of America; as an antidote against the poison of luxury; as the nursery of robust and manly virtue, and as a preventive of a numerous class of citizens becoming indigent, and therefore dependent."

If ever there was an inauspicious time for allowing the mass admission of Europeans, Sedgwick declaimed, it was now. The turbulent derelicts of war—whether from the French or the Allied side—were not fit material for the American way of life, where privileged orders of any sort were unknown. The amendment proposed by Mr. Dexter would not exclude all aliens; it would but sift out the undesirables. Meritorious individuals who were willing to serve a proper apprenticeship could still qualify themselves "to assume the character and discharge the duties of American citizenship." [19]

Sedgwick's speech on this occasion was not only typical of the Federalist attitude towards immigration but foreshadowed the Alien and Sedition Acts which would assist the downfall of the Federalist party. It was an attitude reflective of both partisan politics and sincere prejudice.

The project of restricting the naturalization of aliens took a nasty turn for Sedgwick and his friends when the Virginian William Branch Giles, one of the leading "Democrats" of the House, moved that all titled aliens

19. *Annals*, IV, 1005-1008 (December 22, 1794). This speech was highly regarded and much praised by George Cabot, William Vans Murray, Fisher Ames, John Fenno, Samuel Dexter, and other of Sedgwick's political friends.

solemnly renounce their titles in a court of law before admission to citizenship. The object of this manoeuvre was to have "the federal men" put on record as opponents of the motion and thus as "nobility-loving aristocrats." The Federals raced into the trap.

They insisted that Giles' motion declared for something which was already fully provided for. By taking an oath of citizenship anyone automatically abjured nobility. His title was, to all purposes, dissolved when his allegiance to the country which had granted him that title was dissolved. What was the sense of providing for the same thing twice? The acceptance of the amendment would be a partial justification of the false charge that there was in America a monarchical faction that must not be implemented. Such was the argument of Sedgwick and his colleagues,[20] and theoretically it was sound. Politically it was stupid in the extreme. They should have bent over backwards to avoid giving the appearance of favoring titled orders. However frivolous and trifling the Giles motion was, it would have harmed no one and should have been ignored, not opposed, by his opponents. Oppose it they did, even to the point of Mr. Dexter moving a counter amendment to the effect that any alien who owned a slave must sell it and specifically declare that he held "all men free and equal" before he could become eligible to citizenship.[21]

The Federalists were furious because Giles, according to plan, had called for the yeas and nays on his own amendment. They were in a dilemma. Should they back down "in terrorem" and declare their opposition to this amendment had been wrong, or should they be counted as opposed to the renunciation of titles? There was but one design in calling for a recorded vote, Sedgwick thundered: "to fix a stigma upon gentlemen in that House as friends to a nobility, when they were no such thing, and to raise a popular odium against them. . . . As to himself he did not care. He could not wish to stand better with his constituents than he actually did." [22]

A majority of the Federalists, with that obstinacy which was certainly their weakness as it was possibly their strength, cast their votes against

20. *Annals*, IV, 1035, 1054 (January 1, 2, 1795). Sedgwick opposed the amendment somewhat reluctantly, half foreseeing the danger involved, but felt it would be "ungenerous" not to give aid to his friends.

21. Sedgwick voted for Representative Dexter's Amendment (which lost 28–63) and made an uncomplimentary reference to the incongruity of the master and slave relationship in a republic. He took pains, however, to assert that a proposal for the "abolition of slavery in this country would be the height of madness." *Annals*, IV, 1040, (January 1, 1795).

22. *Ibid.*, IV, 1040, 1054 (January 1, 2, 1795).

the Giles' motion, which passed, January 2, 1795, 59–32, and the "Democrats" gloated openly over the success of their manoeuvre.

What explains Sedgwick's conduct during the debates over the "democratic societies" and the Naturalization Law? Was he motivated exclusively by blind partisanship? Was he inspired chiefly by the desire to retain political office and power?

Sedgwick's stand on these and many other issues can only be understood if one remembers his sincere belief that society was divided into two groups: "the better sort of people" and "the mob." One or the other must be on top, and he had no doubt at all as to which should be granted the honor. In a very real sense, Sedgwick never outgrew Shays' Rebellion. To his dying day, the great enemy was "mob rule"; the great danger, "anarchy." His was a partisanship that stemmed more from political fears than personal ambitions. It was a partisanship nourished, too, by a strong sense of sectional identification. As a New Englander, Sedgwick would find Virginia and Anti-Federalism indistinguishable; as a New Englander, he was perhaps all the more ready to declare Giles reprobate as well as wrong.

It would be idle to deny that Sedgwick enjoyed the prestige of office. The modest poverty he experienced in childhood possibly helps explain his ardent desire to succeed in his profession and carve for himself a place in the social circles of his day and the historical annals of his country. But his ambition was not the kind that could be encompassed by the perquisites of office; his partisanship was not that of the spoilsman. If he hungered for fame, he did so largely as the sincere patriot, one who was convinced he saw the only proper path for his countrymen. He would save them despite themselves. His was a limited vision, surely; but its inspiration was honest patriotism. It was a vision characteristic of the virtues and failings of New England Federalism.

Sedgwick's social activities in the years of his third congressional term were, on the whole, very much of a piece with the engagements and functions of the preceding years—but with one notable modification. For two months in the spring of 1794 his convalescent wife and their eldest daughter Eliza joined Sedgwick in Philadelphia.

Escaped from her confinement to the long and lonely New England winters, Pamela Dwight Sedgwick proved to be a natural-born belle. With her gracious manners and wistful good looks, she captivated Philadelphia society and enjoyed what was perhaps the longest period of unalloyed pleasure of her married life. Sedgwick proudly showed off his wife at "routs," tea parties, and "the play," frolicking generally with such abandon that at least twice they did not return to their lodgings "untill past one o'Clock."

When Sedgwick returned to Philadelphia in November for the second session, it was, he sadly reported, "sans famille." A certain solace was afforded him, however, by the press of engagements that crowded his social calendar. Though occasionally complaining of the frivolity of these occasions, Sedgwick, a man of gregarious and social habit, enjoyed and needed them. The complimentary banter and fine manners of the ladies of Philadelphia eased the loneliness, the self-conscious earnestness of the tense and excitable Massachusetts congressman. If he professed to dislike "the ladies parties," he attended not a few "from mere curiosity." One of his more amusing descriptions of these affairs concerned a reception given by Mrs. Blackwell, the wife of a Philadelphia clergyman, and the sister of "Mr. usually styled Count Bingham":

> The invitations were 10 to 12 days, preceding the evening. The house is very large and was so full that the guests, that is the male part, could neither sit, nor stand without jostling. This is a very convenient way at the close of the year of adjusting all visiting accounts. It had compleatly all the the satisfying [of] two objects —Economy and ostentation. . . . This is the first of Mrs. Blackwell's routs. How it will be received by the Bigotry of Philadelphia I know not. For altho the inhabitants are extremely indulgent to themselves, yet they will allow little to their clergy. They seem to imagine they shall be able to supply their own deficiency from the superabundance of their spiritual guides.[23]

More to his admitted liking than the Blackwell soirée was the evening's entertainment provided by Robert Morris. He described it to Pamela:

> I yesterday dined at Mr. Morris's, and did what I have not before done since I came to town, continue at the bottle till half past 10 oClock. What a rake for a husband you have got? I can only say that I made several attempts but ineffectually to escape. Perhaps it may be some apology that the vice President [Adams] staid as long as I did. . . . I have hardly ever in my life enjoyed more a convivial party. The vice President got himself relaxed and was as jovial as you have seen our friend Van Schaack. But I paid for it all in leaving

23. Sedgwick to Pamela, January 1, 1795. Papers of H. D. Sedgwick, S.P., M.H.S.
The press of social life in Philadelphia at this time is indicated by an earlier complaint of Sedgwick to his wife that though he had paid one hundred calls over a three months period, he was "yet fifty in arrears."

such company and returning to my solitary chamber. No dear wife to receive me to her arms—no delightful domestic comfort.[24]

Sedgwick lodged during the Third Congress in a rooming house on the outskirts of town with Peleg Wadsworth and George Leonard of Massachusetts and Jonathan Trumbull of Connecticut, a gay blade who had not "at the age of 55 discovered that he . . . [was] not a fit companion for Girls and Boys at 15." Sedgwick had become more and more disinclined to have social dealings with southerners and "democrats." His dining companions were now always "good yankees." Paradoxically, the more nationalistic he became, the more provincial he remained. He thought in terms of *national* power, defense, and glory, but felt only an ever smaller band of pure-minded eastern conservatives had the vision and ability to achieve such ends.

Here, as in so many ways, Sedgwick was representative of New England Federalism. Sedgwick, Ames, and other leading Hamiltonians failed to see that provincialism was the enemy of unity. Only by maintaining a political alliance broadly based on adherents in every section could the Federal men remain in power. An experienced and ambitious politician, Sedgwick had once acknowledged this fact; his mounting hatred for the Jacobins, foreign and domestic, now saw him forget it.

24. January 29, 1795. *Ibid.*

X

Sedgwick and the Jay Treaty, 1795–1796

> [A] man . . . [can] give as good evidence of Repub-
> licansim, of virtue, of sincere love of country, who
> should defend the Executive in the exercise of his
> Constitutional rights, as the man who should contend
> for any other department of Government.
>
> Theodore Sedgwick [1]

THE Jay Treaty was the dominating issue of the Fourth Congress [2] and
the chief concern of Theodore Sedgwick during his fifteen months of
service in that body. Jay had embarked in May, 1794, and had concluded
negotiations with British minister Grenville the following November,
but it was not until March 7, 1795, that the President finally received an
authenticated copy of the fateful treaty. Sedgwick found the delay inter-
minable and distressing.

He had been one of the first to favor the Jay mission; as he had
greatly feared the growing surge of hostility towards Britain that was
affecting many "good men," even in New England. The sidetracking of
Mr. Madison's proposals for commercial retaliation was, he felt, but a
temporary alleviation. An agreement must be reached with Britain
settling the varied causes of our mutual irritation—especially those concerning Britain's retention of the Northwest posts and her obnoxious
Orders in Council—if war was to be avoided and the passions of the
people subdued. Sedgwick followed the rumors over the progress of
the negotiations with deep anxiety and fluctuating emotions. He cursed

---

1. *Annals*, V, 515 (March 11, 1796).
2. Sedgwick had been elected to a fourth term in a close campaign with Thompson J. Skinner. He had been most distressed at the narrowness of his victory, and
blamed the apathy of his friends, the "distinterestedness" of his own conduct, and
the ingratitude of the people. The contest was so tight that its issue was not known
for almost a month. Madison wrote Jefferson (November 16, 1794): "Sedgwick's
fate is not known. . . . it is agreed that he will be well sweated." *Letters and Other
Writings of James Madison*, II, 11.

James Monroe, the newly appointed minister to France, for endangering the mission with his "fraternal" address before the French Assembly; he fretted with British minister Hammond over various treaty-defeating plans which Madison might possibly conjure up—especially if the treaty required legislative implementation; worried that the terms of the projected "commercial arrangement" might not be "honorable"; and despaired at the news that the Governor General of Canada was still inciting the Northwest Indians against their American neighbors.

The treaty finally arrived, and the Senate was called into special session on June 8th. After a fortnight of discussion, the treaty was approved, by a bare two-thirds majority (20–10), and subsequently signed and ratified by a troubled and uncertain Washington (August 14, 1795). The senatorial decision was in the long view correct and wise, however unsatisfactory the Jay Treaty was in certain respects. The treaty quite possibly prevented war with Britain, a war we could little have afforded at that period of our growth. It redeemed our territorial integrity by removing the British from our Northwest posts. It gave us certain trade rights in the East Indies, it established various arbitral commissions to deal with Anglo-American disputes that remained from the peace treaty of 1783, and it set up a claims tribunal to fix compensation for illegal British captures. In part, however, it represented a diplomatic retreat.[3]

Jay was probably not expected to obtain every point itemized in his instructions, but few thought he would not gain more than he did. The treaty said nothing about the impressment of our seamen or about compensation for slaves stolen in the Revolutionary War. It extended the contraband list, to provisions especially, in a way most unfair to France. It appeared to violate our Treaty of Alliance with France, overtly by its provision forbidding the sale of French prize goods here, and in spirit by giving up—vis-à-vis the British navy— our doctrine that "free ships make free goods." British claimants were given easier procedural treatment in the pursuit of their claims than were Americans, and, while the Mississippi was freely opened to the British, access to the British West Indies for American ships was in fact further restricted.

3. Two excellent, if occasionally conflicting, analyses of the Jay Treaty and its consequences are Samuel F. Bemis, *Jay's Treaty: A Study in Commerce and Diplomacy* (New York, 1923) and Bradford Perkins, *The First Rapprochement: England and the United States, 1795–1805* (Philadelphia, 1955), 5–79. Professor Perkins argues persuasively that Hamilton did not undercut Jay and that viewed in its long-term results, the Jay Treaty by no means represented a diplomatic defeat for the United States.

America's fast growing shipping industry was not sufficiently considered and a former ally treated badly.

In the final analysis it would appear that the most important consequence of the Jay Treaty was its effect on American politics and public opinion. There was no further pretence of "unity under Washington" once news of the Jay Treaty aroused and divided the American public. Equally with the Alien and Sedition Acts of 1798, the Jay Treaty debate of 1795–1796 can be said to be the event most responsible for the origin of the two party system in America. Because this system has worked to the long-run national benefit is no reason to forget that its original effect was to increase disunity and heighten sectional distrust.

One reason for the angry response excited by the Jay Treaty was the fact that in its inception, negotiation, and terms it was a partisan affair—it was Hamilton's treaty. Hamilton was deeply concerned not only for the national peace and safety, but for the national revenue, for the lucrative commercial interests involved in neutral commerce, for the avoidance of any kind of alliance with revolutionary France, and for our connection with British mercantile and financial interests. Such concerns do much to explain the treaty and its vulnerability to criticism.

For the most part, the merchant community, after a brief flurry of opposition due to the lack of equality granted American ships in Anglo-American trade, came around to accept the treaty. Such acceptance was made easier by the brilliant apologia for the treaty written by Hamilton as "Camillus." The commercial interest had been the core of the Federalists of 1787, leading supporters of the funding system and the national bank, the chief exponents of the neutrality program; now was not the time, they decided, to vent spite and leave the Hamiltonian fold. In Massachusetts, noted Sedgwick, "the disorganizers," "the recipients of secret service money from France," were fast losing many of their new recruits. The Bay State, with its fine core of noble husbandmen and sturdy shipbuilders, would not let itself be deprived of peace and happiness by the rabble mobs of Philadelphia, New York, and elsewhere. Massachusetts was too sensible, reasoned Sedgwick, to ignore the fact that a war would mean not only the end of her profitable, if restricted, trade as a neutral carrier but would lead very possibly to an all-defeating class struggle at home, "French stile." It was not that she had not suffered indignities at the hands of the shortsighted, arrogant Britons. She had, and not in silence. But Massachusetts would wisely accept the half-loaf of compromise and not insist on a total diplomatic victory at the risk of an impoverishing, anarchy-breeding war.[4] The true patriots of Massachusetts saw that the English were sufficiently chastised, that the balance of power in Europe must not be completely destroyed, that America must play a nobler part than that of colonial subservience to France. Thanks to Hamilton, the Congregational clergy, and the extreme violence of the speeches of the Democrats, the Bay State—if not its Governor Sam Adams—was "still sound."

Everyone was not as tractable, however, as the true patriots of Massachusetts. Hotly hated by a majority of the citizens of the country, the Jay Treaty proved such a political irritant that even General Washington was not exempted from criticism and insult, much to Sedgwick's horror. Criticism of the President came to a head in the House debate over the Address to the President in December, 1795. Madison, Sedgwick, and Samuel Sitgreaves of Pennsylvania were a committee of three to draft the reply to the President's annual message. Sedgwick, with the aid of Sitgreaves, inserted into the drafted reply, over Madison's strenuous opposition,[5] a statement expressing the "undiminished confidence of his fellow citizens in the President." By this means he hoped and expected to enlist the authority of the House in scourging the "vile scribblers" who had criticized the administration's pacific British policy. The self-evident optimism of the inserted clause was quickly questioned from the floor of the House, and there ensued an irritable debate of three days' duration. Sedgwick, declaring that the American scene represented an unparalleled spectacle of national happiness derived in large part from the zealous labors of Washington, insisted that the President was warmly supported by virtually all the respectable citizenry of the country. The Jay Treaty had not affected this; that treaty "was less the object of the dislike of some than affording the opportunity for the vent of passion and feelings deep-rooted before." Was the House to pay homage to the infamous attacks of certain licentious newspapers? Surely everyone appreciated that the sanctioning of a vote of confidence

4. Sedgwick had written earlier: ". . . The conduct of the british administration towards America, has undoubtedly been both week and wicked. But the people of that country, are disposed to live on the best terms with this, *because it is their interest to do so.* Why then should we quarrel with them?" Sedgwick to Ephraim Williams, January 28, 1795. *S.P., M.H.S.*

5. See Madison to Jefferson, December 12, 1795. *Letters and Other Writings of James Madison,* II, 63. Madison accused Sedgwick of trying to connect and "confound the treaty with the President." Sedgwick, himself, took snappish pleasure in observing that a gift to Washington of a French flag was made *"since* the Treaty was known for which our Democrats have threatened the just vengeance of our great & good ally." Sedgwick to Ephraim Williams, January 1, 1796. *S.P., M.H.S.*

would by no means "preclude the possibility of a free opinion" if the recent treaty with England "came under the consideration of the House. . . . When the House express their confidence in a public officer, they cannot mean that they believe him infallible, but only his character, grounded on his general conduct, receives their approbation." [6] Sedgwick's efforts, however, were to no avail. The address was finally recommitted and later emerged containing a modest compliment to the President,[7] no mention of "undiminished confidence," and a hesitating endorsement of the recently negotiated "treaties" in so far as they were consistent with the national honor and the Constitution.

The "treaties" comprised the recent Algerian, Spanish, and Indian conventions, as well as that of John Jay. Sedgwick had made an abortive attempt, April 13, 1795, to have the House make a general provision for "executing in good faith" all four treaties at the same time; thus smuggling the Jay Treaty appropriation in with that for the three more popular treaties. This blatant bit of logrolling had been ridiculed and defeated by the Republican majority—now strengthened by Sedgwick's latest *bête noire* Albert Gallatin—and each of the quite independent treaties had to stand forth according to its individual merit.

Sedgwick favored the Algerian Treaty, though displeased that it was so expensive,[8] believing the Mediterranean trade to be profitable and worthy of relief from the Corsair pirates; approved the Spanish Treaty,

---

6. *Annals*, V, 146–147 (December 15, 1795). A "letter from New York" in the Boston *Independent Chronicle* (December 28, 1795) characterized Sedgwick's efforts as follows: "The old womanish whining and sniveling of Sedgwick is become proverbial; he is laughed at, even by his friends."

7. It spoke of "the affectionate attachment" felt for *his character*. Sedgwick took every occasion to point out that the "attachment" was not "diminished." He was pleased to note that on Washington's birthday, in 1796, the Philadelphia Assembly proprietors "engaged the *Circus* for the evening & . . . [went] to an expense for decorations amounting to . . . more than 1,500 dollars. . . . This is the man in whom the *confidence* of the people is *diminished*. This object the feds and antis equally concur in, and indeed vie with each other." Sedgwick to Ephraim Williams, February 20, 1796. S.P., M.H.S.

However unshaken the trust of the Assembly proprietors in the President, it does seem that his popularity was at its lowest ebb.

8. He sharply opposed, however, the recommendations of a committee of his friends that the building of frigates be now discontinued except for two half-completed vessels. Sedgwick foresaw "that in case we should abandon the means of rapulsion we should provoke contempt and a renewal of plunder. Indeed when our commercial navigation exceed [s] probably that of any other nation excepting G.B. we ought not surely to be destitute of all means of protecting it." Sedgwick to Ephraim Williams, February 16, 1796. S.P., M.H.S.

which determined the Georgia-Florida boundary and secured our right to navigate the Mississippi; and heartily applauded General Wayne's treaty, which made peace with some northern Indian tribes. These were, however, admittedly "but the preliminaries." After much "unfortunate delay" and several conferences between the Secretary of State Timothy Pickering and Sedgwick and his friends, the Jay Treaty was sent to the House with a presidential request that the necessary appropriation be voted forthwith. A momentous debate on a fundamental constitutional issue was in the offing, and the importance of the occasion was realized on all sides. Sedgwick dramatically reported: "The storm thickens and the aspect of the house is threatening. If disorganization prevails I see not but that [it] will then be demenstrated that we cannot live in the same family." [9]

The storm broke on March 2, 1796, with the motion of Edward Livingston, Republican from New York, that the President should be required to submit to the House for its study all papers leading up to the Jay Treaty. It was impossible, Livingston declared, for the House to make a correct decision on the propriety of the treaty appropriation if it had not all the available information in hand. The Republicans had decided to fight for the right of the House virtually to participate in the treaty-making process. Sedgwick had been afraid of just this development, but it caught many of his Federalist colleagues quite unprepared.

The burden of the support of the Livingston motion was borne about equally between its author, Madison, Gallatin, and Giles. They contended that they did not demand for the House a right to formulate treaties, but merely a check upon the treaty-making power when that power conflicted with others explicitly vested in the House of Representatives. If the treaty-making power was not to be limited in any way by existing laws, if it automatically repealed all conflicting laws, then the legislature was but the tool of the Executive, and the Executive, with the advice and consent of the Senate, was really the giver as well as the executor of the nation's laws. The President and Senate would

---

9. Sedgwick to unnamed correspondent (probably Ephraim Williams), March 2, 1796. *S.P.*, M.H.S.

Such threats of possible secession were fairly prevalent at this time—see *The Western Star*, April 26, 1796—but in Sedgwick's case were more symptomatic of sound and fury than actual intent. He wrote that "the conversation of a seperation is taking place almost in every company, and even I am obliged to moderate the zeal & cool the passions of more cool and temperate men." Sedgwick to Williams, April 1, 1796. *S.P.*, M.H.S.

be able to promulgate any legislation they pleased "under color of treaty." The authority of Congress, they argued, was legally co-operative "with the treaty power on those legislative subjects submitted to Congress by the Constitution." Treaties were not *necessarily* supreme over national law as they were over state law, and Congress was well within its rights to "call for papers" and deliberate at leisure. A postponement of action on executing the treaty was, moreover, certainly in order, until explicit assurance was received from Britain that she would in the future treat America as a firm friend and full equal. Her conduct since the signing of the treaty had continued most unrepentant. Fresh instances of impressment in the British West Indies were every week occurring.

It would not be reasonable to impute any but the most patriotic and honorable motives to these men. Sedgwick's opinion that they were slaves of the French, desirous of creating chaos in our foreign relations in order that debts owed British citizens might be evaded, the funding system demolished, and the hated merchant capitalists made bankrupt, was assuredly partisan in inspiration. It is true that many of the leading treaty opponents were agrarian minded and did not look upon peace, imposts, and the profits of neutral trade with the loving care of the Federalists, but their opposition seems to have sprung not from partisan politics alone but from a sincere dislike of the treaty, a sincere distrust of executive power, and a sincere belief that only in a government grounded on legislative supremacy could liberty be protected.

What is not generally known is that the Federalists were divided as to the advisability of fighting the initial skirmish represented by the Livingston motion. Now for all intents and purposes a regular party, they had decided in caucus by a majority of a single vote that a full-scale opposition should be offered. Sedgwick had felt it should not. He wished his party merely to vote against the motion, virtually without comment. They were sure to be beaten—the self-pride of the House, alone, would assure that—and they should therefore bide their time and husband their weapons until the discussion on the treaty appropriation itself. Others thought differently, however, Sedgwick reported, and passion rather than "sound discretion" proved victorious.[10] It was decided that the Federalists would make an all-out fight against the call for information. In this fight the best speech on the Federalist side—by general agreement—was that of Theodore Sedgwick. This speech represented most probably "his finest hour." On its occasion he not only expressed concisely the master principles of Hamilton but, speaking to the under-

10. Sedgwick to Ephraim Williams, March 16, 1796. *Ibid.*

lying constitutional questions, struck out powerfully along original lines of thought. Always earnest, industrious, and competent, when Sedgwick arose in the early afternoon of March 11, 1796, before the House in Committee he assumed brilliance as well.

In its principles as in its consequences, Sedgwick declared, this was the most important question which had ever been debated in the House. The point at issue was no less than whether the House should "by construction and implication extend its controlling influence to subjects which were expressly, and he thought exclusively, delegated by the people to another department." Those men who had constantly warned us against "broad construction" and unwarranted implications were now guilty of twisting the Constitution in the most farfetched of interpretations. It was true, of course, that *if* the House had the authority to form treaties, it had "a right to all the means of exercising an intelligent discretion," and therefore the right to the papers concerning the instructions and negotiations upon which the treaties were based. But the House had not this authority.

He was quite aware, he said, how unenviable was the position of a man "who should attempt to limit the extent of power, claimed by an assembly to which he should address himself." Everybody naturally hated any diminishment of their power and glory, but egotism must bow before the constitutional doctrine of "division of powers."

The Constitution had specified that treaties made under the authority of the United States were part of the supreme law. What treaties then were "made under the authority of the United States"? Those treaties indeed which were negotiated under the direction of the President and approved by two-thirds of the Senate; such treaties by their very nature were binding. How could one negotiate to preserve peace, terminate war, enter an alliance, or form a commercial arrangement if one had not the power to pledge his country? There would be many situations in the history of the foreign relations of any country when "unlimited powers of negotiation" would be necessary to prevent "enormous, perhaps ruinous evils." Surely, such a power might be abused, but "a national association required, for the great purpose of preservation, an unlimited confidence on many subjects." Would adding the House to the treaty-making process lessen the amount of power involved? No pattern of governmental arrangements could exclude the possibility of abuse.

The representatives were not the only protectors of the people; the senators were equally so. These gentlemen were "the most enlightened and the most virtuous of our citizens"; they occupied their elevated positions because of the confidence the people had in them individually. They were elected not by "an ignorant herd, who could be cajoled, flattered, and deceived—not even [by] the body of enlightened american citizens; but their legislators, men to whom the real characters of the candidates would be known."

Mr. Madison's theory that "legislative cooperation" was necessary for the execution of any treaty concerning a subject on which the House in the ordinary run of affairs had cognizance, was quite impossible. Why was it never mentioned or evidently considered until the present occasion? If this was the true desire of the Constitutional framers, why was it not expressed in that instrument? [11] Why had these Fathers of the Constitution expressed quite the opposite construction in their state ratification conventions? If the supporters of the Livingston motion were right in their construction, "if this was the understanding of the people at the time they deliberated on and ratified the Constitution, the power of the President and the Senate of making Treaties, which then created the most serious deliberation and alarming apprehensions, was the most innocent thing in nature. It could bind the essential interests of the nation in nothing." He appealed to the reason of the House. "Could any man really believe that the agitation which a discussion of this subject [then] occasioned, more, perhaps, than any other in the Constitution, could have [had] for its object only the power of the President and Senate, in which two-thirds of the latter must concur, to digest schemes of Treaties to be laid before the Legislature for its approbation?"

The Anti-Federalists of 1787–1788 "had stated to their constituents that the power of making Treaties . . . was [just so] extensive as was now contended" by the supporters of the administration. Could anyone "possibly believe that the enemies of the Constitution could have made the charge against it, and that its friends would have admitted the truth of it, on the hypothesis that it was unfounded and false?" This had been "the concurrence of men who could not have united to deceive,

11. Sedgwick declared that it was:
   A fact and must yet be stated if it can be found to be capable of statement from the delicacy of revealing the proceedings of the convention, that a motion was made there to submit treaties to the house for its concurrence, & was rejected, Madison being a principal opponent. How shameful and impudent then is his present conduct?

Sedgwick to unnamed correspondent, March 23, 1796. S.P., M.H.S.

with regard to which it was impossible they should be mistaken." It "formed a guide for our opinion, which could not mislead, which no degree of stupidity could mistake, nor the most ingenious sophistry successfully misrepresent."

The men who had framed the Constitution, the people who had ratified it, alike understood the treaty-making power to be the exclusive province of the Executive and Senate. Further proof of this could be found in certain amendments to the Constitution which had been offered by various state ratification conventions—particularly that of Virginia—complaining of the complete exclusion of the House from the power of making and ratifying treaties. Why had Virginia and the others so complained if the House was actually a party to this power, as the Old Dominion's respected son James Madison would now have it?

A study of the construction of the treaty power which had been given by all branches of our government to the present time further confirmed the exclusion of the House in the ratification of any and all treaties. In 1789 and 1794 Mr. Madison had proposed a discrimination of import duties between nations with whom we had a commercial treaty and those with whom we did not. This was a virtual acknowledgment that those treaties, which had been ratified by the President and Senate alone, were distinctly legitimate. Could it be perhaps that the Constitution gave the government power to treat with every nation on earth but Great Britain? "Might [one] not be permitted . . . to inquire, if this treaty had been formed with any other Power, with the precise stipulations it now contains, whether ever would have existed this doubt of constitutionality?"

Mr. Gallatin's interpretation that any stipulation in a treaty which required legislative provision, or which required the repeal of a previous law, could not become supreme law until it had received legislative sanction, was, if less sweeping, quite as erroneous as that of Mr. Madison, argued Sedgwick. There was surely no limitation expressed in the Constitution on which to found this objection. An historical study of the expression of varying groups at the time of the formulation and ratification of the Constitution, and of the congressional debates of the last seven years, undeniably proved that the authority given by the Constitution to the President and Senate to make treaties was a complete and unrestricted authority. This being so, treaties so formed did in fact become supreme law and, being solemn compacts, *bound* the public faith. A treaty could be "unratified" by the House and the appropriation refused only at the complete disregard of national faith and reputation. The House simply had no business demanding the papers of another department of government in a matter in which its authority was evidently and properly *nominal.*

The fact that certain treaties required legislative action to carry them into effect gave the House no moral right to exercise its discretion as to whether or not it would take the requisite action. The House had no more "right" to refuse to appropriate money to carry into effect this now ratified treaty than it would to refuse to appropriate money for the salary of the President once that salary was ascertained by law. "To promote the public happiness it was essential to hold sacred and to perform the public engagements. In this were included all engagements, whether expressed in the form of Constitution, of laws, or of Treaties; in any way, indeed, in which the people had agreed that their will and their duties might be expressed." No man of honor could or would vote for Mr. Livingston's insidious, unconstitutional resolution.[12]

Sedgwick's long historical analysis of the moral and constitutional inability of the House to refuse to execute a properly ratified treaty was applauded extravagantly by his Federalist friends. Sedgwick demurely described his triumph and an accompanying gift in a letter to his daughters:

[I had] spoken about an hour and an half during which time there was the most profound attention. By my exertions in so full an assembly, and by speaking in a rarified air that by so many breaths was rendered unfit for respiration, I felt so fatigued and exhausted that I was obliged to make a pause. On which Gentlemen, (an occurrence I have never before seen) on both sides rose and expressed their esteem for me and the gratification they recd. from my observations & desired that I would take another day to finish them. This I declined because I knew that it might be imputed to vanity, and might excite envy.—During the pause Miss Patterson beckoned to Mr. Sitgreaves, and gave him a delicious sweetmeat of Orange, neatly folded and accompanyed by a note—"Mr. Sedgwick, as an evidence of the most perfect gratitude, for the pleasure derived from a display of his irresistable eloquence, will accept this with the profound esteem of his friend M. Patterson." I recd. the present and put it in my pocket, but did not open it until returning home after the adjournment.—It is well I did not for it would have confused & embarrassed me exceedingly.—I was last evening for a few minutes at the drawing room, and was covered with confusion by the compliments I recd. & particularly from the ladies.[13]

12. *Annals,* V, 514–530 (March 11, 1796).
13. Sedgwick to Misses Sedgwick, March 12, 1796. Papers of H. D. Sedgwick, S.P. , M.H.S.

The restorative confection was indeed but one of many compliments extended the orator. Vice-President Adams, who was present on the occasion of the speech, shook Sedgwick's hand and declared: "From my heart I thank you, I will not flatter. I never flatter, you least of all men, for I know you would despise it, but your speech for matter, style and delivery exceeds anything I ever heard, and I have heard much good speaking." [14] Rufus King, George Cabot, Uriah Tracy, Christopher Gore, and Oliver Ellsworth all praised it as a model of eloquence and an unanswerable analysis of the treaty-making power, and Robert Morris declared at a public dinner in Philadelphia:

> There have been a great deal of good speaking in all the House on the present subject, but I think that all the speakers ought to join in cursing our friend, for he has so distanced every one that their speeches compared with his appear mere trash. It was precisely such as he [Morris] himself would have delivered if he could speak as he wished,—it was absolutely perfect.[15]

These high-sung praises came, however, from staunch Federalists, and in the House such men were in a minority. The Livingston motion passed, March 24, by a vote of 62–37. The Madisonians were joined by others who judged the call for information harmless or who felt the amour-propre of the House in need of support. Sedgwick was not surprised at the result. He had a week earlier forewarned his friends at home, declaring: "A call for information carries with it so much force as the means of gratifying curiosity that we have always found such motives irresistable." [16] Quite willing to thwart this irresistible curiosity, however, was the President. Firmly assuming the Federalist viewpoint, he refused to honor the House request, criticizing it in a stinging reply as an unconstitutional and dangerous innovation.

The debates on the Livingston motion and on the resolution to appropriate the money necessary to execute the treaty were actually all of a piece. Whether the House would receive the negotiation papers or appropriate funds were questions subsidiary to the main consideration: Did the House have the right to participate in the treaty-making power to the extent of refusing to help execute a treaty properly ratified and previously proclaimed? In the latter phase of the debate, that concerning the appropriation resolution proper, Sedgwick did not take a particularly

14. Berkshire Historical and Scientific Society, *Collections*, III, 99.
15. *Ibid.*, 100.
16. Sedgwick to Ephraim Williams, March 18, 1796. *S.P.*, M.H.S.

active part. Here Fisher Ames was the star, with his impassioned oratory and piteous description of the horrors of the war that would surely follow a refusal to implement the treaty. As self-appointed commandant of the treaty forces, Sedgwick concentrated upon persuading one Bay Stater to change his vote and another not to, and riding herd on an old friend, Jonathan Dayton, and a timid opponent, William Findley.[17] In addition, he rose on at least two occasions to address the House with force and brevity on the *relative* advantages of the treaty, the danger of civil war in America, and the necessity of seeing that the honor of the nation remained untarnished.

The most dangerous of the opposition arguments, in Sedgwick's eyes, continued to be that of Mr. Gallatin—with its seemingly modest request for legislative independence in the case of treaties which required legislative provision or which repealed existing law.[18] Sedgwick believed this interpretation was historically inaccurate, subversive of the doctrine of the "division of powers," and "capable of being easily demolished." [19]

As the debate continued, Sedgwick again attempted to have all recent treaties handled in one great package—certain of the others being not yet fully executed. This shopworn proposal got short shrift. Not discouraged, he continued to hope that the Republicans with but a small majority in the House would not dare declare war on the Senate, the Judiciary, and the Executive, combined, and was soon cheered by the public expressions of support for the treaty which, after some concerted prodding, now began to descend upon Congress. With understandable inconsistency the Federalists now encouraged and indeed actively promoted "popular interference in public matters." Sedgwick received a

17. Sedgwick wrote Loring Andrews, April 5, 1796: "How disgusting is it . . . that on the weakness & wickedness of unprincipled men in a popular government the happiness of millions may frequently depend?" S.P., M.H.S.

18. Sedgwick told Representative Harrison of Virginia: "As an Italian and traitor he [Gallatin] is beneath notice, but as the Representative of your party and its head he deserves attention." Sedgwick to Ephraim Williams, April 13, 1796. S.P., M.H.S.

Gallatin and Sedgwick had at least two sharp encounters during the debate. When Gallatin declared the resolution phrase, "in good faith" to be superfluous, asking sarcastically just how a treaty could be carried into effect with bad faith, Sedgwick rejoined: ". . . he knew what it was to carry a Treaty into effect with good faith, but left the gentleman who made the inquiry to discover the reverse." *Annals,* V, 966 (April 14, 1796).

Later, after Gallatin had made a particularly bitter attack on the Federalist party, Sedgwick called his speech a great "Falsehood." Gallatin's reply "was meek, humble, polite & replete with personal compliments to myself," the martyred warrior reported. Sedgwick to unnamed correspondent, April 22, 1796. S.P., M.H.S.

19. Sedgwick to Ephraim Williams, March 26, 1796. S.P., M.H.S.

copy of a Memorial to Congress from eleven hundred "respectable men" of Boston and memorial petitions from Dalton, Stockbridge, Great Barrington, and nine other Berkshire County towns, all praying that Mr. Jay's treaty be put into immediate effect and many praising Sedgwick's own conduct and statesmanship in the crisis at hand.[20]

Influenced by the dramatic appeal of Fisher Ames, the balance had, by the end of April, gradually swung towards moderation and a Federalist victory. The appropriation resolution passed the Committee of the Whole, 50–49, with Chairman Frederick Muhlenberg casting the deciding vote,[21] and a last ditch attempt by the Republicans to salvage a partial victory died with the defeat, in the House proper, of Massachusetts Representative Henry Dearborn's amendment. The latter was in the form of a preamble to the resolution, and declared that the treaty the House was about to execute was, if necessary, highly objectionable. Sedgwick and the other Federalists would have none of it. Flushed with the imminence of victory, Sedgwick went further than most of his colleagues. The treaty, he said, contained "more advantages than any, than all the treaties ever formed by this country." The Dearborn amendment was a mischievous thing:

> If they passed [it] . . . what language would be strong enough to reprobate the censure which would be cast upon the other branches of Government? Had the President and Senate done more; and if no more than their duty who had given [the] House the authority to comment upon their acts? The proposed amendment declared that they had done the thing that was wrong. Would they bear, ought they to bear this? They ought not to bear it.[22]

By a vote of 49–50 (April 30) the President and Senate were exempted from this mental burden, and the appropriation resolution, without the preamble, then immediately passed the House, 51–48. It was ordered that a bill be brought in pursuant to the resolution, and Messrs. Hillhouse, Gallatin, and Sedgwick were made a committee of three to prepare the same. The bill was quickly prepared and passed, the majority including both those who thought the treaty a good one and that larger group which thought it a necessary evil.

20. Many of the Berkshire County Fourth of July celebrations included toasts to Sedgwick as a "firm upholder of the Constitution." See, for example, *Andrews's Western Star*, July 12, 1796.

21. This courageous act wrote *finis* to Muhlenberg's political popularity and nearly to his life as well. A mentally unbalanced brother-in-law, incensed by Muhlenberg's rescue of the treaty, stabbed him several days afterwards, wounding him severely. Paul Wallace, *Muhlenbergs of Pennsylvania* (Philadelphia, 1951), 287.

22. *Annals*, V, 771 (April 6, 1796).

It would not be correct, of course, to say that the House by passing the Jay Treaty appropriation abdicated its claim to use discretion in the execution of previously ratified treaties, or assented to the theory that senatorial ratification was a "declaration of the public will" binding on every citizen.[23] That issue was still the subject of debate in 1867 [24] and later. But an important precedent for "compliance" had been established, and in its establishment Theodore Sedgwick had played a significant part. In the opinion of the editor of the *Western Star*, Sedgwick's contribution deserved no less than an ode:

. . . . . .

'T was then, resistless, at thy country's call
    Thy voice, O Sedgwick, faction's fatal dread,
In awful accents thunder'd through the hall,
    And wide through empire's utmost limit spread.

In vain Great Gallatin's capacious mind
    Urged all its force the contest to maintain;
Thou gave his efforts to the murmuring wind,—
    Even Giles and Madison were heard in vain.

Edged with keen truths thy powerful accents fly,
    Conviction's pointed dart each word attends;

23. When the House was rebuffed in its call for "the Treaty papers," it passed (57–35) a resolution stating that:

> When a Treaty stipulates regulations on any of the subjects submitted by the Constitution to the power of Congress, it must depend, for its execution, as to such stipulations, on a law or laws to be passed by Congress. And it is the Constitutional right and duty of the House of Representatives, in all such cases, to deliberate on the expediency of carrying such Treaty into effect, and to determine and act thereon, as, in their judgment, may be most conducive to the public good.

Annals, V, 771 (April 6, 1796).

24. The parallel between the treaty appropriation debates of 1796 and 1867 is striking and instructive. During the House discussion over the bill for an appropriation for the annexation of Alaska, in June–July, 1867, a group of "House Constitutionalists" succeeded in attaching an amendment, whereby the House asserted its right to be consulted when matters were contained in a treaty which "involved the exercise of rights" exclusively vested in the legislative department. The Senate refused to submit to this demand and the House finally gave way. See *Congressional Globe*, Fortieth Congress, second session, Part IV, 3621–3625; 4052–4055; Part V, 4392–4394; Part V Appendix, 305–309.

Firm as the unshaken Andes meets the sky,
Thou stand'st the bulwark of thy country's friends.[25]

Although the debate over Jay's Treaty absorbed much of the time
and attention of the Fourth Congress, it did not absorb all. Sedgwick, for
one, found time to damn French Minister Fauchet and "traitor" Edmund
Randolph, continue his fight with Madison and Gallatin over indirect
taxes, and fight an unjust insinuation of personal corruption.[26]

As much as any man, Theodore Sedgwick was the leader of the
Federalist minority in the House during the Fourth Congress. Early in

25. *Andrew's Western Star*, July 12, 1796.

26. This last fight was necessitated by the testimony of two imaginative speculators named Randall and Whitney. These gentlemen and their Canadian merchant
associates wished to receive a grant from Congress of some 60,000 square miles of
land about the Great Lakes. As a means of facilitating matters they planned to reserve certain shares in the venture for interested congressmen. This scheme revealed,
they were brought before the bar of Congress. Early in the testimony, Representative
Christie testified that he understood from Mr. Randall that Representative Sedgwick
had been prepared to help the speculators to draw up the necessary memorial to
Congress.

An enraged Sedgwick was on his feet to give the lie to this allegation. He had
never met Randall and had only met Mr. Whitney at the behest of a Stockbridge
acquaintance, when he had informed him that it would be quite improper for a
member of Congress to be a party to any land purchase necessitating congressional
action. It would be a case of a man making a bargain with himself. He truly believed that there was no congressman more "teazed with applications of this private
kind" than himself, and certainly none more anxious to avoid any proposal at all
suspicious. *Annals*, V, 211 (January 5, 1796); House *Journal*, III, 404–405.

Actually almost no one seems to have given any credence to the hearsay testimony concerning Sedgwick. The whole "trial" disintegrated for lack of proof that
the speculators meant to give rather than sell the "congressional shares," and the
highly ruffled Sedgwick was completely exonerated. Representative Christie backed
down, and Giles of Virginia, meeting Sedgwick at a party shortly afterwards, took
occasion to express his complete confidence in the public morality of his political
enemy:

> Giles who introduced Christie as a Witness came to me & with his hand
> Spread & laid on his breast said "upon my honor, sir, I did not know that
> Christie was to mention your name, and had I known it, I would not have
> moved to have had him sworn." I answered him with equal solemnity, "I am
> very unwilling [not] to *hope* that your declaration is true, for otherwise I must
> hold you an egregious blockhead or a confirm-ate Scoundrel."

Sedgwick to Ephraim Williams, January 10, 1796. *S.P.*, M.H.S.

December, 1795, when the House was being organized, he had been chosen by a caucus of Federalist congressmen to be their candidate for speaker.[27] Because of their slight minority position, these gentlemen had later deemed it more advisable to promote the candidacy of the conciliatory Jonathan Dayton, but it was Sedgwick who led the Federalists in the House Finance Committee, later to be known as the Committee on Ways and Means. This committee was the offspring of the brilliant Republican leader Albert Gallatin, who had originated it as a means of depriving the Secretary of the Treasury of a certain amount of initiative in the formulation of financial policy. It was composed of fourteen members and represented the leadership of both parties. Sedgwick and William Loughton Smith of South Carolina were foremost among the Federalist financial experts who participated in its deliberations, and Madison and Gallatin led its Republican wing.

In Sedgwick's view, Madison, Gallatin, and "the disorganizing faction," despite their protestations, really cherished the national debt for the political capital they hoped to make of it. They assumed the posture of gentlemen eager to retire the debt and accused the Feds of wishing to perpetuate it, but this was clearly but a pose. If they really wished to reduce it, declared Sedgwick, they would co-operate with the supporters of the administration in levying additional excise taxes, promoting the "internal revenues," and establishing a true Sinking Fund.[28]

The conclusive establishment of a Sinking Fund became for Sedgwick a cause as well as a policy. It had succeeded Funding and Assumption as a symbol of concern for the public credit and the fiscal honor of the nation. In the previous Congress he had sought to transform certain temporary excise taxes into a system irrevocable and permanent. Sedgwick had promoted the passage of various excise taxes and duties with the hope that they would insure the public credit against the Jeffersonians of the future as well as the defense requirements of the present. In February, 1795, he had addressed an impassioned plea to the House to make provision for the financing of a Sinking Fund and the orderly retirement of the national debt. Sedgwick sought to mark the forthcoming retirement of Hamilton from the Treasury with the establishment of

27. Sedgwick to Ephraim Williams, December 7, 1795. *Loose Letters* of Theodore Sedgwick, *S.P.*, M.H.S. Two years earlier, Sedgwick had figured prominently in the election of the speaker but the post had then gone to Frederick Muhlenberg, a political independent of sorts. Muhlenberg had been elected over Sedgwick, December 2, 1793, by a majority of ten votes.

28. Sedgwick to Ephraim Williams, February 5, 1796. *Ibid.*

a system that would insure the fiscal accomplishments of Hamilton against future mismanagement or misadventure.[29] Definite provision must be made for retiring the national debt. A permanent Sinking Fund would tend to fix the market price of government securities at home as well as facilitate the nation's credit operations abroad. The debt would become less a subject than an instrument of commerce. It would serve as capital rather than monopolize existing capital. America must secure its citizens against a sudden and excessive tax load in the future, and lessen its possible future dependence upon the money markets of a war-torn Europe, by creating a fund from surplus revenues adequate for the payment of about eight per cent of the six per cent stock annually. Sufficient revenue for this purpose could be gained from such indirect taxes as a stamp duty, a tax on leather, a duty on private carriages, etc. The statements of Madison and Gallatin that additional excise taxes were unfair to the poor husbandman were ridiculous; and their vague talk of a direct tax, false and insincere. The excise taxes in question were neither large nor burdensome, Sedgwick insisted, and would probably annihilate the politically divisive national debt in fifteen years.[30]

Certain bills making partial provision for a Sinking Fund passed the House, February, 1795,[31] but Sedgwick was not satisfied and the Fourth Congress saw him calling, unsuccessfully, for additional excise taxes. He was, in his view, almost alone in his anxiety for the Treasury balances of the future. Even more was he convinced that Madison and his fellow Republicans were determined to thwart him at every turn. Sedgwick viewed the Finance Committee as an arena and saw himself and Madison as contesting champions. Their encounters were frequent and, if one is to judge by Sedgwick's correspondence, after each encounter Madison was "highly discomforted" and the other members of the committee

29. Sedgwick wrote Henry Van Schaack: "If we can establish the sinking fund, we shall have put the security of the government for some time beyond the reach of danger. There are 20 Senators who may be pretty well depended on and the operations of the government will depend almost wholly on mechanical principles." February 3, 1795. S.P., M.H.S.

30. Annals, IV, 1175–1181 (February 5, 1795).

31. Among these was the duty on private carriages that would shortly be the subject of a controversial decision of the Supreme Court to the effect that such an excise was not a direct tax and so need not be levied on an inequitable per capita state basis. According to Sedgwick, William Giles had in December, 1794, made him a proposal that if the Federalists gave up the carriage tax, Giles and his friends would agree to renew various other excise duties. Sedgwick, after consultation with his friends, refused. Sedgwick to Henry Van Schaack, December 27, 1794. S.P., M.H.S.

much impressed by Sedgwick's rough handling of the Virginian.[32] Whatever his forensic success in committee, his legislative triumphs in behalf of further provision for a Sinking Fund were limited to the retention of old excise duties and a modest loan provision for the United States Bank. Sedgwick looked with admiring envy at Mr. Pitt, just completing a new loan for £18,000,000, and at his subjects, those "Wonderful People," the amenable English.[33]

Sedgwick did not complete his fourth congressional term by several months, resigning in June, 1796, upon his election to the United States Senate. To the very last, though, he was as industrious and as consistent a Federalist as any legislator in the House. That is not to say that Sedgwick prostrated himself to the opinions of his party. He voted with the majority of the Federalists about ninety per cent of the time.[34] He did so, however, not as a political Uriah Heep but, rather, as the personification of Federalist thought, virtue, and prejudice. Any conflict between duty to country and to party worried him little, if at all; he was sincerely convinced that what was best for the "good people," "the honest patriots," was best for the nation.

On May 9, 1796, Theodore Sedgwick left the national House of Representatives. His long and tiring journey home was relieved by the warm and cordial welcome which he received at each stage of his travels,[35] and perhaps by the recollection of his contributions to the success of the new government. In his eight years of service in the House he had earned a national political reputation. As pompous and vain as he may sometimes have appeared, it was no foolish coxcomb who had gained the respect, admiration, and affection of such men as Washington, Hamilton,

32. Sedgwick wrote Loring Andrews, the Stockbridge printer, in February, 1796, boasting of his successful effort to call the "bluff" of Mr. Madison and the advocates of direct taxes. He had proposed that a subcommittee be appointed to study the matter of a direct tax and prepare a bill if such seemed feasible. He was certain that it would be impossible for such a group to come forth with a measure either practicable or equitable. He was happy to report that Madison, who had been appointed chairman of the subcommittee, now confessed to him in private that "from a more intimate view of the subject" he had "great doubt of the expediency of doing more than taking some preliminary steps at the present session." Sedgwick to Andrews, February 10, 1796. *Norton Papers*, M.H.S.
33. Sedgwick to Henry Van Schaack, March 4, 1796. S.P., M.H.S.
34. Orin Grant Libby in his *Political Factions in Washington's Administrations* confuses on at least three occasions Sedgwick's votes and consequently classifies him as less of a party stalwart than in fact he was.
35. William Hindman to Sedgwick, May 30, 1796. S.P., M.H.S.

Rutledge, King, C. C. Pinckney, Carroll, and Ames. If he was a good hater, he was also a hard worker; if he was occasionally impetuous and wearily self-righteous, he was also an honest patriot and an able political warrior.

XI

Senator Sedgwick and the French Crisis, 1797–1798

Few reason, & fewer still feel as they ought. That nation which is the most infamous for its breach of faith; detestable for its crimes & which threatens to deluge the world with its atheism, immorality, and tyranny;—which has done every thing in its power to create in every american breast sentiments of disgust; indignation & horror. That nation is the object of the fond attachment of a great portion of our citizens.

Theodore Sedgwick [1]

SEDGWICK has seriously considered quitting the national political scene with the end of the Fourth Congress and devoting his remaining years to his profession and family. His party friends in Massachusetts, however, would have none of it. Sedgwick must remain in the national councils; if not in the House, then in the Senate. Vanity and duty combined to persuade him. He expressed but mild distress when, as has been noted, he was elected, June 11, 1796, to the seat in the United States Senate left vacant by the resignation of Caleb Strong.

There was at this time a complete turnover in the state's representation in the national Senate. Not only Strong but also George Cabot had resigned. There had existed a tacit understanding that one of Massachusetts' senators should be "commercial," the other, "agricultural." Sedgwick was delighted when the "commercial" Mr. Cabot was succeeded by the equally trustworthy and "commercial" Benjamin Goodhue, his old colleague in the national House of Representatives. He had even suggested previously that to effect such a proper end "a new districting of the Commonwealth might be made in such manner as to place the election on a fair footing." [2] Staunch Federalists, Sedgwick and Goodhue were, in fact, only elected after a sharp struggle. The House proposed

1. Letter to Peter Van Schaack, May 4, 1797. S.P., M.H.S.
2. Sedgwick to Ephraim Williams, June 6, 1796. *Ibid.*

that Edward H. Robbins be elected to one or the other of the vacancies, but the Federalist members of the Senate considered him too impartial and independent. As each house in the Massachusetts legislature voted separately, and had a negative over the nominations of the other, Robbins had in fact little chance of election. That gentleman soon simplified matters by signifying his desire not to be considered a candidate. Goodhue was then elected to complete Cabot's present term, that would end March 4, 1797, and also chosen to a full six year term; Sedgwick was elected to complete Strong's term, that would end March 4, 1799.

Whatever pleasure Sedgwick may have taken in his own election was tempered by the failure of his friend and law partner Ephraim Williams to win election as Sedgwick's successor in the House of Representatives. After three angry elections, in which Williams was charged with being a tippling atheist, a royalist, and an individual much too likely to act the part of Sedgwick's puppet,[3] Republican Thompson J. Skinner was elected not only to the uncompleted term but to represent Berkshire in the Fifth Congress as well. Sedgwick's slight faith in the majority of mankind was badly shaken. Hoping, however, that Skinner might be "weaned" to virtue, Sedgwick directed his old House colleagues to flatter Skinner into righteousness.

In the middle of December Sedgwick set out for Philadelphia. He soon found that though the clientele of the Senate was more select than that of the lower chamber, its power was rather less. Afraid that he might be toppled from his hard-won niche of prominence, Sedgwick set about immediately to become one of the most industrious and well-known members of the Senate. He accepted a wide variety of committee posts; helped reorganize the administration of the federal judiciary; voted for further bribes for Algerian pirates and a new salary scale for government officials; and helped deliver a laudatory address from the Massachusetts legislature to the retiring General Washington. His first three months as a senator were, in short, busy if relatively uneventful. They did, however, enable Sedgwick to become accustomed to senatorial ways, and to prepare himself to take a prominent part in the momentous Fifth Congress—the Congress which, with the aid of John Adams of Braintree, would save a nation and divide a party.

Adams, elevated to the Presidency by the election of 1796, was in no

3. *The Western Star,* October 24, 1796, printed a long allegorical piece about a senator-uncle who, by means of whispering pipe and wire, intended to be the voice and raise the arms of a waxen image of his nephew, if the latter was elected congressman—thereby saving the people money and simplifying the legislative process.

way indebted to Theodore Sedgwick for his promotion. To the contrary, Sedgwick, under the influence of Hamilton, seems to have desired that Thomas Pinckney, Adams' running mate, be chosen President. Like his mentor Hamilton, he appears to have hoped that all the northern states would vote solidly for Adams and Pinckney, that South Carolina would perhaps choose Jefferson and Pinckney, a native son, and that the latter, having in consequence the largest number of electoral votes, would be elected President. Although Sedgwick probably wrote a few letters and doubtless engaged in a certain amount of wishful thinking concerning this project,[4] it was, unlike Hamilton's labors, a vague and desultory effort at best.

That Sedgwick's intrigues against Adams were halfhearted is attested by his reply to letters from Jonathan Dayton in which Dayton had hinted that, as it seemed impossible to elect Adams, it might be well to think of supporting Aaron Burr. Sedgwick in a letter of November 19, 1796, politely denounced the suggestion. Although he personally held Burr in considerable "estimation," considered that gentleman by no means Republican, and had favored Burr rather than Monroe as American minister to France, Sedgwick argued that the honor and the future cohesion and success of the Federalists demanded that Adams and Pinckney be supported equally by all Federalists. Only thus would Federalist interests be served. He believed, he told Dayton, that Pennsylvania would give at least some electoral votes to the Federalists, and that the Federalist electors of South Carolina could not "act so faithless and insidious a part as to throw away their votes, preferably to giving them to Mr. Adams." If it should happen that between Adams and Pinckney the latter should "have the greatest number of votes, and of course be the

---

4. See, for example, the letter he wrote to Hamilton, November 19, 1796. *Hamilton MSS.*, Library of Congress.

This is partly, however, in a private code—a mode of correspondence highy popular with the Federalist leaders in these years—and its meaning is far from clear. It refers chiefly to Sedgwick's vigorous electioneering efforts against Burr, vice-presidential candidate of the Republicans, in New Jersey and Massachusetts. See, too, H.G. Otis to Sedgwick, November 25, 1796; Sedgwick to Ephraim Williams, January 7, 1797, *S.P., M.H.S.*

It is true . . . that you have said to me before the existence of the federal government and often . . . since, that a certain man was neither *wise prudent* nor *discreet,* and that you have told many others so I do most assuredly believe—You have therefore abundant reason to console yourself that a certain persons promotion did not acceed with your judgment.

December 26, 1799. *S.P., M.H.S.*

President, contrary to the intention of a great majority of his electors," the party could then console itself "with the purity and federalism of our chief Magistrate" and with the fact that the mischief—if such it was—was the result of the Constitution, not of any breach of faith. He did not think it a likely possibility, in any case; as Adams would very probably get several votes in Virginia.[5]

Sedgwick's main concern was, of course, completely to exclude Jefferson from the executive. If the more amenable and "certain" Pinckney was brought in at the head of the ticket, very well; if not, Adams, however independent, was preferable to any Republican. The refusal of certain suspicious New England electors to give their second vote to Pinckney, and the consequent election of Jefferson as Vice-President outraged Sedgwick. He was similarly inflamed by the brief attempt of the Jeffersonians to win Adams to their side by making capital of the "alleged intrigue" of Hamilton to supplant Adams with Pinckney. Sedgwick insisted that Jefferson's much publicized letter to Madison, praising the superior qualifications of Adams, was but a guileful trick to seduce Adams from his friends, men who have been the "most zealous supporters of the government." Senator Sedgwick trusted that Adams would "not be made the Dupe of their artful falsehoods."[6]

Sedgwick, if not pleased by Adams' election, quickly reconciled himself to it, and by the end of January, 1797, would probably have ridiculed any suggestion that he had ever wished it otherwise. As the Senate's teller of the votes of the electoral college, he took considerable pleasure in sonorously announcing (February 2, 1797) Mr. Adams' election to the Presidency by a majority of three votes.

In Sedgwick's view the new Chief Executive conducted himself with great dignity at the "august and sublime" inauguration, and he described Adams' initial address to Congress as one that gave "much satisfaction" to the friends of the government. But Sedgwick's unconscious estimate of Adams may have been reflected in the fulsome praise he lavished on ex-President Washington's conduct at the "sublime" inauguration:

5. Copies of these letters are among the *Hamilton MSS.*, Library of Congress, #4002–#4004, 151–153.

Sedgwick did not, at this time, doubt the strength of Adams' Federalism; rather, under the influence of Hamilton, he was suspicious of Adams' "independence of counsel." The present author cannot agree with Professor Dauer that Adams represented *at this time* the Moderate Federalists and Conservative Agrarians. There is no clear-cut and distinct division among the Federalists until the defense debates of 1798. See Manning J. Dauer, *The Adams Federalists* (Baltimore, 1953), 54, 63–64, 77–79.

6. Sedgwick to Ephraim Williams, January 9, 1797. S.P., M.H.S.

The company was numerous, respectable, and behaved with that decent gravity which the solemn occasion demanded; but the circumstance the most interesting was the presence of the late President. He came unattended and on foot, with the modest appearance of a private citizen. No sooner was his person seen, than a burst of applause such as I had never before known, and which it would be as impossible for me to describe, as my own sensations produced by it, saluted the venerable Hero and Patriot, while the animation of countenance which accompanied it gave the most pleasing, as well as the most convincing evidence, that all the lies which malice had invented, have been ineffectual to injure the character of this great and good man.[7]

The Election of 1796 saw considerable changes in the membership of Congress, which Sedgwick declared were for the better. The Federalists had maintained their supremacy in the Senate, and in the House had perhaps a wavering majority, if the southern Federalists could be held in line. Sedgwick estimated that 54 out of 106 representatives "professed attachment to the government." Many of the new men from the southern states were, however, little better than their predecessors, and "not to be counted on." The optimistic forecasts of certain Virginian Federalists that the Old Dominion would send a Federalist senator had proved erroneous, and the "man Anderson from Tennessee who . . . had been represented as federal . . . [is] a fool & therefore must be a Jacobin."[8] Sedgwick, nevertheless, was happy to note that the Republican membership and leadership had weakened perceptibly. Fortunate this was, in his view; for a decisive confrontation was obviously impending "with the nation the Jacobins so love," France.

The French by a series of harsh and illegal decrees had forced matters to the point of crisis. Declaring (July 2, 1796) that any neutral nation that would allow itself to be bullied by Britain would be treated in similar fashion by France, they had decreed (March 2, 1797) that all types of enemy goods found on an American ship would be confiscated; that Americans serving in British ships would be treated as pirates; and that any American ship not having a fully and properly prepared *rôle d'équipage* would be confiscated.[9] The French perhaps had good reason to be displeased with various American acts and with certain provisions

7. Sedgwick to King, March 12, 1797. King, *King*, II, 156.
8. Sedgwick to Henry Van Schaack, December 14, 1797. S.P., M.H.S.
9. *American State Papers.* Class 1: Foreign Relations, II, 496 ff.

of the Jay Treaty, but had little excuse to demand that the acts of a sovereign nation promote exclusively the interests of France. The fact that we had, for the sake of much needed peace, treated with England did not make us *per se* the enemy of France. The enforcement of our rights was our concern. Our seeming inability at times to take proper note of that concern did not give France cause to confiscate ships destined for neutral ports, lay a paper blockade, and, in short, wage unofficial war against us. The French government if not out to subdue America by physical conquest, as Sedgwick believed, certainly wished to incorporate this country into its sphere of influence. By means of diplomatic baiting, punitive action on the high seas, and intervention in American internal affairs and politics, the French sought to turn this country against England and into the fraternal arms of her sister republic. Though they did not wish to incite a war with the United States, they did hope to scare this country into discarding the Federalists and revoking the Jay Treaty.

To take measures against ever increasing French arrogance, Adams called Congress into extra session on May 15, 1797. Almost immediately guerilla warfare between the parties began. The Jeffersonians, insisting that France wished nothing but equal treatment with England, declared that the Federalists were creating imaginary dragons in hopes of increasing the executive power. They wished to manufacture a war with France, the better to transform this glorious republic into a system of Anglo-Federalist despotism. The Jeffersonians opposed therefore the Address to the President, which spoke of the impartial treatment accorded all belligerents; opposed extensive military or naval rearmament; and fought all proposals to discontinue commercial intercourse with France.

Sedgwick was incensed by "this rascality." [10] His own suspicions of the French and of their American "adherents" had increased immeasurably during the last year. He had followed the erratic but generally victorious course of France with despair, and gradually had come to think

---

9. (cont.)

Gardner W. Allen gives the best short resumé and analysis of the various French decrees. Gardner W. Allen, *Our Naval War with France* (Boston, 1909), 33–37. In January, 1798, the French went so far as to declare that all neutral vessels that had enemy goods aboard were proper prize.

10. Sedgwick's friend Uriah Tracy of Connecticut was so outraged as to suggest, "Separating the Union immediately," if the perverse "do-nothing" Republicans in the House did not rapidly turn a new leaf. Tracy to Sedgwick, March 29, 1797. *S.P.*, M.H.S.

of Britain and her navy as the sole remaining obstacle to probable world domination by the French. In Britain, indeed, was "the last recourse for the protection of a civilized society." [11] Sedgwick felt, not without some reason, that the French were encouraged to maltreat the United States by the fervor with which the Jeffersonians expressed their partiality for France and the animosity which they displayed toward the federal administration. The French, he declared, were virtually invited to make capital of the internal dissensions of the country, to intrigue in its elections, and to incite its people to turn against their legally chosen representatives. He saw much less clearly that Britain had interfered, and was yet interfering, in the domestic politics of the new nation.

France was the enemy, but Sedgwick believed that before America committed itself to war an attempt should be made to negotiate. Unlike the extremist fringe of his party, he did not advocate an immediate full-scale war with France. Peace must be preserved as long as honorably possible.[12] It was perhaps not merely coincidental that his views were those of Hamilton, who had written Sedgwick advocating concurrent negotiation and preparedness. Hamilton had cautioned that it was very important for the sake of national unity to prove to the people that the administration had omitted no endeavor that might have brought America an honorable peace, and had suggested that an extraordinary commission should be sent to treat with the French Republic. These commissioners (Hamilton recommended Madison, George Cabot, and C. C. Pinckney) "should be charged to make explanations, to remonstrate, to ask indemnifications; and they should be empowered to make a new treaty of commerce, not inconsistent with our other treaties." [13]

Sedgwick, though angered by the refusal of the French Directory to receive Charles C. Pinckney as the new American ambassador, agreed. He very much doubted if France would ever be satisfied with anything less than "a complete control over our Government," and felt that the French "relying on their influence to divide our people &, distract our council . . . held our resistance in contempt." Still, if conceding them the advantages granted Britain "respecting free bottoms not making free

11. Sedgwick to Henry Van Schaack, January 7, 1798. S.P., M.H.S.
12. Many historians have exaggerated the "grim determination," to use Claude Bowers' graphic phrase, of the majority of Federalists for war, at least so far as the months preceding the XYZ exposé are concerned. (*Jefferson and Hamilton,* 345). See, also, J. S. Bassett, *Federalist System,* 225; Joseph Charles, *Origins of American Party System,* 419; 441.
13. Hamilton to Sedgwick, January 20, 1797; February 26, 1797. *Hamilton MSS.,* Library of Congress.

goods, extending further the list of contraband, and the provision article" would cause them to desist from their piratical actions, such concessions should be made. He seriously doubted whether such an "amiable adjustment" was possible,[14] but time would be gained, "time to build our sadly inadequate defenses and to unite our people and to liberate them from the influence of their leaders."[15]

When Adams, like Hamilton, decided that negotiations were preferable to hostilities and proposed to send a special commission to treat with France, Sedgwick expressed strong approval.[16] Pleased with signs of an increased "display of an American spirit," Sedgwick set about to inform his friends of the means he considered necessary to put the fear of God in the "atheist" French. He wanted to give the President authority to lay a temporary embargo on American shipping, to raise a force of 90,000 militia, and to fortify our ports and harbors. He wished to have Congress authorize 20 or 30 cruisers for convoy purposes, raise 3,000 artillerists and cavalrymen, institute a provisional force of 30,000 men, and create additional revenues of about $2,500,000 per annum to support these projects. These defense measures, he felt, would be both conducive to peace and essential in case of war. They owed much to the sugges-

14. Sedgwick to Increase Sumner, May 23, 1797. *Photostat Collection*, M.H.S.
15. Sedgwick to Henry Van Schaack, June 16, 1797. *S.P.*, M.H.S.
16. Adams first nominated C. C. Pinckney, John Marshall, and Nathan Dane. When Dane refused his appointment, Adams appointed Elbridge Gerry, whom Sedgwick considered "a probable Republican" and very "unsteady." Risking Adams' displeasure, Sedgwick, with five other senators, voted against confirmation of the appointment. The remembrance of this vote gave him much satisfaction when Gerry elected to remain in France after the negotiators had been ordered to leave the country.

This was the first open disagreement between Sedgwick and Adams. Samuel Otis, secretary to the Senate, informed Sedgwick of Adams' reaction to the six negative votes as Sedgwick recounted in a letter to Ephraim Williams, June 23, 1797:

The Secy. told me that when he waited on the President with the act of the Senate he expressed much regret that his conduct was disapproved by his friends. On which Otis says he told him that I said he ought to have consulted his council, & respected the opinion of his friends in the Senate & in the U. S. none of whom had any confidence in Gerry, that the former administration had invariably so conducted & that there was no other way in which the Executive could expect support. He said the Prest. appeared astonished at this—said he was sorry Mr. Sedgwick felt hurt & wished he could have an opportunity to converse with him on the subject—He shall have it; and if by sacrificing his regard I shall be able to correct so dangerous an evil as his undertaking to act without concert I shall deem the purchase well made.

S.P., M.H.S.

tions of Hamilton. Indeed, Sedgwick was at this point Hamilton's chief lieutenant in the Senate, serving in that body a role similar to that of Pickering in the cabinet.

Whatever the origin of Sedgwick's defense recommendations, they gained little congressional support when first broached.[17] The Bay State senator felt that the news of the late French military successes in Europe had frightened and "torpedoed many weak but honest minds." Some men even evinced a disposition to repay the French loans without delay, a disposition which to Sedgwick was a "damnable heresy."[18] He concluded that Congress—especially the House—was slipping into disgusting apathy; "we must receive more stripes before we shall suitably resent the chastisement."[19]

Sedgwick's impatience with delay led him to exaggerate the "do-nothingness" of Congress in the spring and summer of 1797. There was some basis for his impatience, for the House had refused to agree to raise a small corps of artillerists and engineers or to take action "authorizing an arming of vessels, the property of individuals" (merchantmen), and the Senate turned down a provisional army bill, authored by a special committee dominated by Sedgwick. But certain recommendations incorporated in the President's message on military defense had fared somewhat better—a bill to prohibit the exportation of arms finally squeezed through, and authority was given the President to equip and man nine sloops of war of twenty guns each. These might be steps in the right direction, Sedgwick declared, but they represented only a paltry beginning.

Sedgwick's chagrin over congressional laxness was based on his assessment of the European situation. He refused to believe that peace in Europe was close at hand, and doubted that, even if European hostilities were suddenly to cease, France would try to restore her commerce by peaceful co-operation with the United States—as the Jeffersonians argued. He conceded that France might in such circumstances be occasionally conciliatory for the sake of provisioning her West Indies, but it was more likely that she would continue to concentrate on Europe and consequently despise America. Nor could he understand the loathing of many in Congress to spend money for defense preparations. They did not seem able to appreciate, he complained, that France respected

17. A "temporary embargo" proposal, authored by Sedgwick, did come before the Senate, but was defeated, March 1, 1797, by an equi-vote of 15-15.
18. Sedgwick to unnamed correspondent, June 14, 1797. *S.P., M.H.S.*
19. Sedgwick to Pamela, June 21, 1797. Papers of H. D. Sedgwick, *S.P., M.H.S.*

strength alone. The enemy—both foreign and domestic—was quite prepared to take advantage of weakness. He claimed to have it on secret authority that France would not alter her conduct until we absolutely rescinded the Jay Treaty, and that Jefferson had intended to hoist the French flag at a dinner extended the returned "Citizen Monroe" but had abandoned the idea for "want of nerve." [20] But he nevertheless hoped that the situation would soon improve, and "Americanism" come out of the shadows, for as he wrote his law partner: "If France should reject our Minister[s], of which in my opinion there is a probability, indeed I have confidence that a spirit of resistance will be roused, and that the nerves of some of us will be more tensely strong." [21]

Within less than a year his expectations were borne out, but in the interim Sedgwick's wrath at the "appeasing men" increased. His anger was directed primarily at the continued refusal of the Fifth Congress (whose second session opened in November, 1797) to advance American preparedness. He did not believe, as did other High Federalists, that France was about to declare war on the United States, but he thought it "a question whether open and undisguised enmity . . . [was] not preferable to professions of friendship from those unprincipled Scoundrels." [22] Certainly we must not be lulled into a disastrous trap by recent conciliatory speeches by that chameleon Talleyrand. Only if we made it clear that we had the power to retaliate would France be conciliatory in earnest. We should support the diplomatic endeavors of our three ministers to France—Pinckney, Marshall, and Gerry—by further strengthening our defenses against that nation. Otherwise their negotiations must surely fail.

The southern Federalists delayed in "adopting a system," however, and without their support, Sedgwick admitted, the eastern wing of the party could do nothing.

As Sedgwick's disgust with Congress deepened, so did his impatience

20. Sedgwick was at this time particularly incensed by what he considered a viciously underhanded blow dealt Alexander Hamilton by the partisans of Jefferson. A Jeffersonian underling John Beckley had not been re-elected clerk of the House, and in revenge this Beckley had written a pamphlet broadcasting the indiscretions of Hamilton with a Mrs. Reynolds. The evidence on which Beckley had based his charges were papers in the hands of James Monroe, which, in accord with a gentleman's agreement reached between Hamilton, Muhlenberg, Venables, and Monroe, were supposedly to have been kept in complete confidence. Sedgwick, a great admirer of Hamilton's beautiful wife, was sincerely horrified by this instance of "diabolical malice." See Sedgwick to King, June 24, 1797. King, *King*, II, 193.
21. Sedgwick to Ephraim Williams, June 28, 1797. *S.P., M.H.S.*
22. Sedgwick to Henry Van Schaack, December 11, 1797. *Ibid.*

for news from France. When after a passage of some months no word was heard from the three commissioners, he was certain that either they were confined or their correspondence was being intercepted by French spies. Apprised of the Franco-Austrian Treaty of Campoformio and the proposed French invasion of Britain, Sedgwick gloomily declared that actual armed resistance would soon become inevitable:

> When we reflect how soon after they [the French] had disposed of the war with Austria, they assumed a new tone to Switzerland, and totally altered their conduct towards Portugal—When we reflect that enmity to England was among their most powerful motives to these enormities; and when, too we take into consideration, how much more important to G.B. we are than both these countries; and when we know that their insatiable ambition is unrestrained by morality or even decency—we have reason to expect, from these and other considerations that she will demand of us to break our "incomprehensible treaty." We shall have, then, presented to us, in the one scale the rights of self-government, national honor, public faith, and in the other degredation, immorality, atheism, infamy and an established system of colonization. I trust there will be no suspense in the preponderation. . . .
>
> A rupture with France seems almost impossible to be avoided. Nothing which could have been done has been omited & if we must again put on the harness I trust that in the sight of Heaven & Earth we shall stand requited of blame.[23]

Philadelphia heard rumors as early as January, 1798, that the French had refused to receive the American commissioners, but still the Jeffersonians fought "the great measures of defense." Sedgwick was certain that their conduct would end in rending the country in two, and making it easy prey to the conquering French.[24] Sedgwick wished the President to rescind the executive order in restraint of the arming of merchantmen, and to permit individuals to exercise a right of self-defense. This would compel the House to rouse itself and take matters in hand. If more spirit was not shown quickly, he would resign his seat, refusing to be a mem-

23. Sedgwick to Peter Van Schaack, January 7, 1798. *S.P.*, M.H.S.; Sedgwick to Pamela, January 9, 1798, Papers of H. D. Sedgwick, *S.P.*, M.H.S.

24. Sedgwick considered the spitting and poker-wielding brawl of Representatives Griswold and Lyon as previewing the civil war that might soon rend the country. He felt, however, that the fault of that fracas lay entirely with the Vermont Republican Lyon—a "filthy & insignificant Beast." Griswold "behaved like a prince" and "administered the chastisement with the most temperate dignity." Sedgwick to Ephraim Williams, February 10, 1798; Sedgwick to Henry Van Schaack, February 22, 1798. *S.P.*, M.H.S.

ber of a legislative body which because of its cowardly apathy would be an object of detestation to all men of honor and good sense. His personal position was, he admitted, not unenviable. "I am treated, by the Citizens of Philadelphia, with a distinction that few if any can boast. By the gentlemen of the Legislature with a confidence which is grateful, and by the President and Gentlemen in the executive administration with a more familiar & reposing intercourse than any other person in or out of Congress." [25] Being more dogmatic than prideful, however, he preferred agreement and action to confidence and reposing intercourse.

Finally, early in March, the Senate received the long-delayed first report of the commissioners. This report merely confirmed the initial inability of the Americans to gain an audience, but that alone was of salutary influence in Sedgwick's view. The Jacobins felt quite "done over," he reported; they had but weakly opposed publication of the dispatch, and that "out of a tender regard to the safety of our Envoys." [26] The other dispatches which the President had received were not quickly forthcoming, however, and this Sedgwick considered poor policy. Adams had told certain senators in confidence that a partial deciphering of their contents led him to believe that no further communication could be made to the Senate "because the ministers had expressed such just sentiments and so much indignation upon the gross insults inflicted on themselves & their country, that he feared the publication would expose them to assassination." [27] Sedgwick, by now a political professional, foresaw danger to his party in this humanitarian course. The Republicans, he insisted, will say that the President does not dare publish the recent dispatches for fear of revealing that there never has been any intention on the part of the administration to negotiate amicably with France.

He was cheered, however, by the news that orders would be given the envoys immediately to quit France, and he was quite positive that there would then "be told a tale at which every ear will tingle; and unless . . . [he were] mistaken . . . [would] give a most fatal blow to the Jacobins." [28] By March 21, he was certain of this happy result, for he then knew the contents of the last dispatches and was, he believed, the only member of Congress who did.[29] He now agreed with Adams that Pinckney, Marshall, and possibly even Gerry should be allowed to

25. Sedgwick to Pamela, January 30, 1798. Papers of H. D. Sedgwick, S.P., M.H.S.
26. Sedgwick to unnamed correspondent, March 7, 1798. S.P., M.H.S.
27. Sedgwick to unnamed correspondent, March, 17, 1798. Ibid.
28. Sedgwick to Henry Van Schaack, March 17, 1798. Ibid.
29. Sedgwick to Henry Van Schaack, March 21, 1798. Ibid.

leave "that land of perdition" before publication of the dispatches. The latter were the XYZ dispatches, disclosing the attempt of agents of the Directory to extract large sums of tribute money from the Americans before deigning to negotiate. With this foreknowledge, Sedgwick was able to contain his anger at the vehement criticism directed by the opposition at the President. The Republicans understandably, if unwisely, demanded to see the dispatches. Congress, they declared, would have to decide whether war should be declared, and it was therefore essential it be given all relevant information. Accordingly, Senator Anderson—at Jefferson's instigation, deduced Sedgwick [30]—requested Adams to lay before the Senate all the instructions he had given the commission, and all the information he had received of their conduct under these instructions.[31]

Had the Federalists been allowed to map their opponents' strategy they could hardly have done better. The request of the Republicans that Congress be permitted to see the XYZ dispatches was granted. With this disclosure came the first signs of a popular wave of animosity against the French and their more outspoken American sympathizers. In an effort to further this shift in the popular temper, Sedgwick wrote long letters to his friends urging that the recent revelations—the dispatches were not officially printed until June—be given wide dissemination. He advised that stress should be placed particularly on "those parts which confess the means by which [the French] expect to preserve their influence—their diplomatic agents—their threats, and their acknowledgement of the injustice practiced towards us." [32] The Jacobins were initially stunned and penitent, Sedgwick reported, but after a bit they rallied and took the tack that the Directory had had nothing to do with this international scandal. It was the unauthorized work of a few blackguards in the pay of that unreformed royalist Talleyrand.[33]

30. Sedgwick described Jefferson, whom he considered "the very life and soul of the opposition," as "the greatest rascal & Traitor in the United States." Sedgwick to King, April 9, 1798 (Copy); Sedgwick to Henry Van Schaack, March 27, 1798, *S.P.*, M.H.S.

31. With respect to the first request, Sedgwick pronounced it purely mischievous: "That the instructions weer liberal and authorized many sacrifices to avoid war, every man of common sense, with reasonable confidence in the Presid. must beleive." As to the second, all communications of the envoys would be given the public—the Republicans need not fear—but not while *two* men of great worth were "within the reach of the monsters whose iniquity" they had disclosed. Sedgwick to Henry Van Schaack, March 21, 1798. *S.P.*, M.H.S.

32. Sedgwick to Peter Van Schaack, April 7, 1798. *Ibid.*

33. Sedgwick to King, April 9, 1798. (Copy) *S.P.*, M.H.S.

The Jeffersonians, self-acknowledged Francophiles, found themselves in an uncomfortable position and one that posed increasing political hazard. The wildest of rumors floated about. A Rhode Island newspaper intimated that France had demanded as the price of peace "the annullment of our Constitution, the dismission of our President & that of . . . [the] honble House, the Surrender of Newport or Portsmouth . . . and the payment of 100,000 Dollars." [34] Fast days were observed, in which Federalist ministers exhorted their congregations to unity and patriotic adherence to the administration. *Hail Columbia* became the virtual national anthem; Adams was given an ovation by a Philadelphia crowd when he attended Mr. Sailson's circus; anti-French toasts dominated every banquet.[35]

During the spring and summer of 1798 a number of warlike measures passed Congress, to the delight of Theodore Sedgwick. As has been noted, Sedgwick was among the first to cry for reprisals and measures of defense, and by early April he had fully evolved "the system" he wished to see adopted.[36] He outlined it in full in a letter to Rufus King in London, April 19, 1798. After noting that prospects were good for the passage of the frigate-convoy bill [37] and a measure for the establishment of an iron foundry, he went on as follows:

The measures which I hope will take place are the passage of those two bills; the procuring of arms, ammunition & cannon. A fortification of our ports, raising immediately a corps of artillerists & another of cavalry, an authority to raise 30,000 men to be added to the Military establishment & to accept the tender of voluntary Corps. (This last a measure of security to the great towns principally.) To authorize the capture of any French armed Vessels which shall attack any of ours, & all such as shall be found within 20 leagues of our coasts. A legislative declaration that all treaties with France are become

34. Benjamin Bourne to Sedgwick, April 8, 1798. S.P., M.H.S.
35. The Fourth of July celebration in Springfield, Massachusetts, was highlighted in 1796 by various toasts lauding "our French brethren"; two years later it was signalized by many toasts vehemently damning those "outragers of liberty." *Hampshire & Berkshire Chronicle* (Springfield), July 5, 1796; *The Federal Spy* (Springfield), July 10, 1798.
36. Hamilton's assistance in this evolution was considerable. Compare Hamilton to Sedgwick, n.d., S.P., M.H.S. with the letter to King and with Sedgwick's letter to Henry Van Schaack, April 21, 1798, S.P., M.H.S.
37. The American navy was virtually non-existent at this time. No vessel of the Revolutionary navy had survived, and America had but three newly christened frigates to her name: the *United States* (44 guns), the *Constitution* (44 guns), and the *Constellation* (32 guns), all authorized in 1794 when the British war scare was at its height.

void. A comprehensive alien act, and revenue sufft. to sustain the necessary expenditure and preserve the public credit. If something like this cannot be done, I shall not deem the public safety provided for.[38]

Sedgwick set about to lend every aid to the accomplishment of this grand design. He headed a committee that secured passage of the bill to continue in force the prohibition against export of arms and ammunition; he spoke for the "artillery bill"; he voted for an act "to provide an additional armament for the further protection of the trade of the United States"; and he helped defeat an amendment to that act which would have provided that all American conduct be solely "applicable to a state of neutrality." Sedgwick served also as the chief spokesman for the provisional army bill. A sharp attack of gout necessitated his absence during the decisions to suspend commercial intercourse with France, to arm merchant ships, and to authorize the President to build or purchase certain frigates and smaller vessels, but he was back in Congress in time to vote for the climaxing legislation of the session: the act declaring the French treaties of 1778 null and void.[39] All of these measures had become law by early July, but another, near and dear to Sedgwick's heart, had not. This was the bill encouraging capture of French armed vessels by ships owned by citizens of the United States. It sailed through the Senate, but the less bellicose House refused to concur.

Sedgwick fought for additional revenue as vigorously as for additional frigates or foot soldiers. He voted (July 14, 1798) for a direct tax of $2,000,000 to be levied by state quotas on lands, dwelling houses,[40] and slaves—though hating all direct taxation in principle. Opposing Gallatin's drive for "economy" and detailed appropriations, and fighting the tendency of certain House Federalists "to act the little sneaking part of calculation for personal safety & popularity,"[41] Sedgwick labored steadily for additional customs charges and excise taxes. The Treasury must be strengthened, he declared, and the Sinking Fund commissioners

38. (Copy) *S.P.*, M.H.S.

39. A majority of the Federalists now took the view that as France had continually violated the treaties for the last five years, they were without any binding effect whatsoever. See George Cabot to Theodore Sedgwick, May 11, 1798. *S.P.*, M.H.S.

40. Hamilton often utilized Sedgwick to help press his views of proper fiscal policy on Wolcott. He sent him, for example, a detailed scheme for a house tax, and declared that Sedgwick might "show it to the Secretary and confer." Hamilton to Sedgwick, n.d., quoted by Hamilton, *History of the Republic*, VI, 592. See, too, Sedgwick to Ephraim Williams, May 22, 1797. *S.P.*, M.H.S.

41. Sedgwick to Ephraim Williams, January 28, 1797. *S.P.*, M.H.S.

continue to retire the debt. He defended, against the attacks of the Republicans, Secretary Wolcott's authorization of an interest rate of eight per cent on the public loan floated in 1798, and continuously battled for quick and generous action on all military measures.

Pleased as he was with the quick passage accorded most of these army measures, Sedgwick's pleasure was soon characteristically replaced by annoyance. The new object of his anger was Secretary of War McHenry, who, Sedgwick charged, was unpardonably tardy in putting these bills into execution. He complained to Timothy Pickering, Secretary of State and strong man of the cabinet, that such organizational delay was certain "to damp the public ardor." [42] Sedgwick appreciated that America was much more apt to accept a navy than to countenance that democratic bugbear, a standing army, and he concluded that the longer recruiting was delayed, the longer the people would have to conjure up imaginary evils. Adams' conduct, he charged, was most dilatory; by the end of January, 1799, he had not issued one enlistment order. [43] Sedgwick favored devoting the current session of the Fifth Congress exclusively to "invigorating the system adopted at the last." They should not press for any increase in the numbers of authorized troops but concentrate on renewing the authority to raise a "provisional army" of 20,000 and making a flesh and blood reality of the blueprinted corps of volunteer "regulars."

Alexander Hamilton and Sedgwick were in full agreement. Hamilton, indeed, took unofficial charge of "the new army," even before he was appointed Inspector General and second in command to Washington, and it was at Hamilton's request that Sedgwick convened the Massachusetts congressional delegation and got their views on "the most eligible division of that state for the purpose of recruiting on your plan." Sedgwick was in complete sympathy with Hamilton's successful effort to gain precedence of commission and rank in the new army, despite the claims of Henry Knox and the angry resistance of Adams. [44] Increasingly, support of the proposals of Hamilton implied opposition to Adams, and it is

42. Sedgwick to Timothy Pickering, October 23, 1798. *Pickering Papers*, XXIII, 254, M.H.S.
    Sedgwick's anxiety on this score was, of course, more than matched by that of his mentor, Hamilton.
43. Sedgwick found little fault with Adams on the score of naval rearmament, where the President, interested in protection rather than retaliation and doubting the probability of a French invasion, concentrated his energies. Dockyards were built, timber purchased, and ships constructed with little fuss or fury.
44. Sedgwick to Hamilton, February 22, 1799. Hamilton, *Works of Hamilton*, V, 216.
    The sorry tangle of the major generals, if pettish in character, is significant as

now that Sedgwick and his friends begin definitely to turn against the President and a fundamental division as to proper Federalist policy becomes apparent.

Legislative activity in the Fifth Congress came to a climax with February, 1799. The Senate passed bills allowing American traders when attacked to retaliate in kind (February 8), reauthorizing a provisional army, and empowering the President "to employ the volunteer corps to repel invasion & suppress insurrection" (February 18).[45] With reference to the last bill, Sedgwick declared that: "No act of Congress has ever struck the Jacobins with more horror; and I believe they have at last thought of force against the government as a possible event." [46]

The Republicans had throughout, of course, intimated that the motivating force behind the Federalist drive for "defense measures" had been their wish so to increase the executive authority and the nation's military might that they could stamp out all domestic opposition and make permanent their control of the national administration. But the evidence suggests that they were mistaken. Through the summer of 1798 the main consideration of Sedgwick and his friends was to put the country in a position of defense should there be war with France. It is true that after their fear of imminent French invasion wore off, they were reluctant to reduce or disband the army which had been raised; the possible usefulness of these troops in suppressing insurrection was doubtless not lost on them. These troops, however, had been initially raised to combat the French, not the Jeffersonians.[47] Sedgwick and his

---

44. (cont.)
a contributing factor in dividing the Federalist Party between the High (or Hamiltonian) Federalists and the Moderate (or Adams') Federalists.

It would appear to this writer, incidentally, that there was no deep-dyed conspiracy involved in the efforts of Sedgwick and his friends to have Hamilton selected as the ranking major general. Such a conspiracy has been implied by several writers, but the more obvious explanation would appear to be that Sedgwick, Pickering, and Company sincerely—and correctly—believed Hamilton to be vastly more able than Henry Knox. They promoted Hamilton's claims not as a means towards some mysterious and evil end but primarily because they were convinced that he was the best man for the job at hand. See, in this connection, Timothy Pickering to Alexander Hamilton, August 22, 1798. *Hamilton Papers*, Library of Congress.

45. Sedgwick to unnamed correspondent, February 18, 1799. S.P., M.H.S.

46. *Ibid.*

47. For a strongly contrary judgment, see Stephen G. Kurtz, *The Presidency of John Adams* (Philadelphia, 1957), 308–330. Professor Kurtz is convinced that the Hamiltonians were vindictively determined to use the army for political ends and anticipated a civil war. Henry Adams and Manning J. Dauer also suspect the

colleagues proclaimed throughout 1797 and 1798 that the invasion of America by French troops was a definite possibility; that they were wrong does not disprove their sincerity.

As so often in their short history, the Federalists eventually perverted a righteous cause. Extremism was continually their weakness. Valiantly fighting for national honor and security through the first half of the Fifth Congress, they became intoxicated with their popularity after the XYZ dénouement. In turn they called for a declaration of war, opposed Adams' decision to make another try for peace, and utilized their popularity and power in an effort to crush domestic opposition. The latter two instances of extremism will be discussed in subsequent chapters. The desire of certain Federalists—Sedgwick among them—to declare war on France may be briefly related here.

Unlike certain Federalist hotheads such as Harper, Tracy, and William L. Smith, Sedgwick had advocated, if he had not always had great confidence in, the Pinckney-Marshall-Gerry attempt at amicable negotiation. As has been noted, their insulting treatment at the hands of France infuriated him. Throughout the spring of 1798 he pondered the wisdom of waging out-and-out war with France, but it was not until early summer—after Congress had failed to arm the country to the extent and with the celerity that Sedgwick felt necessary—that he actually favored such a radical course. Unable to see the necessity of peace for this weak young country with the vision that had been his when the conduct of non-democratic England was involved, Sedgwick by July 1, 1798, openly advocated a declaration of war against France. He rejected the advice of Caleb Strong and others, that such a move would damn the Federalist party as "the war party." Sedgwick insisted that further delay in declaring war on France would by no means serve the political fortunes of the Federalists:

> If Congress adjourns without a declaration I am persuaded, it will have a directly contrary effect. In that case the people will be addressed with some plausibility & more effect, and induced to believe, that the friends of peace [the Republicans] may save them from the calamity of war. But, on the other hand, if war be inevitable, it may reasonably be hoped, that the people, in their selection of characters,

47. (cont.)
original motivation behind the defense measures of 1798. Henry Adams, *Life of Albert Gallatin* (Philadelphia, 1880), 199, 211; Dauer, *Adams Federalists*, 209–210.

will choose those who are best qualified to conduct it. Unless, among our most respectable friends in the house, there is an absolute despair of success; the measure will be brought forward. . . . Should it pass the House there is no doubt it will prevail in the Senate.[48]

The House fortunately refused to push matters in such drastic fashion, and Sedgwick was left to complain of "that most dangerous species of warfare, for the seduction of our people, 'diplomatic skill.' " [49] By January, 1799, he was insisting that war should have been declared against Spain, as well as "her principal," France:

Spain had given us sufficient cause, by innumerable aggressions, to justify our conduct. Having assumed the character of Enemy, as such, I would have rendered myself respectable by a prompt and decided blow. The mouth of the Mississippi & the countries connected with and dependent on it should have been immediately seized. The immense benefits to have been derived from that position, whether for treaty, or a continuance of the war, are obvious. In the mean time we should have superseded the necessity of alien & sedition laws—without them we might have hanged traitors and exported frenchmen. This was the policy I would have pursued instantly after the publication of the dispatches. But it was ordered otherwise.[50]

Such outbursts as this, however, were reserved for epistolary exercises with his fellow Federalists. In the Senate itself, Sedgwick was content to "fortify and invigorate" the plans already adopted, and to push forward the augmentation of the army. Urged on by Hamilton, Sedgwick belabored McHenry to overcome the bottlenecks that were causing delays in the military department. When that official bemoaned the failure of contractors to obtain clothing, Sedgwick retorted that by an immediate employment of all the tailors in Philadelphia and New York clothes could be procured faster than they could ever be wanted. This was the season to secure enlistments; if it passed, no one could foresee the evil consequences which might result.[51] Believing that the authorized

48. Sedgwick to Rufus King, July 1, 1798. (Copy) *S.P.*, M.H.S.
King, surprisingly, rather praised these sentiments. King to Sedgwick, October 27, 1798. *S.P.*, M.H.S.
49. Sedgwick to King, January 20, 1799. (Copy) *S.P.*, M.H.S.
50. *Ibid.*
51. Sedgwick to Hamilton, February 7, 1799. Hamilton, *Works of Hamilton,* VI, 393.
McHenry's decision to push "the eventual army" force at the expense of the recruitment of Hamilton's "emergency" troops especially incensed Sedgwick. Sedgwick to Oliver Wolcott, May 8, 1799, cited in George Gibbs, *Memoirs of the*

force of twelve infantry regiments was none too large in view of possible domestic disorders, Sedgwick saw hope only in the figure of Alexander Hamilton and the latter's increasing direction of the recruitment of the projected regiments.

Sedgwick's anger and efforts were, however, fruitless and outdated. Adams had decided on peace. With the senatorial ratification of the Vans Murray commission (February 27, 1799), the possibility of gallant American troops driving the French back into the sea, or chasing the Spaniards over the New Orleans levees, or even chastising domestic troublemakers was diminished if not erased. Sedgwick, persuaded by the intoxicating power of popularity to transform a righteous crusade for national defense into policies of purely partisan advantage, was thwarted by a fellow citizen of Massachusetts, a man with a will as strong as his own and a grasp of history far firmer—President John Adams.

---

51. (cont.)
Administrations of Washington and John Adams. . . . (New York, 1842), II, 239. See, too, Sedgwick to McHenry, May 26, 1799. *MSS. Letters,* Henry F. Huntington Library.

FEDERALIST EXTREMISM AND FEDERALIST DEFEAT

XII

Sedgwick Attacks the Executive

Had the foulest heart and the ablest head in the world
have been permitted to select the most embarrassing
and ruinous measure, perhaps it would have been pre-
cisely the one which has been adopted.
                                    Theodore Sedgwick [1]

THEODORE SEDGWICK's break with President Adams, in the early days
of the year 1799, represented a marked change in the political career of
Berkshire's leading statesman. During Washington's administrations
Sedgwick had taken great pride in being "an administration man," "a
friend of the executive," and he reserved his harshest strictures for those
who sought to diminish the power or defile the good name of the President. That break reflected, too, a widening division within the Federalist
party, one that would see Sedgwick represent but an extremist minority
of his beloved party.

The story of Sedgwick's break with the majority of his party is the
story in miniature of the failure of our first major political party. In the
autumn of 1798 the Federalists were at the height of their popularity.
Due partly to the bellicosity of the French and partly to the blunders of
the Republicans, the Federalists had managed to become the party of
patriotism. Their tenure in office appeared to be secure, their opponents
discredited. Yet in little more than two years time they would lose control of the Presidency and Congress and by the election of 1804 would
win the vote of only two states. By the latter year it was obvious to all
but the most politically obtuse (and Sedgwick would be among them)
that the Federalist party had disintegrated. Sedgwick, Pickering, Ames,
et al. may have bemoaned its death, but they had unwittingly contributed to it. In attacking John Adams they delivered fatal blows to
Federalism.

1. Letter to Hamilton, February 19, 1799. Hamilton, *Works of Hamilton*, VI,
396.

The course of relations between Sedgwick and Adams had always been a bit strained and curious, but, up to the spring of 1798, Sedgwick had respected Adams and generally approved his conduct. Sedgwick had headed the committee that had prepared an address lauding Adams' service as Vice-President (February, 1797); he had helped secure senatorial ratification of John Quincy Adams' nomination as minister plenipotentiary to Prussia; he had approved most of Adams' Massachusetts' appointees; and he was a warm admirer of Abigail Adams—"one of the most exalted characters I have seen." [2] Sedgwick was, moreover, during the first half of the Fifth Congress a most frequent guest at the Adams' Sunday "family dinners," and on one occasion declared: "Was I a son or brother the family would not treat me with more affectionate regard." [3] Indeed, such sympathetic regard existed between the two men at this time, at least in Sedgwick's judgment, that he hesitated to inform Adams of a tentative decision to soon retire from public life, "knowing how difficult it would be to silence his arguments, and how painful to resist his importunity." [4] Sedgwick sympathized over the high rent Adams was required to pay in Philadelphia (£ 1,000, annually); spoke admiringly of his "firmness," "manly fortitude," and "dignified composure"; and dismissed his appointment of Dr. Benjamin Rush as treasurer of the mint as simply an eccentricity that "must be expected & pardoned —in great things he will do right." [5] Memorials to Adams from various towns in Berkshire, praising the President's firm course with the French, were forwarded by Sedgwick with "respectful attachment, & sincere personal regard," though with the reminder that "the policy of *town meeting* addresses . . . is not, generally approved by the most enlightened and best disposed in this county." [6]

As Adams and Sedgwick were temperamentally quite opposite, their co-operation was never perhaps without a certain sense of strain. If neither was a democrat, Adams had a certain sense of balance and proportion that kept him from fearing the people as did Sedgwick. On one occasion he told Sedgwick that if Congress would only do its part the country had nothing to fear. He had known "the people" for twenty-

2. Sedgwick to Pamela, June 7, 1797. Papers of H. D. Sedgwick, *S.P.*, M.H.S.
3. Sedgwick to Pamela, December 12, 1797. *Ibid.*
4. *Ibid.* In May, 1798, Sedgwick, on leave of absence from Congress due to a severe case of gout, wrote Adams of his recovery and his plans soon to return to Philadelphia. Sedgwick to Adams, May 21, 1798. *Papers of John Adams*, Microfilm #388, M.H.S.
5. Sedgwick to Henry Van Schaack, December 14, 1797. *S.P.*, M.H.S.
6. Sedgwick to Adams, May 21, 1798. *op. cit.*

three years, and they had "always been better disposed & more to be relied on than their governors." [7]

Adams, as Sedgwick doubtless appreciated, was a complicated person. A self-made aristocrat himself, he believed that the aristocracy as well as the mob must be held in check. He considered the Jeffersonian view that human nature was innately good completely erroneous, and Rousseau's belief in the moral perfection of man in a state of nature quite without foundation. He was not, however, as sometimes charged, an exponent of a system of benevolent despotism. An honest "republican," he wished to see the executive, the representative of the public interest at its "purest," strong—even with a final veto power—but not unchecked. Like Washington, he felt that the trappings of office should be carefully promoted, but only as a means of giving dignity to responsible officers. A mixed government, ever watchful of both anarchy and tyranny, was to Adams the only salvation of liberty.

Adams was an undeniably profound student of government and human psychology and an unquestioned patriot, but he was an unsuccessful politician. Vain and touchy,[8] he was easily irritated, usually blunt and undiplomatic, and occasionally unable to appreciate how his friends or his enemies would respond to his actions. Surprisingly enough, he was also a poor administrator, either giving too free rein to his subordinates or wasting his executive energies by personally assuming their duties. He unwisely retained Washington's cabinet and thereby took as members of his official family, Timothy Pickering, Oliver Wolcott, and James McHenry—ardent Hamiltonians who looked for their orders to New York. Aided by the newly originated congressional party caucus system, these men tried to reduce the personal authority of Adams and virtually to ignore the unpleasant fact of his incumbency. As did Sedgwick, these men would to the end persist in considering themselves supporters of the administration, the Hamilton administration.

February 18, 1799, can be designated as the date of Adams' open rebellion against the Hamiltonians. On that day Adams nominated William Vans Murray as peace envoy and minister to France. On that day, too, Adams, in conversation with Sedgwick, scoffed at High Federalist fears of an insurrection, and openly accused the senator and his colleagues of attempting to supersede the President as the supreme military commander. Sedgwick returned from the interview unjustifiably indignant

7. Sedgwick to Pamela, March 11, 1798. Papers of H. D. Sedgwick, *S.P.*, M.H.S.

8. Adams refused to attend the Washington Birthday Ball in 1798, as he felt the chief magistrate was "entitled to a precedence in public attention." Sedgwick to Henry Van Schaack, February 22, 1798. *S.P.*, M.H.S.

and understandably angry. The next morning he wrote Hamilton a full account of his "astonishing" reception:

> I last evening called to pay my respects to the President. He was alone, and, as I hoped, soon introduced the subject of our military. I gave him my view on the subject. . . . He replied, and nearly in the following words:—"As to the Virginians, sir, it is weakness to apprehend any thing from them; but, if you must have an army, I will give it to you; but, remember, it will make the government more unpopular than all their other acts. They have submitted with more patience than any people ever did to the burden of taxes, which have been *liberally laid* on but their patience will not last always." This was the text on which he dilated extensively. I cannot say that I was astonished. Astonishment is a sentiment which he has for some time lost the power to excite.
>
> During the time that I was with him, the bill before the Senate for the organization of the army was mentioned. He asked me what additional authority it was proposed to give the commander-in-chief?[9] I answered none; that all that was proposed was to give him a new title—that of general. "What," said he, "are you going to appoint him general over the President? I have not been so blind but I have seen a combined effort among those who call themselves the friends of government, to annihilate the essential powers given to the President. This, sir, (raising his voice) my understanding has perceived, and my heart felt." After an expression of surprise, and a declaration of belief that he was mistaken, with *all humility* I prayed him to mention the facts from which he had made this inference. He answered, that if I had not seen *it,* it was improper for him to go into the detail.
>
> This shows that we are afflicted with an evil for which certainly no complete remedy can be applied, but it might be paliated, perhaps, by bringing into the administration a man of talents, and of that peculiar kind which gives an ascendency without its being perceived.[10]

Sedgwick was, indeed, led by his rage to admit Adams' very charge— that the Hamiltonians were trying to diminish as well as by-pass his per-

9. Upon Washington's insistence, Adams had most reluctantly commissioned Hamilton as ranking major general and second in command to Washington. Washington was to be a lieutenant general and "the Commander-in-Chief."

10. Sedgwick to Hamilton, February 19, 1799. Hamilton, *Works of Hamilton,* VI, 393–394. Professor Dodd has Sedgwick giving Hamilton an oral report of his interview with Adams, but this is incorrect. William E. Dodd, *The Life of Nathaniel Macon* (Raleigh, N.C., 1903), 141.

sonal authority.[11] Adams' "unconquerable intrepidity" which Sedgwick had so recommended to Hamilton in 1788, during the discussion on Adams' fitness for the vice-presidency, now came to plague Sedgwick. He had unwittingly advocated to Hamilton the very man who would thwart the New Yorker's plans of party command and possible military conquest.

Far more disastrous in Sedgwick's view than Adams' sloth in recruiting the army was his nomination of Vans Murray as minister plenipotentiary to France. Although Adams told Sedgwick that if he and his friends "must have an army," he would give it to them, he had already decided to hazard one final effort to make it unnecessary for that expensive and potentially troublemaking force ever to progress past infancy. Encouraged by word from Vans Murray, Minister to Holland, that Talleyrand and the Directory were talking peace and were ready to promise honorable treatment for any American envoys, Adams sent the name of Vans Murray to the Senate. The diplomat was to negotiate an amicable settlement with the now penitent French, if that nation would give assurance that he would be properly received. The approaches of the French, if unofficial, provided, Adams believed, a sufficient basis for reopening negotiations.

Sedgwick was enraged. Penitent! Pichon's vague promise to Vans Murray, he charged, was just another trick of those rascally French. Exactly what degree of evidence was Adams' "plausible appearance of probability"? What court of law had ever heard of it? Nothing would be accomplished by this mission except the utter destruction of all current armament efforts. The nation would lose its unity and purpose. The Jacobins would come out of hiding, incite civil war, and, once victorious, greet the French invader with a fraternal embrace as he landed on these, the last shores of liberty.

Sedgwick sought Hamilton's advice. Assuring him that this unexpected announcement was solely "the result of Presidential wisdom" and had been kept completely secret from the cabinet, Sedgwick announced that it was his solemn judgment that "had the foulest heart and

---

11. Professor Zechariah Chafee in his generally excellent biographical sketch of Sedgwick is surely in error when he labels Sedgwick a "Federalist of the Adams wing." Allen Johnson and Dumas Malone, eds., *Dictionary of American Biography*, XVI, 550.

Adams' growing resentment of Hamilton was quickly echoed by his wife. See Abigail Adams to John Adams, January 13, 1799. *Adams Papers* (Microfilm #393) M.H.S.

the ablest head in the world have been permitted to select the most embarrassing and ruinous measure, perhaps it would have been precisely the one which has been adopted." He and his friends were, he declared, in the deepest of dilemmas. Whether the nomination was approved or rejected, incalculable evils were in store. This was certain if Vans Murray was "the ablest negotiator in Christendom"; how much more so when he was "feeble, unguarded, credulous, and unimpressive." Declaring that he had not yet decided whether to risk dividing the Federalist party by publicly fighting the nomination, Sedgwick tacitly asked for counsel.[12] Hamilton, as well to advise Sedgwick as to counsel the President's Cabinet, answered by return post. He advised his friends to compromise with disagreeable necessity, but went on to suggest that "my present impression is that the measure must go into effect with the additional idea of a Commission of three. The mode must be accommodated with the President—Murray is certainly not strong enough for so immensely important a mission." [13]

Hamilton's advice was sent to the right man, for the Senate had just appointed Sedgwick to head a committee to consider the Vans Murray appointment. The New Yorker's suggestions coincided with the opinion of this committee and of other leading Federalists in Congress.

Sedgwick's committee, composed of Federalists Ross and Bingham of Pennsylvania, Read of South Carolina, Stockton of New Jersey, and Sedgwick, met on February 21. It decided, after some internal debate and dissension, to solicit an interview with the President [14] in order to induce him to alter the mission "as it respects the person; and instead of an individual, to propose a commission,—as it respects the principles on which the negotiation shall commence,—and as it respects the scene within which it shall be carried on." [15] Sedgwick's first reaction, to reject

12. Sedgwick to Hamilton, February 19, 1799. Hamilton, *Works of Hamilton,* VI, 396.

13. Hamilton to Sedgwick, February 21, 1799. *S.P.,* M.H.S.

14. Sedgwick to Hamilton, February 22, 1799. *Hamilton Papers,* Library of Congress. Sedgwick grieved: "It is one of the misfortunes to which we are subjected by the wild and irregular starts of a vain, jealous, and half frantic mind, that we are obliged to practice an infraction of correct principles, a direct communication between the President and the Senate."

15. *Ibid.* Leonard D. White intimates that the Sedgwick committee was simply parroting Hamilton in its insistence on a commission. Hamilton's letter of February 21 probably reached Sedgwick on the afternoon of the 22nd, but the committee had decided a day earlier to insist that Vans Murray be but one of three envoys. Leonard D. White, *The Federalists* (New York, 1948), 248.

out of hand the whole idea of the mission, had evidently been tempered by cooler senatorial heads, and then by Hamilton's letter. But he was not altogether convinced, for he concluded that if Adams proved "unaccommodating," and Sedgwick was almost certain he would, then he "must vote against the appointment," whatever his friends did.[16]

Adams granted Sedgwick's request for a conference between the President and the committee, specifying that it should not be mentioned in their report or considered a precedent. The interview was held Saturday evening, February 23. What transpired is the subject of considerable dispute. Sedgwick's letter to Hamilton of February 25 is the only extant contemporary account. Not unexpectedly it strongly emphasizes Adams' obduracy:

> During the conversation he [Adams] declared, repeatedly, that to defend the executive against oligarchic influence, it was indispensable that he should insist on a decision on the nomination; and he added: "I have, on mature reflection made up my mind, & I will neither withdraw nor modify the nomination." He was, however, pleased to let us know, that if Murray was negatived, he would then propose a commission, two of the members of which should be gentlemen within the United States . . . and that in no case should the Gentlemen be permitted to leave the country, until the positive assurances mentioned in his message of the 21st June shall have been given. In consequence of these declarations, at a meeting of the federal members, it was agreed to reject the nomination.[17]

Adams, ten years later, depicted himself as much more "accommodating," even as quite willing to modify the nomination *before* it came to a vote:

> The gentlemen thought that a commission would be more satisfactory to the Senate and to the public. I said, although this was not perfectly consonant to my own opinion, I could . . . easily give up my own to the public; and if they advised it, I would send another message, and nominate a commission of three. . . .
> The gentlemen acquiesced, and one of them, whom I took to be

16. Sedgwick to Hamilton, February 22, 1799. *Hamilton Papers,* Library of Congress.
   Adams was well aware that the proposal of a new mission to France had "stirred the Passions" of such High Federalists as Sedgwick—"Rivalries have been irritated to madness." Adams to Abigail Adams, February 22, 1799. *Adams Papers* (Microfilm #393) M.H.S.
17. Sedgwick to Hamilton, February 25, 1799. *Hamilton Papers,* Library of Congress.

the chairman, was pleased to say, "after this very enlightened explanation of the whole business, I am perfectly satisfied." [18]

Adams' memory surely was playing tricks on him. Sedgwick, the chairman, was not "perfectly satisfied"; the Federalists caucused at Mr. Bingham's palatial Philadelphia residence and decided on rejection, and Sedgwick drafted a committee report recommending that the Senate, though wishing to restore tranquility, "do not advise & consent that the said William Vans Murray be sole minister plenipotentiary of the U. S. to the french republic." [19] It would appear that Adams met the committee with all politeness, and that Sedgwick, after proposing a commission of three, had insinuated that perhaps Adams' friend Gerry had had a hand in the nomination. Adams, much incensed at this allegation, had then declared it his irrevocable decision that he would never modify the proposed mission unless Vans Murray was out-and-out rejected. Sedgwick thereupon had left the President's residence, bitterly angry and vowing to defeat the nomination. [20]

18. From one of Adams' letters to the *Boston Patriot* in 1809 as quoted by Charles Francis Adams, ed., *The Works of John Adams.* . . . (Boston, 1850–1856), IX, 250.

19. An unsigned draft of this report in Sedgwick's hand is in S.P., M.H.S.

20. See letters of Stockton and either Ross or Bingham to Pickering in the year 1822, when the last-named was seeking material for a history of the Adams' administration. Quoted in Octavius Pickering and Charles W. Upham, *The Life of Timothy Pickering* (Boston, 1867–1873), III, 439.

There is in the *Adams Papers* (Microfilm #393, M.H.S.) a letter from Sedgwick to John Rutherfurd, former senator from New Jersey, that appears at first glance to cast doubt upon the above account. This letter was written, however, on March 1, 1799, after the Senate had approved Adams' three nominations and confuses in part the initial struggle and subsequent compromise. It consequently minimizes the initial deadlock between Adams and Sedgwick's committee. Perhaps its most interesting feature is its revelation of disunity within this committee prior to its meeting with Adams.

My dear Sir—
    The sentiments which were excited in you by the nomination of Mr. Murray were just & natural and I am sorry to add that they would have been stronger if you knew precisely, the communications between him & Pichon, no *direct* assurances . . . and those which were given, contained continuous exceptions & reservations . . . excluding *all those who had been seduced by England, were the friends of royalty, or the enemies of France*—or as we should express it *the friends of our government & administration* from being appointed as our negotiators—The approbation of the nomination, from the inconsistencies of the case as well as from the character of Mr. Murray was impossible. The task imposed on the committee was a delicate one and the difficulty of executing it was increased by a real difference of opinion among the members of it—

The previewed showdown did not, however, take place. Adams, once he heard the result of the Sunday night caucas and saw that the majority of Federalist senators were positively determined to reject Vans Murray, decided to compromise. He sent a messenger to inform Sedgwick that the President wished he would postpone his report, as a second presidential communication on the mission to France was then being prepared. That afternoon (Monday, February 25) this second message, nominating a commission of three—Oliver Ellsworth, Patrick Henry, and Vans Murray—was received by the Senate. Sedgwick's committee was discharged, and its report never read. It was a wise decision on Adams' part. He had the substance: one final attempt at peace was to be made. For the sake of even nominal party unity, the decision as to form might be awarded the Hamiltonians. Adams would see to it that the new form of the mission did not unduly retard its progress.

Sedgwick, who voted for all three nominations, felt that the Federalists had gotten "out of this vile scrape" as well as could be expected and was greatly pleased with the instrumental part he had played. To an unnamed correspondent he wrote: "If ever I have deserved well of my country it was on this occasion.[21] Sedgwick was also pleased with the record of the congressional session now coming to a close. It was, he said, a glorious one, excepting only "the *faux pas* of the great man." [22] He saw, however, that "the *faux pas*" went far to undermine the armament efforts and to weaken the martial spirit that had made the session so "glorious." "Nothing," he wrote, could have been "more unfortunate than this measure":

---

20. (cont.)

the majority beleiving, that it is competent to the Senate to decide not only on the fitness of the man nominated but also *on the expediency* & terms of negotiation. . . . it was finally agreed, unanimously, to confine ourselves in any intercourse we might have with the executive, merely to the man. So restricted and pledged to each other, a conversation took place and nothing but the character of Mr. Murray was hinted at by any of the committee, but as introduced & proposed by the President, nor afterwards discussed by us but *as private individuals;* and it was also agreed that no notice should, in any event, be taken of the interview with the President. . . . The President was informed by the Chairman of the object of the desired interview, and on that principle assented to it, but he did in fact present the subject in all its relations to the committee—We perfectly concurred as to the means of being extricated from the embarrassment, & *he* has ultimately adopted our views, *but with much apparent reluctance.*

Obligated as I am to write in haste & unable to correct . . . I fear that what I have written is not inteligible.

21. February 26, 1799. *S.P., M.H.S.*

22. Sedgwick to Henry Van Schaack, March 4, 1799. *Ibid.*

After infinite embarrassments we had obtained a point of . . . open and declared hostility, the most desirable, and which should not, but on great consideration, have been relinquished. The state of our affairs as well at home as in Europe required a firm adherence to the system which had been adopted.[23]

The appointment of Gerry to the earlier French mission in 1798, and the President's "slothfulness" in forwarding "the new army," had in combination caused a rift between Adams and Sedgwick; the Vans Murray appointment made the break irreparable. Their separation had also been furthered by Adams' rejection of Sedgwick's request for a seat on the United States Supreme Court. Sedgwick had written Adams in the preceding September, humbly suggesting that he was available for the vacancy caused by the death of Associate Justice James Wilson.[24] Such

23. Sedgwick to King, March 20, 1799. (Copy) S.P., M.H.S.
King, probably reflecting Sedgwick's sentiments, wrote that gentleman, in strictest confidence, as follows:

> How weak, how . . . criminal we are, to believe for an instant, that after the Resistance we have *dared* to make that France will ever return moderation. . . . you and I and our children, with those of every other man who has foresight and firmness to descry and to denounce the Danger, are marked; and if the occasion unhappily arrives, will be given as offerings to appease the anger of the offended Directory.

King to Sedgwick, March 21, 1799. S.P., M.H.S.
The perceptive Abigail Adams wrote her husband that "the appointment of Mr. Murray" had stirred "the whole community . . . like a flock of frightened pigions." March 3, 1799. *Adams Papers,* (Microfilm #393) M.H.S. Henry Knox and John Marshall, however, stood firmly by the President and supported the new mission to France. Knox to Adams, March 5, 1799; Charles Lee to Adams, March 14, 1799. *Ibid.*
24. Sedgwick to Adams, September 25, 1798:

Sir

> By the death of Judge Willson [sic] there is a vacancy on the bench of the supreme court. Whether I may be deemed competent to supply that vacancy, or whether it may be thought proper to appoint another Judge, from this State, I am ignorant, so Pardon, Sir, my thus suggesting a wish—I should not have done it, but from a fear, that my friends, will compel me, again, to serve in the house of Representatives. The sacrifices which I have made, and which are exacted of me, are more than the just claims of a numerous family will authorise. I would have preferred a station wholly private to any other; but this the friends of the government, will not permit, without, (what is impossible,) an absolute denial on my part & an office, incompatible with a legislative appointment, is the only mean of my escape. Again I pray you, Sir, pardon this address which I fear will be thought improper or presumptious; and beleive me to be, with great esteem and sincere personal attachment, Sir.

Papers of John Adams, (Microfilm #391), M.H.S.

an appointment would enable him, he had declared, to honorably refuse the expected request of his friends that he continue to serve the nation in a legislative capacity. There is no record that Adams ever answered this request; if he did it was only to reject Sedgwick's offer.

After the appointment of Vans Murray, Sedgwick still communicated with the President; he even recommended to him certain officers who might be appointed in "the eventual Army," [25] but from February, 1799, on, Sedgwick in fact despised Adams. Not appreciating that the wedge which was splitting the Federalist party was being wielded chiefly by Hamilton, Pickering, McHenry, and Theodore Sedgwick, Sedgwick cast all blame on the heavy hands of John Adams. He analyzed the party's plight for the benefit of Rufus King in London:

> The P———t by a fortunate concurrence of circumstances had obtained an elevation, which certainly his friends did not expect. The principal cause of this was a supposed just appreciation of the conduct of France toward our country, a strong resentment of our wrongs and a dignified firmness in supporting our honor and steadily adhering to that system, such as it is, which had been adopted by the friends of Government. The foundation on which confidence rested has been, by this strange measure, destroyed, and the consequences disagreeable and may be more so. I do not undertake even to conjecture their nature or extent, but it is impossible to reoccupy the ground which has been lost.[26]

Adams, a "good hater" in the best tradition of Dr. Johnson, reciprocated the feelings of Senator Sedgwick. Some sixteen years after the event, he wrote that peace had been essential in 1799 because of the bitter and near equal division of the nation into two parties, and because of the extreme feebleness of "the administration men" in Congress. He rhetorically asked: "And what was my support in the Senate? . . . Mr. Sedgwick, without dignity, never able to win the complacency, or command the attention of his hearers in either house, but ever ready to meet in private caucuses and secret intrigues to oppose me." [27]

After Adams, in May, 1800, declared his independence of the Hamiltonians by demanding the resignation of his secretaries of State and War,[28] and after Sedgwick began intriguing to bring in Charles Cotes-

25. Sedgwick to Adams, May 3, 1799. (Microfilm #394) *Ibid.*
26. Sedgwick to King, July 26, 1799. (Copy) S.P., M.H.S.
27. Adams to James Lloyd, January, 1815. Adams, *Works of Adams*, X, 113.
28. Sedgwick wrote Hamilton: "Every tormenting passion rankles in the bosom of that weak and frantic old man . . . I have good reason for believing that Pick-

worth Pinckney ahead of Adams in the election of 1800, the two New Englanders seem never to have written a line nor spoken a word to one another. The delightful Sunday family dinners with the amiable Adams and his "admirable wife" were like something from the distant past.

The same extremism and lack of perspective, the same fear of losing power, that characterized Sedgwick's behavior during the latter months of the French crisis had been exhibited also in the late spring and summer of 1798, when the Fifth Congress passed two laws that were partisan and unwise: the Naturalization Law and the Alien Friends Act, and one which was possibly unconstitutional, the Sedition Act.

---

28. (cont.)

ering and McHenry have been sacraficed as peace offerings." Sedgwick to Hamilton, May 13, 1800. *Hamilton Papers,* Library of Congress.

McHenry probably showed Sedgwick a copy of his formal "recollection" of a conversation with Adams, May 5, 1800—on the evening prior to McHenry's forced resignation. In this recollection (that took the form of a long letter to Adams, May 31, 1800) McHenry remembered Adams' charges that Hamilton "ruled" Washington and that the latter "saddled me with three secretaries who would controul me." *Adams Papers,* (Microfilm #397) M.H.S.

Pickering initially refused to accept "the opportunity of resigning." Pickering to Adams, May 12, 1800. *Ibid.*

XIII

The Alien and Sedition Acts

*I never like half measures, and at present I think them
disgraceful and dangerous.*
Theodore Sedgwick [1]

To such Federalists as Sedgwick political prospects had never seemed
brighter nor the evils of disloyalty more evident than in the year 1798.
A glorious future awaited nation and party if only disloyalty could be
extinguished. Sedgwick and the other high priests of Federalism believed this goal could be accomplished through legislation. By legislation, present and future aliens could be carefully regulated, and licentious Jacobins deprived of their power to incite sedition and defame
constituted authority.

Though Theodore Sedgwick was ill at home when the first Alien Act
was passed, he was one of its leading authors. On the twenty-sixth of
April, 1798, he had been appointed a member of a committee to consider the problem of "dangerous aliens," and on the twenty-eighth he had
informed his wife that he was in the process of "framing a bill to authorize the President to send out of the country the French rascals who disturb our repose." His draft was utilized by the Senate committee which
reported (May 1, 1798) a bill authorizing the President, for a period of
two years, to order aliens whom he judged "dangerous to the peace and
safety of the United States" to leave the country. During Sedgwick's absence a motion that the courts, rather than the President, be allowed to
grant aliens exemptionary permits was defeated (May 10), and the bill
passed, 16–7 (June 9th). Sedgwick was gratified by the passage of this
"Alien Friends Act," though disappointed that the House saw fit to
soften a provision demanding "hard labor for and during life" for an
alien remaining in the country after sentence of transportation was pronounced. He applauded without qualification senatorial approval (June

1. Letter to Rufus King, July 26, 1799. King, *King*, III, 147.

18) of the naturalization bill hindering potential Republican voters from becoming citizens by extending the residence period required for citizenship from five to fourteen years.

The Alien Friends Act and the Naturalization Act may have been partisan, foolish, and opposed to the best interests of the country, but they were undoubtedly constitutional and, viewed in the perspective of subsequent immigrant exclusion, understandable. So, also, was the Alien Enemies Act passed by Congress on June 25, 1798, several days after Sedgwick's return to Congress. This measure enpowered the President in time of war or invasion to imprison or transport any alien enemy whose presence might endanger the public safety.[2]

Far more stringent than these measures dealing with aliens was the Sedition Act, possibly the most repressive and the most controversial act in American legislative history.

Lacking any conception whatsoever of the true nature of the growing two party system of politics, Sedgwick and his friends regarded the Jeffersonians in the same way that certain propertied citizens in 1920 regarded the Socialist party of Eugene Debs. Sedgwick did not think of the Republicans as a rival party but as a vicious band of anarchists. They were godless lovers of the atheistic French; they were defamers of everything he loved and treasured; they were revolutionaries, utilizing the freedoms granted by the Constitution to destroy the Constitution. Perhaps more to the point, they ridiculed him and his friends in their vile sheets. These Jacobin papers were purveyors of poison, not information, and should be destroyed. Now grown more extreme in his partisanship, Sedgwick told his friends to subscribe to no papers unless assured that their editors were "well disposed—Not Impartial printers —such are always seditious."[3]

A single-minded and emotional partisan, Sedgwick had taken the denunciatory warnings of Hamilton to heart and would hold them long after his more flexible and pragmatic friend had modified them to meet existing circumstances. Sedgwick, possessing little ability to stand apart

2. No one was actually deported under the two alien acts, but Volney, the scientist, whom Sedgwick believed to be a master spy, and certain other Frenchmen were frightened into leaving the country. It was the possession of the "club" rather than its continuous use that was chiefly desired by Sedgwick and his friends.

3. Sedgwick to Henry Van Schaack, February 22; April 21, 1798. S.P., M.H.S.

Sedgwick had evidently forgotten his strong opposition to certain harsh anti-Tory measures passed by Massachusetts some sixteen years earlier. Then he had declared: "It may. . . . be asked whether I would have no Restraint? I answer, yes; Restraints upon Actions but none on Thought." Sedgwick to Timothy Edwards, n.d. Papers of H. D. Sedgwick, S.P., M.H.S.

from events at hand, and less ability to adapt himself to new ideological currents, thought of the Federalists as the government. The idea of the United States supporting two political parties, each honest and sincere, the idea of any sort of inter-party co-operation, he would have dismissed as patently absurd.[4] Believing as he did that the Jeffersonians were the "disorganizers of our Government" rather than the political opposition, he felt it proper to attack them with any weapon available. Not to pass a stringent, all-inclusive Sedition Act would be a betrayal of our hard-won independence and glorious Constitution.

Sedgwick had called for measures respecting "our internal police" many months before the XYZ Affair made them possible.[5] Though such demands had been submitted in private letters, his political opponents both suspected and exaggerated his desires. Jefferson had written William Giles early in the spring of 1796 that he understood that Sedgwick "one of the Federal 'great men' " was contemplating a sedition act aimed at the democratic societies.[6] Certainly by the summer of 1798 Sedgwick was convinced that an internal police measure was essential and he strongly supported a motion, June 26, 1798, which granted Senator James Lloyd of Maryland permission to bring in "a treason and sedition bill." Such a bill was quickly reported and passed the Senate on Independence Day by a vote of 18–6. Sedgwick voted, of course, with the majority, and it was the opinion of certain Jeffersonians that he was, with James Hillhouse of Connecticut, the bill's chief author.[7] Several Federalist senators helped draft the measure, however, and Sedgwick's role was rather less instrumental than his enemies allowed.

As originally drafted, the Sedition Law would have made it illegal to imply that the administration acted in any way contrary to the Constitution or the liberties of the people, or even to speak in any way favorable of the French nation. Passed in this form, it might have been the signal for an American Reign of Terror. In its final form, however, the Sedition Act was less stringent. It specified fine and imprisonment for anyone attempting to hinder the operations of the government, and pun-

4. Sedgwick rebuffed the attempt of Jonathan Hunter to "pair" with him in May, 1798, on the occasion of the ratification of certain presidential nominations. Hunter to Sedgwick, May 4, 1798. *S.P.*, M.H.S.

5. Sedgwick to King, March 12, 1797. King, *King*, II, 158. King heartily concurred with Sedgwick's suspicion of the "aliens who are among us." See King to Sedgwick, June 6, 1798. *S.P.*, M.H.S.

6. Jefferson to Giles, March 19, 1796, as quoted by Henry S. Randall, *The Life of Thomas Jefferson* (New York, 1858), II, 290.

7. John Wood, *History of the Administration of John Adams, esq. . . .* (New York, 1802), 182.

ishment for any individual who made or published "false, scandalous, and malicious" statements in defamation of the President or Congress, or who tended "to stir up sedition within the United States." Under this act some fifteen Republican printers and agitators were indicted, and Representative Lyon was fined and imprisoned.

The Sedition Act was surely opposed to the *spirit* of the Constitution and, many believe, to the *letter* of the First and Fifth amendments. The accused was given a trial and allowed to prove the truth of the "libel," but as Federalist judges influenced the selection of juries in highly partisan fashion, and as "libelled" officials of the government could not be subpoenaed, the supposed fairness of the judicial process was largely a mockery. It was an attempt to give the national courts common-law jurisdiction in criminal cases. The offenses listed in the Sedition Act were admittedly already punishable in the state courts but had been rendered obsolete in application. The *federal* statutory enactment of the common-law principle in question emphasized, invigorated and renewed it to such an extent that new offenses and punishments were in effect created.[8]

Sedgwick insisted, of course, that Congress had a right to punish seditious libel under our heritage of the English common law. He asserted that the First Amendment protected the freedom of a responsible press, not the character assassinations of licentious Jacobin editors.[9] If the Federalists had set up clearer and more limiting standards of sedition and libel, he might have had a better point. But so loose was the legislative terminology, so feeble were the judicial safeguards, and so wide was the net cast, generally, that not only were men subject to imprisonment who plotted to subvert and overthrow the government, but also those who plotted no more than the electoral defeat of Theodore Sedgwick.

Sedgwick, positive that only by exterminating "Jacobins" could the nation survive, was quite shocked at the distaste shown by certain south-

8. For an able and incisive analysis of the Sedition Act see James Morton Smith, *Freedom's Fetters* (Ithaca, 1956), 418–433. The present author cannot agree, however, that the XYZ Affair had no causative influence on the Alien and Sedition Acts, that it afforded but a convenient "occasion." *Ibid.*, 21.

9. Professor Leonard Levy in his brilliant and revisionist analysis of the evolution and early history of the First Amendment freedoms, *Legacy of Suppression: Freedom of Speech and Press in Early American History* (Cambridge, 1960), convincingly demonstrates that *both* Republicans and Federalists believed that suppression of political criticism deemed subversive or irresponsible was legitimate and proper. Surely, however, the Federalists, the group in power, were more extreme in their interpretation and application of this doctrine.

ern Federalists for the Alien and Sedition Acts. John Marshall's answer to the "Queries of a free-holder" of Virginia he considered especially "reprehensible." Archfool Gerry, he said, had never behaved more mischievously. He did not believe that "a man who stood so high in the confidence & respect of the worthy part of his fellow citizens, should have degraded himself by a mean & paltry electioneering trick." Sedgwick was neither fully convinced by Pickering's letter vouching for the honorable character of Marshall, nor persuaded by George Cabot's defense of the Virginian in the *Columbian Centinel*. Senator Sedgwick had increasingly little use for "moderates." [10]

A strong dislike of halfway measures and men characterized Sedgwick's response to the Kentucky and Virginia Resolutions, passed in protest against the "unconstitutionality" of the Alien and Sedition Acts. Sedgwick was eager to put the fear if not of God at least of the Federalists into the intransigent hearts of the citizens of these two states, and when the cautious counsel of more temperate colleagues prevailed, he mourned their disgraceful "lack of spirit."

The Virginia and Kentucky Resolutions varied both in the vehemence of their protest and the radical quality of their recommendations. Madison, author of the Virginia Resolution, was content to call the new statutes unconstitutional, and to assert that the *people* of the states *collectively* had the power to take corrective measures. Collectively, he argued, they could completely ignore the federal laws and call a convention of the states, or do what they would. Jefferson, author of the Kentucky Resolution, boldly declared that *each state* had a right to judge violations of the Constitution for itself and to take necessary corrective measures. He heartily approved when the Kentucky legislature—not its citizens in popular convention—declared the Alien and Sedition Acts of no effect whatsoever in Kentucky, and invited the support of other right-thinking states.[11]

These resolutions by no means represented the best constitutional thought of their day. However widely accepted the "compact theory" and the theory of "co-ordinate sovereignty" were at this time, it would seem doubtful if either was ever meant to extend to extremes which

10. Sedgwick to Pickering, October 23, 1798. *Pickering Papers*, XXIII, 253. M.H.S. Pickering to Sedgwick, November 6, 1798. *Ibid.*, IX, 570–571.

11. For an excellent comparison of the two resolutions, see Irving Brant, *James Madison, Father of the Constitution* (New York, 1950), 462.

For an interesting analysis of "Contemporary Opinion of the Kentucky and Virginia Resolutions," see Frank M. Anderson's articles in the *American Historical Review*, V, 45–63, 225–252.

might destroy the Union. Madison's explanation of the relationships of the federal and state governments, and of the limited sphere of *supremacy* of the federal government, in numbers 44–46 of *The Federalist*, was surely a more practical and convincing commentary on the Constitution than his and Jefferson's attempt ten years later. These resolutions did not, probably, represent the predominant political theory of the Republican party in 1798 or even, possibly, that of Thomas Jefferson. As much as anything else they were a skilled political manoeuvre, designed to bring dramatically before the voters the partisan motivation and nature of the Alien and Sedition Acts. With the fading of the Jay Treaty issue from the public consciousness, Jefferson's loosely organized Republican party had stood in life-and-death need of a new issue, a new battle standard. The Federalists had obliged with the Alien and Sedition Acts.

Sedgwick refused to see matters in this light. On the contrary, he felt that not the Alien and Sedition Acts but the Kentucky and Virginia Resolutions might well prove decisive in the forthcoming presidential election. If they could not in themselves, then a little salutary publicity and punishment might help matters along. A detailed proposal of how this might best be done came from his friend Hamilton.

Hamilton suggested that "the first thing in all great operations of such a Government as ours is to secure the opinion of the people." To this end a special committee should be set up by Congress to consider the proceedings of the legislatures of Virginia and Kentucky, and the Alien and Sedition Laws of which they had complained. "That Committee should make a report exhibiting with great luminousness and particularity the reasons which support the constitutionality and expediency of those laws." It should point out "the tendency of the doctrines advanced by Virginia and Kentucky to destroy the Constitution of the United States—and, with . . . calm dignity united with pathos, the full evidence which they afford of a regular conspiracy to overturn the government." They likewise should "dwell upon the inevitable effect and probably the intention of these proceedings to encourage a hostile foreign power to decline accommodation and proceed in hostility." The government must arraign its enemies as well as defend itself. "But in all this, there should be great care to distinguish the people of Virginia from their legislature and even the greater part of those who may have concurred in the legislature from their chiefs." The report should conclude with a statement that there was no cause whatsoever for a repeal of the federal laws in question. "If however on examination any modifications consistent with the general design of the laws, but instituting better guard, can be devised it may [be] well to propose them" as a means of affording an honorable retreat to those susceptible to redemption. "Concessions of the kind adroitly made have a good rather than a bad effect. On a recent, though hasty revision of the Alien law it seems to me deficient in precautions against abuse and for the security of Citizens." The report should be disseminated as widely as humanly possible. "A little pamphlet containing it should find its way into every house in Virginia. This should be left to work and nothing to court a shock should be adopted."

In rather contradictory fashion Hamilton then proceeded to explain how a salutary "shock" might be produced. "In the mean time the measures for raising the Military force should proceed with activity." It was to be greatly regretted that execution of these measures had been marked with such delay. "In times like the present not a moment ought to have been lost to secure the Government so powerful an auxiliary. Wherever the experiment shall be made to subdue a refractory & powerful state by Militia, the event shall shame the advocates of their sufficiency." Once a proper military force had been brought together it should be drawn towards Virginia "for which there is an obvious pretext—& then let measures be taken to act upon the laws & put Virginia to the Test of resistance." Such a plan would serve the country well. It would "give time for the fervour of the moment to subside, for reason to resume the reins, and by dividing its enemies . . . [would] enable the Government to triumph with ease." [12]

Hamilton's plan was congenial to Sedgwick, who had similar opinions on the necessity of Federalist counterattack upon the Virginia and Kentucky Resolutions. He replied that, some time before, he had consulted with "the apparent leaders in the House of Representatives," and attempted to convince them that an able committee should be appointed "to refer the addresses on the subject with an intention of making a report." The House, as the more popular body and one whose conduct "would excite more attention," was to be preferred for this task. The House, however, exhibited a sad lack of unity. "I spoke to no gentleman who did not explicitly concur with me in opinion, but nothing has been done, because, as I understand the gentlemen cannot agree on the precise mode in which it is to be done." [13]

The final result was a House Committee Report of February 25, 1799, which, while avoiding specific mention of the Kentucky and Vir-

12. Hamilton to Sedgwick, February 2, 1799. *Hamilton MSS.*, Houghton Library, Harvard University.
13. Sedgwick to Hamilton, February 7, 1799. Hamilton, *Works of Hamilton*, VI, 392.

ginia Resolutions, reiterated the Federalist claims that the Alien and
Sedition Acts were justified as national defense legislation.[14]

Senator Sedgwick, increasingly extreme in his devotion to Federal
men and principles, was all for massing a number of troops on the borders
of Virginia and frightening the Virginians into submission.[15] Reports of
Judge Bushrod Washington and others that a very large group of Virginians were totally opposed to the views of Madison and Jefferson,
failed to sway him. Sedgwick did not feel sanguine about the ability of
the Virginia Federalists to clean house unaided. He was certain that the

14. Sedgwick never accepted the idea that the Sedition Act was either politically unwise or unduly severe. He opposed all attempts by the Republicans to wipe
it from the statute books and as Speaker of the House of Representatives was later
instrumental in delaying its demise. In January, 1801, the recommendation of a
special committee to continue the Sedition Act was accepted by the tie-breaking vote
of Speaker Sedgwick, and in February, 1801, a bill to repeal most of the Sedition
Act was defeated when, on a vote of 50–49, Sedgwick declared himself with the
nays. *Annals,* X, 975, 1038 (January 23, February 19, 1801).

Sedgwick, indeed, seems to have believed that the only thing wrong with the
Sedition Act was its execution by the courts:

> Juries are returned by sheriffs & sheriffs are chosen by the people—universal
> suffrage. . . . There is an action commenced by the Secy. of State [Pickering]
> agt. the editor of the Aurora [Duane]. This will be tried by a democratic Jury
> & altho the Slander was as malignant as could have been conceived, and as
> false as malignant yet I should not be astonished if he did not recovered [*sic*] a
> fiftieth part so much as the Physician [Dr. Benjamin Rush] has got agt. [Wil-
> liam] Corbett.

Sedgwick to Henry Van Schaack, n.d. *S.P.,* M.H.S.

15. Sedgwick to Henry Van Schaack, February 18, 1799. *Loose Letters* of
Theodore Sedgwick, *S.P.,* M.H.S.

The subsequent dispatch of the Vans Murray mission did not, in Sedgwick's
eyes, lessen the true danger or give cause for "disbanding" the army. Throughout
the winter of 1799–1800 Sedgwick continued to insist that domestic and foreign
dangers demanded nothing less than a re-enlistment of the army on a new basis. To
dismiss the army at present would be "extremely dangerous, if not absolutely ruinous." At the very least, it would mean sending home "as many, with few exceptions,
active & resentful agents to disseminate discord, as there are persons that at present
compose it." More importantly, it would leave the government defenseless against
foreign and domestic foe alike. It was unfortunately true that Congress had specified
that all enlistments would "terminate with the differences between the United States
and France," but the dispatch of the foolish Vans Murray mission had surely not
ended such "differences." Not only did the French continue to display a "spirit of
turbulent ambition," but so did Kentucky. Kentucky appeared determined to reduce
the national government "to a mere diplomatic association." See Sedgwick to King,
December 12, 29, 1799; February 11, 1800 (Copies), and Sedgwick to Henry Van
Schaack, December 14, 1799, *S.P.,* M.H.S.

Virginians were actively preparing for resistance "by arming the People," and asserted that the majority address of the Virginia legislature was "little, if at all, short of a declaration of war." [16] A retaliatory display of national military strength was obviously required. If such was impossible, however—and he soon saw that it was—the next best thing was legislative declarations by the other states, spurning Virginia's plea for united action in opposition to the Alien and Sedition Acts. If pacific measures were all that the temper of the times would afford, "infinitely more beneficial" than any action by the Federalist minority in Virginia was an exhibition of "firm, dignified & patriotic conduct of the other State legislatures, whose *unanimity* will in some degree redeem our character, disgraced by Virginia democracy; and . . . [arrest] the progress of the designs of the leaders in that state." [17]

Sedgwick was happy to see that Massachusetts was foremost among the states rejecting the insidious invitation of Virginia. His own state had been a little tardy with its resolutions, Sedgwick thought, but, once aroused, had behaved handsomely. In the upper house of the General Court only that "incindiary" Republican from Stockbridge, John Bacon, had dared to be counted as an advocate of the Virginian theories. But if Massachusetts was on the side of the angels, Sedgwick feared that New York might join the devil. Accordingly, Sedgwick advocated accession there to a compromise declaration proposed by Aaron Burr. It was highly important that a real test of strength of the Federal and Republican parties in New York not take place at this time, and the possible presence in New York of a sizeable faction "engaged in the business of disorganization" not be disclosed for the encouragement of Virginia and Kentucky. The Burr proposal *did* mildly chide the Virginians, and Sedgwick felt that it was best under the circumstances to accept the half loaf. The declaration would, in any case, do excellent service in separating Burr from the southern elements of the Republican party.[18]

Eventually nine legislatures commented on the Kentucky and Virginia resolutions, all of them unfavorably. With this response to "warmongers" Jefferson and Madison, Senator Sedgwick had to be satisfied.

Apart from his noteworthy endeavors in 1797 and early 1798 to defend the nation's honor and strengthen its military defense against France, perhaps the most creditable activities of Sedgwick as a senator concerned the more routine duties that fell his way. An efficient organ-

16. Sedgwick to King, March 20, 1799. (Copy) *S.P., M.H.S.*
17. *Ibid.*
18. Sedgwick to Henry Van Schaack, February 18, 1799. *S.P., M.H.S.*

izer of his time and a man of tremendous energy, Sedgwick held more committee assignments in the Fifth Congress than any other senator.[19] But whatever the committee or debate at hand—whether it concerned the Yazoo Lands of Georgia or the destitute refugees from Nova Scotia— Senator Sedgwick was first and foremost a party man. Sedgwick was convinced that only in party regularity was there a hope of stemming the tide of Jeffersonian democracy. When the Logan Act [20] was before the Senate, Sedgwick, though doubting the "policy as well as the utility" of the measure, felt that "after it became a question of party" it should be supported without question. Such loyalty had, of course, its rewards. Among them was Sedgwick's election, June 27, 1798, as President *pro tempore* of the Senate. Vice-President Jefferson had excused himself for the remainder of the second session, and Sedgwick was awarded the privilege of presiding over the Senate for the following nineteen days.

There were rewards, too, in academic and social spheres. The College of New Jersey, later to become Princeton, awarded him in 1799 its honorary degree of Doctor of Laws,[21] and the wife of the British minister allegedly "marshalled all her attractions" in an effort to insure Sedgwick's attendance at her dances and routs.[22]

19. In March, 1798, Sedgwick had described a typical day's work to his friend Henry Van Schaack:

> I was called out of bed in the morning by the Secretary of war, with whom I spent all the time till I was summoned to a committee. There I continued until at eleven I was summoned to the Senate where I labored till three oclock. I then waited on the President with whom I spent the interval till dinner. After dinner I spent an hour with some members of the house, the speaker included. From them I went to the Secretary of the Treasury & from him again to the President. I am now returned home at half past nine to employ the half hour that my eyes will bear application in writing.

March 27, 1798. S.P., M.H.S.

Also included in Sedgwick's day would be such miscellaneous duties as his attempt, in October, 1798, to secure a patent for a Mr. Charles Whiting, who had discovered a method of "extracting an useful oil from the seed of cotton." Sedgwick to Timothy Pickering, October 23, 1798. *Pickering Papers*, XXIII, 253. M.H.S.

20. An act, introduced by Senator Griswold of Connecticut and inspired by the visit of the Quaker pacifist George Logan to France, which declared it to be a penal offense for a private citizen to engage in any type of diplomatic negotiation with a foreign nation.

21. Republican Samuel Smith of Maryland, a trustee, forwarded Sedgwick's degree in March, 1800 with many effusive compliments. Samuel L. Smith to Sedgwick, March 3, 1800. S.P., M.H.S. In 1810, Sedgwick also received the honorary degree of Doctor of Laws from Harvard University.

22. Sedgwick to his daughter, Frances, March 31, 1798. Papers of H. D. Sedgwick, S.P., M.H.S.

About to lose its status as the nation's capital, Philadelphia attempted in these years a brisk social pace—with uneven success. A fever epidemic in the summer of 1797 served to sober the citizenry, and an even worse attack the following year extinguished all social activity for a time. Then there was the nuisance of the "Banditti: or Robbers," who had caused special havoc in the winter of 1797, and, more importantly, the shadow cast by the collapse of the speculation boom. On this last count, Sedgwick had been mildly sorry for his one-time friend Robert Morris and certain other Federalists but, with the righteousness of a teetotaler at a debauch, he decried the recent "rage to get rich without industry or economy."[23] He felt that cleaner souls would rise from the financial pyres then dotting Philadelphia and lesser financial centers. "The greatest mischief, politically considered . . . [was] that in too many instances ruined speculators" became zealous Republicans.[24]

The Philadelphia scene was on the whole, however, agreeable and interesting; and the period, one of excitment and challenge. Portents of the bitter and decisive presidential election of 1800 continually intruded; the outcome of the latest negotiation with France remained undecided; the climax of the battle between the Hamiltonian and Adams factions of the Federalist party awaited its cue. Sedgwick, incurably bitten with the disease of politics and fast held by the noble glamour of statesmanship, could not bear to retire. When with the adjournment of the Fifth Congress he returned home, via New York and the new Bennington stage, he was happy with the knowledge that a seat in the new House of Representatives was his; thanks to the dependable rectitude of a majority of the electors of Berkshire County.

He had not given in without a struggle. After having faithfully promised his wife that he would retire with the end of his senatorial term, and having refused to consider re-election as a senator by the Massachusetts General Court,[25] he had succumbed to a reasonably spontaneous draft sparked by close friends in Stockbridge, Sheffield, and Great Barrington. The Berkshire Federalists had previously agreed, with Sedgwick's warm approval, to support the candidacy of Ephraim Williams but, discovering that Sedgwick was himself "available," gladly revised their plans. They met in informal convention and drafted a laudatory address, begging Mr. Sedgwick once again to postpone his retirement from politics.

23. Sedgwick to King, July 1, 1798. King, *King*, II, 353.
24. Sedgwick to King, March 20, 1799. (Copy) S.P., M.H.S.
25. Samuel Dexter was chosen in Sedgwick's stead, only to resign in May, 1800, to accept the post of Secretary of War. Sedgwick wrote Rufus King, July 1, 1798, that "had there been any doubt that a good man would have been chosen, I certainly would not have declined." King, *King*, II, 353.

Sedgwick's answer was, quite typically, a combination of mock modesty and deep sincerity:

I have been honored, by receiving your polite address . . . in which you inform me, of the wish, of a respectable meeting of Gentlemen, that I would permit myself to be considered as a candidate, in the approaching election, to represent this district in Congress.

You, gentlemen, are certainly right in believing that it will require the sacrafice of personal considerations on my part to meet your wishes on this subject—The application, for my consent, was unexpected. . . . But at this time of imminent political danger,—at this awful crisis, when the liberties & independence of our country are wantonly attacked, it is the duty of all to subordinate personal & inferior, to public considerations. Painful therefore as it is [to] embark on the troubled sea of politics I dare not reject your request. . . .

That the electors may have a perfect knowledge of the course of conduct which I deem it my duty to persue I think it proper to declare that I have an entire confidence in the wisdom, virtue & integrity of the executive admininistration [sic] of our Govt., and that I have an undoubting belief that the prosperity, happiness, liberty and religion of our country cannot be defended against the united atacks of foreign ambition and domestic faction without its energetic support.[26]

With the congressional elections of 1798 the Federalist party gained it greatest electoral success. Even in the South it procured a majority of the newly elected congressmen. For the first time in several years the House would have a decided Federal majority. Sedgwick was greatly elated to hear of this "amelioration." Hints had been floating about for some time that if the Federalists were able to organize the House of Representatives, a deserving Berkshire man who had resisted the lure of private life would gain proper reward.

26. Sedgwick to unnamed correspondents, September 14, 1798. S.P., M.H.S.

XIV

Speaker Sedgwick and the Election of 1800

My opinion is that Genl Pinckney will be President.
Theodore Sedgwick [1]

FOR Theodore Sergwick the Sixth Congress began on a note of personal triumph and then proceeded from disappointment to disaster. Elected Speaker of the House of Representatives, it was Sedgwick's unhappy fate to witness the success of Adams' peace mission to France and the gradual collapse of all plans to augment the military and exorcise the seditious. Placed in a position of official honor, it was his galling lot to experience a steady loss of influence upon the policies of the administration and country. Increasingly concerned with the techniques and tools of politics, he was to witness the party he loved suffer widening division and then decisive defeat. The Sixth Congress sustained the theme of mounting Federalist frustration and gained its natural climax with the victory of the Republicans in the election of 1800.

Paradoxically, Sedgwick's assumption of a position previously associated with relative non-partisanship was the means of accentuating the partisan temper of his own conduct. The years 1799-1800 saw Sedgwick increasingly involved in political manoeuvre and factional struggle. In some part this was the result of the natural if erratic adaptation of the speakership to the two party system. In greater part, it was the result of the pervasive influence cast by the forthcoming presidential election on all activities and men of the Sixth Congress. But the increasingly partisan character of the speakership was certainly accelerated by the temperament and personality of Sedgwick himself and his personal involvement in the political schemes that preceded and followed that election. Sedgwick's elevation to the speakership was the result of party manoeuvre and his entire tenure of office bore witness to his association with those who—in the eyes of friend and foe alike—

1. Letter to Theodore Jr., December 5, 1800. S.P., M.H.S.

came increasingly to deserve the appellation of the High Federalists. Sedgwick was elected speaker only after a stiff struggle with Nathaniel Macon of Georgia and by a bare majority of 44 votes out of 86. Although his acceptance speech emphasized his obligation to the "enlightened and virtuous representatives" of all his countrymen,[2] he was quite aware that this support had come but from one party and indeed but from one section of that party. In a letter to his admiring friend Peter Van Schaack, he attributed the narrowness of his victory to the "local prejudice" of southern Federalists:

> My friends by too early publishing their intention had created all the opposition in their power; and of consequence every antifederalist on the other side of the potommach attended while nine or ten federalists were absent. But the new members from that division of the country were so impressed with local prejudice that they did not chuse to vote for me, and I am told I had not more than three votes in the whole of that country. They ... would not, however, vote for Macon the antifederalist candidate.[3]

Sedgwick was unable to make the speakership a focal point of political power as he would undoubtedly have liked; his increasing estrangement from the Executive and the inertia of tradition thwarted him here. Surely, however, his conduct as speaker was more political in orientation and tone than was true of his predecessors. Though he never subverted the rules of parliamentary procedure, his best efforts to curb dilatory tactics and expedite congressional business were reserved for federal measures. He spoke rather more during debate in the Committee of the Whole than had his predecessors and was more active in a behind-the-scenes capacity. He also utilized his appointing power to promote the Federalist faith as he conceived it. He admitted quite frankly that he had appointed John Marshall as chairman of a committee to report on the French mission only because he had supposed he "could perfectly rely, that General Marshall entertained the same opinion of the mission"

2. *Annals,* X, 186 (December 2, 1799).
3. December 8, 1799, *S.P.,* M.H.S.
Harrison Gray Otis, now a Federalist leader himself and less respectful of Sedgwick than formerly, wrote his wife, "Old Sedgwick is chosen Speaker, & much delighted with the appointment—We were however obligated to manage a little to secure this object." S. E. Morison, *Life and Letters of Harrison Gray Otis. . . .* (Boston, 1913), 1, 177.
The preceding speakers, Muhlenberg, Trumbull, and Dayton, were all less politically stalwart than Sedgwick. Sedgwick was perhaps the first speaker elected on purely partisan grounds.

as himself.[4] The relative mildness of that committee's report gave Sedgwick cause to question the wisdom of his choice but not its motivation.

Possibly the most criticized action of Sedgwick as Speaker and that most liable to the charge of impropriety involved his long battle with two reporters of the new Jeffersonian organ, the *National Intelligencer*. When these gentlemen applied to Sedgwick for seats on the floor of the House their petition was curtly refused. Forever displeased with the brevity and innaccuracy of the reporting of his own speeches, Sedgwick had little use for any stenographers, and none for those of Republican persuasion. He asserted that to allow their request, because of "the structure of the room and the arrangement of the furniture," would be contrary to the dignity and convenience of the House.

Refused admittance "to the bar" of the House, the editors of the *Intelligencer* were not slow to retaliate. When a few weeks later Sedgwick instructed the sergeant-at-arms to "see to" an intoxicated member of the gallery and this rambunctious gentlemen saw fit subsequently to sue the sergeant for assault, the *Intelligencer* happily took sides. The editors portrayed Sedgwick as short-tempered, autocratic, and worse, and when the Speaker complained before Congress of the paper's "gross misrepresentation," they proclaimed him to be incoherent as well. They had tried to report faithfully the Speaker's words and actions but could not deny an occasional inability to understand their meaning. Their consolation was, however, that the "misfortune" was not peculiar to themselves; many members of the House also seemed to suffer this inability.

Sedgwick exploded at this example of insult compounded. He expelled the editor-reporter of the *Intelligencer* first from the area "outside the bar" and then from the gallery where he had retreated. For this action the Republican members of the House tried to censure the Speaker for "usurping" the authority of the House but failed in the attempt. Sedgwick's friends succeeded in delaying a vote and the motion was finally forgotten by common consent.[5]

Forgotten but not forgiven. The reaction of the Republican congressmen to the occasionally partisan conduct of Sedgwick exemplified the old saw concerning pots and kettles. The Republicans were forever sniping at Sedgwick, culminating their expressions of distrust in an unprecedented attempt at the conclusion of his term as Speaker to defeat the customary resolution of thanks. This resolution passed by the narrow

4. Sedgwick to Peter Van Schaack, December 8, 1799. S.P., M.H.S.

5. *Annals*, X, 797, 806, 814–816, 865–866, 880, 886, 890 (December 4, 8, 30, 1800; January 6, 1801), and Richard Hildreth, *The History of the United States of America* (New York, 1871-1874), rev. ed., V, 411–412.

margin of 40–35, and only after Representative Gabriel Christie's tirade against the improprieties, inconsistencies, and rudeness of the Speaker was drowned out by wounded Federalist cries of "Order! Order!" [6]

Was Sedgwick a discredit to the post, as such Republicans as Christie proclaimed so vigorously? A careful analysis of their complaints and of Sedgwick's conduct in his capacity as Speaker would indicate that at least ninety per cent of the opposition Sedgwick aroused was the result of the perfervidly partisan atmosphere of the Sixth Congress.[7] Sedgwick brought to the speakership an excellent knowledge of parliamentary procedure, he moderated debate for the most part in fair and judicious style, and he performed the mechanical operations of the post— such as his service as congressional paymaster—in exemplary fashion. Sedgwick obviously did not conceive of the speakership as non-partisan; rather he believed his only obligation was not to pervert the rules of procedure when applying them to his political opponents. Acting under this belief he was occasionally guilty of favoritism but never of illegality. A man of great integrity in his private life, Sedgwick could better be charged with intolerance than impropriety in his public career. The tirade of Republican abuse which met the motion for a vote of thanks is chiefly attributable to the bitter aftermath of the election of 1800 and to Sedgwick's labors in behalf of the Burr candidacy. As that election dominated the years of the Sixth Congress, so too did Sedgwick's official performance as Speaker become confused with his unofficial labors to thwart the Republicans, sabotage the candidacy of Mr. Adams, and, finally, select Burr over Jefferson.

Sedgwick's electioneering activities in the winter, spring, and summer of 1800 embraced an intelligent but largely unsuccessful effort to

6. *Annals*, X, 1079 (March 3, 1801). See also *Aurora For the Country*, March 7, 1801.

7. Sedgwick had mourned throughout his term that the difficulties of his office were doubled "in consequence of the hatred with which the Jacobins honor me." Sedgwick to Henry Van Schaack, February 9, 1800. S.P., M.H.S.

Sedgwick's manner would on occasion irritate even those of the Federalist faith. Former minister to France, Gouverneur Morris was displeased when Sedgwick "swinging in a seat with his heels on the table" continued "his attitude and occupation" unchanged during a visit Morris had paid him in Philadelpha. Anne C. Morris, ed., *The Diaries and Letters of Gouverneur Morris* (New York, 1888), II, 386.

induce Congress to pass certain "national measures" which he felt would aid the popularity of his party, a less intelligent but equally unsuccessful effort to dictate electioneering policy for such "Moderate Federalists" as John Marshall, and a very unintelligent and self-defeating effort to gain the Presidency for the presumed vice-presidential candidate of the Federalist party, General Charles Cotesworth Pinckney.

A true Hamiltonian, Sedgwick was well aware of the connection between economic prosperity and political popularity. By promoting certain measures which would advance, in his phrase, "the national economy," he saw opportunity further to bind together the nation and so promote the electoral success of that party most associated with nationalist aims and ambitions. He drew up an elaborate plan for extending the turnpike roads throughout the country, and expressed sharp disappointment that this project came to nothing. He wrote his political friends that both canal and turnpike construction should be encouraged in order that communication between the different parts of the country might be facilitated and a heightened sense of nationality engendered. Such a heightened sense of nationality would be good for the country and excellent for the party. For similar reasons he promoted a national bankruptcy law, and this successfully. He declared that such a law would make the government "the active agency of commercial interests and passions" by submitting to it all relations of creditors and debtors and, equally important, would decrease opposition to the existing government from the more "clamorous description of persons"—debtors finding an interest in its support.[8]

Disappointed that the Sixth Congress proved relatively uninterested in constructive "national measures,"[9] Sedgwick was even more disturbed by the growing division of the Federalist members of Congress. He appreciated the political danger embodied in this division but

8. Sedgwick to King, November 15, 1799, King, *King* III, 147; Sedgwick to Henry Van Schaack, January 15, 1800, S.P., M.H.S.

In the House Sedgwick cast the tie-breaking vote that secured passage for the bill "establishing a uniform system of bankruptcy throughout the United States." *Annals*, X, 534 (February 21, 1800).

9. At one point Sedgwick was ready to declare that most of the few laws passed by the first session of the Sixth Congress were "hardly worth the parchment on which they . . . [were] written." Sedgwick to King, May 11, 1800. (Copy) S.P., M.H.S.

Sedgwick believed the act accepting the cession of the Western Reserve, the act prohibiting Americans from engaging in the slave trade, and the bankruptcy law were alone "commendable."

attributed all blame to President Adams and the weakness of certain men whose Federalism had been rendered tepid by their residence "south of the Potommach."

The growing division between the "High" and "Moderate" Federalists was sharpened by their diverse reactions to the Franco-American Convention of 1800 and made public by their differences over electioneering strategy in the summer and fall of that year. In fair part, that division was typified by the differing attitudes and strained alliance of Theodore Sedgwick and John Marshall.

When, in the spring of 1800, Adams dismissed Sedgwick's fellow Hamiltonians Pickering and McHenry from his cabinet, Sedgwick had expressed anger and frustration. A rump caucus of certain Federalist congressmen had been held, but they had been forced to admit they could do nothing about Adams' emancipation. After having warned Marshall against joining the new cabinet, Sedgwick was obliged to congratulate him on his appointment as Secretary of State.[10] Sedgwick and other of the High Federalists were similarly frustrated when faced with the necessity of discarding all plans to resist the French Convention of 1800. Sedgwick was disgusted by the Convention—indeed, was certain that his friend Oliver Ellsworth, one of the American commissioners, had been "rendered feeble by disease"—but discussion with Marshall reluctantly convinced him that to attempt to reject the convention would "utterly ruin the federal party, and endanger our internal tranquility." [11]

Faced with the danger of Republican victory in the presidential campaign under way, Marshall and Sedgwick never formally acknowl-

10. See Sedgwick to King, September 26, 1800. King, *King*, III, 309.

11. Sedgwick to Hamilton, December 17, 1800. Hamilton, *Works of Hamilton*, VI, 491–495.

Ellsworth had written Sedgwick, somewhat apologetically, that he hoped the latter would not be too displeased with certain small sacrifices that had to be made. "I hope you will think, as the reign of Jacobinism in France is over, and appearances are strong in favor of a general peace, that it was better to sign a Convention than to do nothing." Ellsworth to Sedgwick, October 10, 1800. Transferred Volume 18 (1751–1810), S.P., M.H.S. His propitiatory hope was ill-founded, as Sedgwick believed the agreement did nothing less than give our seal of approval to French "principles of Navigation."

Sedgwick did not, incidentally, agree with Ellsworth that the end of "the reign of Jacobinism" meant the return of stability in France. He judged Napoleon to be just another of the successive tyrants to which the idiotic French had tamely submitted. He had, however, derived some pleasure in the discomforture of certain Republicans when their fellow revolutionaries across the seas had welcomed a military dictatorship. See Sedgwick to King, December 12, 1799. (Copy) S.P., M.H.S.

edged the growing division between their wings of the party and, indeed, maintained to the very end of the Sixth Congress a posture of political intimacy and friendly regard,[12] but their relationship was subject to increasing strain as the election year of 1800 wore on. Marshall's influence with the southern Federalists had been quickly remarked by Sedgwick as soon as the Virginian had entered Congress, and he had made a concerted attempt to re-educate his new colleague and bring him into the charmed circle of "the true patriots." He had begged Rufus King to use his influence with Marshall, and on several occasions admitted that Marshall possessed "great powers and has much dexterity in the application of them." Marshall was, indeed, "highly and deservedly respected by the friends of the Government from the South" and as a result its friends from New England could "do nothing without him." An able man, he would have been a "more decided man had his education been on the other side of the Delaware."[13]

In a letter to Rufus King, May 11, 1800, Sedgwick gave what is perhaps the most interesting of all contemporary descriptions of Marshall. It is a description which reveals both subject and writer:

> He is a man of very affectionate disposition, of great simplicity of manners and honest & honorable in all his conduct. . . . He has a strong attachment to popularity but indisposed to sacrafice to it his integrity; hence it is that he is disposed on all popular subjects to feel the public pulse and hence results indecision and *an expression of doubt*. Doubts suggested by him create in more feeble minds those which are irremovable. He is disposed to the erotic refinement, and to express great respect for the sovereign people, and to quote their opinions as an evidence of truth. The latter is of all things the most destructive of personal independence & of that weight of character which a great man ought to possess. This Gentleman, when aroused, has strong reasoning powers; they are indeed almost un-

12. Marshall wrote Sedgwick in September, 1800: "By union we can securely maintain our ground—without it we must sink & with us all sound, correct American principles." Sedgwick to King, September 26, 1800. King, *King*, III, 309.

13. Sedgwick to Rufus King, December 29, 1799. (Copy) S.P., M.H.S.
Sedgwick wrote Henry Van Schaack on the same day that Marshall's powers were great and that:

> In the main, they will be usefully employed. He has an ascendancy in the whole district south of the Potommach which is astonishing. There are but two men who will not in all things be guided by him; Rutledge [of South Carolina] who is one of the finest fellows in the world, and Harper [Robert Goodloe Harper of Maryland] whom no one can controul.

S.P., M.H.S.

equalled. But before they are excited, he has frequently nearly destroyed any impression from them.[14]

Marshall's criticism of the Alien and Sedition Acts as inexpedient of course irritated Sedgwick, and Marshall's respect for the wishes of his constituents was, as noted, judged an unfortunate weakness. Sedgwick entertained the British view that a legislator represented the nation, rather than any single group of voters, and so should work for the best interests of the country as he *personally* saw those interests. The conflicting attitudes of Sedgwick and Marshall on this and other questions where High and Moderate Federalists divided was highlighted by the effort of Sedgwick and his friends in the spring of 1800 to inveigle Marshall into giving his approval to a deservedly unsuccessful scheme to damage the presidential chances of Jefferson—especially in Pennsylvania.

This scheme revolved about the mode of deciding disputed contests for presidential electors. Sedgwick wished to see a law passed submitting such disputes for final decision to a special committee consisting of thirteen members, six each from the Senate and House and the Chief Justice of the Supreme Court, who would serve as presiding officer.[15] Sedgwick had several long talks with Marshall, attempting to convince him of the propriety of the measure and the necessity of presenting a solid Federalist phalanx against the Jeffersonians. Marshall was tactful but obdurate. First he questioned the constitutionality of the legislature delegating such authority to a committee, and then, when Sedgwick seemed to have persuaded him on this point, he began increasingly to insist that the people expected members of Congress to decide such an important matter severally and personally. Sedgwick had finally to complain that Marshall's "attenuated and unsubstantial" objection had so delayed matters that the expected majority "had dissipated" and the time gone by when the measure might have passed.[16]

If Marshall and his wing of the Federalist party were reluctant to support projects designed to tamper with the electoral machinery, they

14. (Copy) S.P., M.H.S.

15. Sedgwick wrote William Loughton Smith, then minister to Portugal: "Our Senate has a bill before them the object of which is, to canvas the votes given for President and vice President; which will succeed & secure us against their [the Republicans'] designs." March 24, 1800. *William Loughton Smith Papers*, Library of Congress.

16. Sedgwick to King, May 11, 1800. (Copy) S.P., M.H.S. Bowers has this scheme being discussed and defeated nearly a year earlier. Bowers, *Jefferson and Hamilton*, 441. Actually the proposal was demolished by a dramatic exposé in William Duane's *Aurora*.

were clearly opposed to all schemes for undermining the party primacy
of Mr. Adams. Sedgwick and other Hamiltonians had consequently to
pursue their designs in clumsy secrecy.

Theodore Sedgwick viewed the election of 1800 not only as a contest
between two political parties but as a struggle between the forces of
good and evil as well. He felt almost a sense of mission as he worked
to defeat Jefferson, whom he believed intent on destroying the whole
political and social structure of America. There were no rules when
fighting the demons of Jacobinism. Speak not to him of being a good
loser; to lose was to be destroyed. Sedgwick's was a view not easily
comprehensible to the present-day American mind, but it was far from
exceptional at the time. The political pendulum is a relatively new
notion; the concept of good fighting evil with no holds barred was more
in keeping with the background and experience of Sedgwick's contemporaries—both Federalist and Republican. Even the more temperate
of these contemporaries viewed the election of 1800 as a milestone in the
political history of the new country. They did not believe the party
contest of 1800 to be exclusively economic in character—the mercantile
interests versus the agrarian—but understood that it had a large political
content.[17]

To a deadly earnestness about politics—so understandable for the
politician of a new nation but recently forged in the fires of revolution—
Sedgwick added a personal narrowness of mind. He conscientiously
believed that anyone who thought or acted differently from himself was
inspired by only the very worse motives. He lived to do honor to his
country, and was positive that every action he took and belief he held
furthered the good of that country. Therefore, every opposing action

17. Jefferson's platform of agrarian liberalism was perhaps negative in approach, but it bespoke a close sympathy with various concerns and prejudices of
the American people. Jefferson saw the augmentation of executive authority and
the centralization of federal authority as threats to the representative and popular
features of our constitutional government. As they limited the freedom, so they
would hamper the natural development of the American people. That people was
threatened, not by sedition and license, but by sedition laws, political justices, secret monarchists, burdensome taxation, and politically powerful monied interests.
To resist these real threats, let the national government be more responsible to simple majority rule. A vote for Jefferson, the Republicans would trumpet, was a vote
for lower taxes, a properly strict construction of the Constitution, and protection
from the forces of militarism and tyranny.

and belief was *per se* damaging to the national welfare and consequently disgraceful. Of very excitable disposition, Sedgwick was often led to utter statements which, taken at their face value, make him appear the most mischievous of malcontents. When he declared, after the election of Jefferson appeared probable, that a "dissolution of the Union" was imminent, he was reflecting to some extent a feeling of insecurity regarding the duration of the government—not uncommon at the time —but even more a personal tendency to enjoy moments of exaggerated despair.

Sedgwick's sorrow upon receiving news that seemed to augur the presidential success of Jefferson was not matched by any elation at conflicting reports prophesying a victory for Mr. Adams. The nomination of Adams by a congressional caucus of Federalists early in May, 1800,[18] was accepted by Sedgwick, if at all, as a highly disagreeable necessity. The state of his relations with Adams at this time is well illustrated by a letter Sedgwick wrote Henry Van Schaack in February, 1800:

> I very rarely visit the president. I have been there but twice during the session, (except on perticular invitation;) and then his conduct was as cold as his heart. This is not peculiar to me—it is the same towards all those men in whom he used formerly to confide. His jealousy is extreme, and I believe, incurable. The men who have succeeded are industrious in blowing up the flames of discord, and his vanity affords inexhaustible fuel. Notwithstanding all this we are told that he must be our candidate at the next election.[19]

Hamilton's pamphlet attacking Adams' character and presidential performance was the final blow needed to rend the Federalist party in two. Its division found Sedgwick firmly in the anti-Adams wing. He appears in the winter of 1800 to have rather favored the candidacy of Ellsworth,[20] but the improbability of electing that gentleman, and his

18. This caucus was held in the Senate Chamber. The Republicans in Congress nominated Jefferson and Burr in the same manner. These were probably the first instances of organized presidential caucus nominations, but "the caucus" was quite well established in local politics, especially in New England, by the middle 1780's. See Frederick W. Dallinger, *Nominations for Elective Office in The United States* (New York, 1897), 12–16.

19. February 9, 1800. *S.P.*, M.H.S.

20. An anonymous letter to Adams of March 19, 1800, declared Sedgwick to be among those working for the success of Oliver Ellsworth. The author of this letter attributes to Sedgwick a leading role in plots against the re-election of Adams and it would be interesting to know his identity.

> Your opponents are every day becoming more bold & sanguine. General Hamilton & Mr. Wolcot are organizing their plan of supporting Mr. Ellsworth,

approval of the convention with France, quickly turned Sedgwick's thoughts in other directions. By the time of the nominating caucus, however, these directions had not materialized to a sufficient extent to prevent the good sense of certain Federalist leaders, and the known preference of the rank and file of the party, from again choosing Adams as the Federalist standard-bearer. Sedgwick reported to King that it had been "agreed that we will support, *bona fide,* Mr. Adams and General [Charles Cotesworth] Pinckney. If this agreement shall be faithfully executed we shall succeed, but otherwise we cannot escape the fangs of Jefferson.[21]

The description, *"bona fide"* support referred to the agreement made at the caucus that each Federalist elector would vote uniformly for both Adams and Pinckney, with the understanding that the first named would be the presidential candidate and the latter, the vice-presidential candidate. Sedgwick was quite correct in proclaiming to King that only in this honest fashion would they succeed, but secretly he and the majority of Hamiltonians wished to see Pinckney brought in ahead of Adams. Sedgwick seems to have favored supporting the two Federalists equally, so there would be no chance of Jefferson gaining office, and at the same time to have hugged the thought that a tie vote in the electoral

---

20. (cont.)

& the military & revenue officers under the direction of their respective chiefs are to be arrayed against you. The fear of your disbanding the army has of late given them much uneasiness—this measure would they know render you popular amongst the great mass of people, & take from them a powerful engine which directed by its General will they think be very operative. This fear however has passed by, & Sedgewick's [*sic*] party do not now think you will disband the army previous to the election. Mr. Dayton, who talks openly of opposing your election, pledges himself that Patterson Howell & Stockton will support Ellsworth—Dayton says Sedgewick answers for Mssrs Strong Hitchborn & Ames —*He* also says that Maryland will be managed by McHenry Craik Carrol & Harper—*He* further says the southern States will unite [with] the Hamilton party when they are *shewn* that you stand no chance of succeeding. This, Sir, is the present State & Prospect of the Party. I pray to god you may be able to frustrate their diabolical projects!

If circumstances will not shortly admit of your disbanding the 12 Regiments . . . or doing some other very popular measure, the men who plot against you ought to be conciliated, or *they will succeed.* Pray sir do not neglect my advice because I cannot *now* give you my name. Those who are most near to your person are your most bitter enemies. Beware of the confidence of Cesar [*sic*] lest you share his fate: He had as much confidence in Brutus as you have in your Secretaries your Generals or in Dayton Sedgwick or Bayard.

yr friend

Adams Papers, (Microfilm #397), M.H.S.

21. Sedgwick to King, May 11, 1800. (Copy) S.P., M.H.S.

college would throw the election into the House. Once it was deposited there, Sedgwick planned to convince the Federalist congressional majority that Pinckney had been as much the chief Federalist candidate as the unfit Mr. Adams.[22] There was, moreover, the comforting possibility that the Republican electors of South Carolina might solve everything by giving their second votes to Pinckney, a native son.[23]

Like most gentlemen engaged in intrigue, Sedgwick was incensed by any revelation of his plans and intentions. He was deeply angered when Harrison Gray Otis charged that the "Pickering faction"—Sedgwick among them—planned to oppose Adams' re-election, whatever their pretensions to the contrary. The threat voiced by Otis, that certain of Massachusetts' electors, suspecting foul play, would refuse to give Pinckney one of their two votes, was a source of great worry.[24] Sedgwick had a premonition that the respective supporters of the two Federalist candidates would so undermine each other that Jefferson would be returned to head the Senate, or even occupy the White House. He was amazed at the lack of adaptability shown by men of "small minds," such as Otis. Even Sedgwick's good friend Samuel Dexter seemed to have no appreciation of the relative importance of Hamiltonian suggestion and popular mandate, and had refused to agree that Pinckney should have an equal chance with Adams in the electoral college.[25] Sedgwick, determinedly ignoring the popularity of Adams with the rank and file of Federalists, hammered away at Adams' "last mission to France," his unjust treatment of his "manly ministers," his strange and "most furious indignation" at the eminently proper "recommendation of the whole Federal party, of

22. See Sedgwick to King, November 15, December 12, 1799. King, *King*, III, 146, 156.

King advocated wholehearted support for Adams' candidacy. King to Sedgwick, February 24, June 6, 1800 (Copies) S.P., M.H.S.

23. Sedgwick to King, September 26, 1800. King, *King*, III, 309.

Sedgwick expressed surprise that Burr rather than Chancellor Livingston of New York had been nominated for the second place on the Republican ticket.

24. See Sedgwick to Pickering, December 22, 1799. *Pickering Papers*, XXV, 317. M.H.S.

25. Sedgwick to Hamilton, May 7, 1800. *Pickering Papers*, XLVII, 237–239. M.H.S.

Hamilton wrote Sedgwick, May 8, 1800, that New York, if Federalist, would not vote for Adams unless Pinckney was supported by New England in "faithful adherence to the plan which has been adopted." Two days later, in another letter to his Massachusetts supporter, Hamilton declared: "For my individual part my mind is made up. I will never be responsible for him [Adams] by my direct support, even though the consequences should be the election of Jefferson." Hamilton, *Works of Hamilton*, VI, 440–441.

General Pinckney as a joint and *equal* candidate with him for the office of President." Sedgwick was sure that Adams' misconception of the part played by his friends in the election of 1796 was the basis of his late denunciation of the most praiseworthy Federalists as:

> [An] oligarchish faction, who are combined to drive him from office, because they cannot govern him, and to appoint Pinckney, by whose agency, under the controul of this faction & particularly of Hamilton its head, the country is to be driven into a war with france & a more intimate, if not an indissoluble, union with great Britain.[26]

Merely because the Federalists at that time had favored the succession of Adams "with different modifications," complained Sedgwick, Adams had proceeded to listen to the flattery of personal retainers and to court popularity with his enemies, the French-loving Jacobins, until now the federal character of his administration was hardly to be retrieved. "By the most painful industry, and the most perfect union, the friends of the Government had attained a height on which they appeared to be impregnably intrenched; but by the conduct of an individual, the whole force is disheartened, on one hand, and on the other the adversary is inspired with fresh confidence." [27]

Writing to correspondents in New York, New Jersey, Rhode Island, South Carolina, and Maryland, Sedgwick proclaimed that both Adams and Pinckney should receive the unanimous votes of all Federalists, and privately wondered whether, even if they chose to oppose Mr. Adams, some Georgia or South Carolina electors might not be induced to bestow a vote or two on Pinckney.[28] As late as December 5, 1800, Sedgwick could declare that "my opinion is that Genl Pinckney will be President." [29] Pinckney, though on friendly terms with Sedgwick and the latter's confidants, gave no countenance or support to their plans.

Jefferson's election was perhaps to be anticipated once the threat of a full-scale war with France faded. The probability of the outcome was surely not lessened, however, by the electioneering campaign waged by the Federalists. Those gentlemen relied on intrigues and dire prophecies, and seem to have forgotten those powers of close reasoning

26. Sedgwick to King, September 26, 1800. (Copy) *S.P., M.H.S.*
27. *Ibid.*
28. See letter of Richard Stockton of November 29, 1800, in answer to Sedgwick's "friendly letter of the 24th." *S.P., M.H.S.*

The Republicans tried to make considerable capital of this Federalist "inconsistency," especially in the South Carolina elections. See Fisher Ames to Sedgwick, December 4, 1800. *S.P., M.H.S.*
29. Sedgwick to Theodore Jr., December 5, 1800. *S.P., M.H.S.*

and moderate argument which marked much of their campaign liter-
ature on previous occasions. They aimed more at scaring than persuading the people. Jefferson, they cried, was a mad physiocrat who would
destroy New England's commerce and shipbuilding industry. He was an
atheist, a mob-lover, ready to set class upon class—witness how he had
robbed the Virginia aristocracy when governor. The abject servant of
the French nation, he would do everything in his power to drag the
United States into a war with England.

Sedgwick was in the thick of it all, worrying over one crucial state
after another, despairing and exulting by turns. He gave especial attention to the possibility of manipulating the election laws to favor the
Federalist cause. Election laws were, of course, a matter of state regulation. In most states, presidential electors were either selected popularly,
usually on a district basis, or by the state legislature on a general ticket.
Sedgwick was one of fourteen federal representatives and senators from
Massachusetts who addressed the state's governor, urgently advising him
to shift Massachusetts from the popular to the legislative form of selection.[30] There must be no possibility that any of the Massachusetts electors would entertain Republican sympathies. In imitation of "Jacobin"
Virginia, the General Court of Massachusetts proceeded to rearrange its
electoral laws, much to Sedgwick's delight. "The laudable conduct of
the Legislature," he wrote, "in retaining to themselves the choice of
electors was intended to prevent the scattering of votes." [31]

More questionable on ethical grounds was the evident desire of
Federalist friends of Sedgwick to prevent Pennsylvania, with its Republican sympathies, from participating in the election at all. The Federalist senate of that commonwealth and its Republican lower house stood
deadlocked over the proper method of choosing presidential electors.
The Federalist party labored to see that this deadlock was not broken.[32]

Throughout the summer and fall of 1800 news of the probable in-

30. Circular letter from Massachusetts Delegates in Congress, January 31, 1800.
J. M. Robbins Collection, M.H.S.
31. Sedgwick to King, September 26, 1800 (Copy) *S.P.*, M.H.S.
The Federalists in Maryland also obtained a law enabling the state legislature
to select the state's electors. See Robert Goodloe Harper to Sedgwick, August 11,
1800. *MSS. Collection*, New-York Historical Society.
In Virginia, though Jefferson's initial idea was to have the General Assembly
select the presidential electors, it was ultimately determined to allow the freeholders
to vote a *general ticket*.
32. This deadlock was finally settled to the definite advantage of the Federalists. Seven out of the fifteen electors allotted Pennsylvania would be chosen by the
Federalist-dominated state senate.

tentions of the doubtful states held the attention of citizens everywhere. Slowly the electoral count was tabulated. Only when the votes of South Carolina went to Jefferson and Burr uniformly, and only when nothing but the foreseen Republican sweep of the new states of Tennessee and Kentucky remained to be announced, did Sedgwick finally concede defeat. Jefferson and Burr, with 73 electoral votes each, were elected; Adams and Pinckney trailed with 65 and 64 ballots, respectively. Much of Sedgwick's own western Massachusetts, with its social and religious homogeneity, had remained true; New England, as a whole, had maintained its Federalist character,[33] but the combination of agrarian republicanism below the Potomac, sedition trials in the doubtful Middle States, and Burr's Tammany politics in New York City had brought the overthrow of the old régime.[34] The Republicans, through fortuitous circumstances and clever strategy, had rapidly altered the popular conception of themselves as "the French party." They were now the opponents of military extravagance and direct taxes, the victims of Federalist persecution, the proper inheritors of the Revolutionary tradition of individual liberty, the supporters of the interests of all as opposed to the advocates of the privileges of the few. Reacting from the stimulus of the French war scare of 1798, many people, tired of high taxes and fearful of a standing army, had desired a change and turned in consequence to the Republican party. Such factors, combined with brilliant

33. Sedgwick was very interested in the Massachusetts state elections of 1800. For governor he favored moderate Federalist Caleb Strong of Northhampton as an old friend who, though he would not "on some accounts, be quite so good as . . . [he] could wish," possessed "that strange thing called popularity." Strong was nominated by the Federalists and subsequently elected. Sedgwick to Henry Van Schaack, February 9, 1800; Sedgwick to King, Sept. 26, 1800, (Copy) *S.P.*, M.H.S.

The defeat of Ephraim Williams by John Bacon for the post of Berkshire delegate to the national House of Representatives incensed Sedgwick. He told Rufus King that if he had known that John Bacon, a Republican, would win, he would not have declined to run for another congressional term. Sedgwick to King, May 24, 1801. King, *King*, III, 456.

Aurora For The Country (March 2, 1801) reported: "Mr. Sedgwick regrets very much that he has relinquished his election for next congress—as he thinks he could *cut a figure* at the head of [the] opposition—some one observed he cuts a very *droll figure* already!"

34. For an interesting geographical breakdown of the election of 1800, see Libby, *A Sketch of the Early Political Parties*, 228–230.

Nathan Schachner sharply repudiates the idea that the election of 1800 represented a "revolution." Schachner, *The Founding Fathers* (New York, 1954), 548–549. It would appear that the election of 1800 was a "revolution" primarily on the score that it marked the final termination of Federalist control of the national government.

political tactics, brought the Republicans to power but five short years after the Jay Treaty debates had succeeded in forming the friends of Jefferson into something approaching an organized political party.

The Republicans were surely victorious, but after the first stunning impact of the blow had passed, Sedgwick and his friends began to see a way of salvaging some gain from their defeat. Not only had Jefferson received a majority of all votes cast but so had Burr; both had 73 electoral votes. Owing to a defect of the Constitution, the electors had cast their ballots for the two men without designating the office desired for each; indeed, without any differentiation whatever. Such a tie vote meant the election had to be thrown into the House of Representatives.

Speaker Sedgwick was one of the first to sense the opportunity afforded the Federalist party.

XV

The Sedgwick Federalists and the Burr Intrigue, 1801

To what evils shall we expose ourselves by the choice of Burr, which we would escape by the election of Jefferson?

Theodore Sedgwick [1]

THOUGH Theodore Sedgwick was one of the first to sense the opportunity afforded the Federalist party by the tie between Jefferson and Burr, he was not at first eager to support a man of Burr's character and reputation. Sedgwick wrote Hamilton, December 17, 1800, that it seemed certain that Jefferson and Burr would have equal votes and that in consequence "the Jacobins in the House . . . [are] more civil in their attentions than I have ever known them." He went on to add, significantly, that "should the House have to decide between these rivals, my opinion would prefer the former [*i.e.,* Jefferson] for reasons which will readily occur to you. In this, many of my friends differ from me." [2] Hamilton, who had previously written Oliver Wolcott, warning him against preferring a man as dangerous as Burr and asking that his letter be communicated to Marshall and Sedgwick, [3] hastened to reply. He heartily agreed that the Federalists must never be responsible for the elevation of that "Catiline of America," Aaron Burr. Frightened and troubled that his friends could even think of being party to such a national betrayal, Hamilton wrote: "The appointment of Burr as President would disgrace our country abroad. No agreement with him could be

1. Sedgwick to Hamilton, January 10, 1801. Hamilton, *Works of Hamilton* VII, 451.
2. Sedgwick to Hamilton, December 17, 1800. Hamilton, *Works of Hamilton* VI, 492.
3. Hamilton to Wolcott, December 16, 1800. Henry Cabot Lodge, ed., *Works of Alexander Hamilton* (New York, 1886), VIII, 565. Hamilton did suggest that it might "be well enough to throw out a lure for him [Burr], in order to tempt him to start for the plate, and then [thus-?] lay the foundation of dissension between the two chiefs."

relied upon. His private circumstances render disorder a necessary recourse. His public principles offer no obstacle. His ambition aims at nothing short of personal power and wealth in his own person." [4]

Hamilton, however, had taught too well. He had informed his disciples for years that Jefferson was the most evil and dangerous man in America. Now these disciples—extremely literal-minded gentlemen—could not understand why any means that would prevent this human devil from assuming control of the nation would not be high-minded and patriotic. "The voice of the people" was but a phrase; the salvation of the people was, in their minds, the issue. The corruption of power had had its effect on the Federalist party. Partisanship was confused with patriotism; the maintenance of power, with the welfare of the nation.

Sedgwick was quickly drawn into the group of Federalists advocating the choice of Burr. About a week after Sedgwick first wrote Hamilton, Oliver Wolcott informed Hamilton that he had passed the latter's note of December 16 on to Sedgwick, and that that gentleman seemed "inclined to support Mr. Burr." [5] Wolcott's conjecture is supported in part by a letter written Sedgwick, December 27, by his admiring and emulating son Theodore, Jr. Sedgwick's heir wrote that it would be "a pretty thing" to reproach the Republicans with the fact "that a republican candidate may be made a Federal President. . . . If your predictions should prove true we are secured for four years from the horrors of anarchy and misrule." [6]

Fisher Ames, one of the most influential, if least physically active, of the Federalists seems to have confirmed Sedgwick in his decision. His arguments strengthened Sedgwick to disregard, for almost the first time, the advice and wishes of Alexander Hamilton. In two letters, which Sedgwick was requested to read and burn immediately, Ames analyzed the relative safety that would be afforded the Federalists by the elevation of Burr. The fact that no one in America had any trust in Burr's morals was, Ames insisted, an advantage. This fact, and "the dread inspired by his known ambition," and his "mode" of "coming in by hit," all tended to disarm him, and consequently to make him more amenable to Federalist guidance. Coming from New York, one of the more central states, it was doubtful if he would ever attempt to divide

4. Hamilton to Sedgwick, December 22, 1800. Hamilton, Works of Hamilton, VI, 498.
5. Wolcott to Hamilton, December 25, 1800. Ibid., VI, 498.
6. S.P., M.H.S.

the Union; being bold, he was the "more likely to preserve the union." As for the "violent counsels" which a man of his character was liable to entertain, even "if they tended to personal advantage, or even to usurpation," they could only prove temporary. "During their progress some tone would be given. It would be better that a fever should give it than that the lazy blood shood sleep and turn putrid in the veins. . . . I strongly incline to your opinion that B. is the preferable man." Burr should, however, be made to understand that Federalist support came only at a price; "terms must be well understood." Ames wanted to see four provisions insisted upon: that the country be neither "sold given nor lent to France;" that pacific relations be retained with Britain; that credit and banks be considered inviolable; and that our trade "not be tampered with—nor regulated Madison-wise." [7]

Ames and Sedgwick were but two of a large body of Federalists who, despite their unquestioned personal honesty and private integrity,[8] were prepared to place Aaron Burr at the head of the federal government. The intention and reasoning of these Federalists is understandable. These were no immoral men desirous of committing some conscious deviltry but, rather, a group of individuals who believed with certain justification that they had a perfect right to make a free choice between Burr and Jefferson, and who so hated Jefferson that they felt that no greater evil could befall the country than his election as President. They had no precedent to guide them and could not be said to be bound by any constitutional theory or provision. The original framers of the Constitution, indeed, having no foreknowledge of the place the party system would soon play in American politics, seem to have felt that the electoral college would have virtual *carte blanche* in its choice of a President.

7. Ames to Sedgwick, December 31, 1800; January 7, 1801. S.P., M.H.S.

8. Sedgwick was in his private life a man of the highest morals and strictest scruples. Bowers' comment to the effect that "it was a day of rather loose morals, and the press made free with the gossip concerning Harper and Sedgwick" seems rather wide of the mark, certainly in so far as it reflects on Sedgwick's faithfulness as a husband. Unduly harsh, too, is that writer's reflection on Sedgwick's heightened interest in religious matters: "Everywhere the Federalist leaders were assuming a pious pose, even Sedgwick and Ames and Otis were becoming religious, and the Democrats greeted their pose with ribald mirth." Bowers, *Jefferson and Hamilton*, 449, 476.

A parishioner, though not a "member," of the Stockbridge Congregational Church, Sedgwick was a man who had throughout his life supported religion as a source of civic virtue. He was far less dogmatic in his religious views than in his political beliefs, but if his temperament was not pietistic, neither surely was it that of the hedonist.

In 1801 the Federalists could make a case for the position that the House was serving in lieu of the electoral college and thereby had similar freedom of choice. They were in no sense, they declared, obliged to heed the undoubted preference of the Republican voters of the nation. They were under no moral, ethical, or constitutional compunction to do anything but exercise their own independent judgment.

Their defense is indisputable to a point. The two party system and the concept of party leadership were very new, and, as they impinged on original constitutional theory rather than derived from it, one can surely not charge Sedgwick and his friends with unconstitutional conduct in the winter of 1801. It would seem, however, that they may not so easily be exonerated from a charge of unpatriotic conduct. While it is true that the idea of the inviolability of the will of the majority was by no means clear-cut in Sedgwick's day, it is also true that even by 1800 the device of the electoral college was known to be largely a formality. When the legislatures of New York and Georgia, for example, chose their electors in 1800, they had no idea that these electors would vote otherwise than for Jefferson and Burr. These electors, in turn, undoubtedly wished to see Jefferson President and Burr Vice-President. Sedgwick appreciated this was true. Even more to the point is the fact that Sedgwick and his friends believed—even asserted—that Burr was a dangerous character, a man of little principle, a man whose hunger for power far outweighed in all probability his patriotism. They were promoting the candidacy of a man whom they themselves labelled as profligate and without character. If they could not have brought themselves to cast a vote for their old enemy Jefferson, at least they might have avoided electioneering for the amoral Aaron Burr.[9]

It was not, however, only the Federalist leaders who allowed their bias to becloud their judgment at this time. There was within the ranks of the party, as well, a large group that eventually came to think that any legal manipulation that would upset Jefferson's victory was right and proper. Sedgwick's Berkshire friends were delegated to sound opinion in western Massachusetts. They reported an increasing sentiment in favor of Burr. Certain "small Federalists" were balking at this latest decision of the "enlightened and decided part of the community"; the declared distaste of Governor Strong for the scheme was occasioning

9. There is no real parallel here with the contested election of 1824. In that year the Clay men could show that they had a free choice, as both Adams and Jackson had received the first votes of many electors. Burr, it was appreciated by everyone, was not really the first choice of any elector. He was, in any case, a man of quite different character and morals than John Quincy Adams.

some wavering; [10] and the forthright opposition of such Federalist editors as Isaiah Thomas of the *Massachusetts Spy* was not without influence. On the whole, however, the bulk of the Federalist party in Berkshire was quite ready docilely to follow their leaders in the national capital.[11]

Their unaccustomed revolt against the commands and desire of Hamilton, the nexus of their political party and faith, greatly disturbed Sedgwick and his friends, and a great many letters were sped to New York in an attempt to explain their position and appease their old chief. Foremost among these was Sedgwick's of January 10, a long and carefully reasoned epistle, most probably the work of several minds. It deserves to be quoted in full, for it reveals not only the rationalized doubts and secret uneasiness of its writer but the very workings of his mind:

> No decision is yet had though there is, I believe, a strong preponderance of opinion against Jefferson. In his favor, it is said, that it was the intention, that he should be elected President, of a large majority of those who voted for him. But wherefore was this preference given him? Because it is answered, he was known to be hostile to all those great systems of administration, the combined effect of which is our national prosperity and all we possess of national character and respectability; because he is a sincere and enthusiastic Democrat in principle, plausible in manners, crafty in conduct, persevering in the pursuit of his object, regardless of the means by which it is attained, and equally regardless of an adherence to truth, as is demonstrated by his letter to Mazzei, his declarations in the Senate, on his first taking his seat, there, &c., &c.; because he is known to be devoted to the views of those men, in his State, whose unceasing effort, it has been, and is, to reduce in *practice,* the ad-

10. Strong tactfully explained to Sedgwick the innate stupidity of the belief that Burr would ever redeem any pledges he might make the Federalists, or ever allow them to control his actions when President:

> I can hardly suppose that Mr. B. would make any Speculation before hand which would ruin him with his Party or that after his Election he will forget that there is to be another Choice in four years and that if he is to be rechosen it must be by the States which have now supported him for he must know that the others will never take him up—you will consider then whether his Patriotism will be likely so far as to prevail against his Interest as to induce him to persue federal measures.

Strong to Sedgwick, December 21, 1800. S.P., M.H.S.

11. See, especially, Henry Van Schaack to Sedgwick, undated, 1801. S.P., M.H.S.

ministration of this government to the principles of the old Confederation, in which that state by her numerous representation, and the influence she has on surrounding States, will be the directrix. Because he is known to be servilely devoted to one foreign nation under any form of Government, and pursuing any system of measures, however hostile to this country, and unrelentingly hostile to another nation, and those the two nations on earth with which we have the most interesting relations, and with which it is most important to preserve an equal and impartial regard. Ought we then to respect the preference which is given to this man from such *motives* and by such *friends?*

As to the other candidate, there is no disagreement as to his character. He is ambitious—selfish—profligate. His ambition is of the worst kind; it is a mere love of power, regardless of fame, but as its instrument; his selfishness excludes all social affections, and his profligacy unrestrained by any moral sentiment, and defying all decency. This is agreed, but then it is known that his manners are plausible—that he is dexterous in the acquisition and the use of the means necessary to effect his wishes. Nothing can be a stronger evidence of this than the situation in which he stands at this moment—without any pretension from connections, fame, or services—elevated by his own independent means to the highest point to which all those can carry the most meritorious man in the nation. He holds to no pernicious theories, but is a mere matter-of-fact man. His very selfishness prevents his entertaining any mischievous predilection for foreign nations. The situation in which he lives has enabled him to discern and justly appreciate the benefits resulting from our commercial and other national systems; and this same selfishness will afford some security, that he will not only patronize their support, but their invigoration.

There are other considerations. It is very evident that the Jacobins dislike Mr. Burr as President—that they dread his appointment more than even that of General Pinckney.

On his part, he hates them for the preference given to his rival. He has expressed his displeasure at the publication of his letter by General Smith.[12] This jealousy and distrust, and dislike, will every day more and more increase, and more and more widen the breach between them. If then, Burr should be elected by the Federalists against the hearty opposition of the Jacobins, the wounds mutually

12. The letter to General Samuel Smith was one written by Burr, December 16, 1800, in which he declared he had no thought or desire to rival Jefferson for the first place. For a laudatory appraisal of Burr's conduct at this time, see Nathan Schachner, *Aaron Burr* (New York, 1937), 188–204.

given and received will probably be incurable. Each will have committed the unpardonable sin. Burr must depend on good men for his support, and that support he cannot receive but by a conformity to their views.

In these circumstances, then, to what evils shall we expose ourselves by the choice of Burr, which we would escape by the election of Jefferson? It is said, that it would be more disgraceful to our country and to the principles of our government. For myself, I declare I think it is impossible to preserve the honor of our country or the principles of our Constitution, by a mode of election, which was intended to secure to preeminent talent and virtues the first honors of our country, and for ever to disgrace the barbarous institution by which executive power is to be *transmitted through the organs* of generation. We have at one election placed at the head of our government a semi-maniac [Adams], and who in his soberest senses, is the greatest marplot in nature; and at the next a feeble and false, enthusiastic theorist [Jefferson], and a profligate [Burr] without character and without property, bankrupt in both.

But, if there remains any thing for us, in this respect, to regard, it is with the minority in the Presidential election; and can they be more disgraced than by assenting to the election of Jefferson?—the man who has proclaimed them to the world as debased in principles and as detestable and traitorous in conduct? Burr is indeed unworthy, but the evidence of his unworthiness is neither so extensively known, nor so conclusive as that of the other man. It must be confessed that there is part of the character of Burr more dangerous than that of Jefferson. Give to the former a probable chance, and he would become an usurper. The latter might not incline, he certainly would not dare to make the attempt. I do not believe that either would succeed, and I am even confident that such a project would be rejected by Burr, as visionary. At first, I confess, I was strongly disposed to give Jefferson the preference; but the more I have reflected, the more I have inclined to the other; yet, however, I remain unpledged, even to my friends, though I believe, I shall not separate from them.[13]

13. Sedgwick to Hamilton, January 10, 1801, Hamilton, *Works of Hamilton*, VII, 450–452; James A. Parton, *Life of Aaron Burr* (New York, 1848), 275–278.

See also, Sedgwick to King, May 24, 1801 (King, *King*, III, 455), for a concise digest of the Federalist reasons for supporting Burr. Jefferson would, unlike Burr, have the full confidence of his party, and, therefore, be able to carry into effect his "mischievous designs."

See, too, the interesting letter from Sedgwick to his son Theodore Jr. of January 11, 1801, in which he admitted that the considerations in favor of the choice of Burr were "of a negative nature, principally, and drawn from the greater unfitness of Jefferson." S.P., M.H.S. Sedgwick, though quite friendly with Burr in the 1780's, and

Without the least consciousness of wrongdoing, Sedgwick was prepared to make President a man whom virtually no American in the election of 1800 had selected or wanted as *chief* executive. The sharp sense of justice which had characterized his behavior in assisting the slave Mumbet, in protecting the "neutralist" Tories of Berkshire during and after the Revolution, and in defending the executive discretion of Washington at the time of the Jay Treaty, was now dimmed by an absorbing preoccupation with the evils of Jefferson and French philosophy. He did not appreciate the decided stupidity of tarnishing the reputation of a great party by lending its name to an opportunist of unsavory reputation.

Hamilton, appreciating that the motives and reasoning of his old confidant Sedgwick were typical of the Federalist majority in the House, made one last desperate appeal. Writing Sedgwick, January 21, 1801, he referred him to a letter he had just dispatched to Bayard of Delaware, in which he had again detailed his objections to Burr, and begged Sedgwick: "as you love your country, your friends, and yourself . . . reconsider dispassionately the opinion you have expressed in favor of Burr. . . . I never was so much mistaken, as I shall be, if your friends in the event of their success, do not rue the preference they will give to that Cataline." [14] Hamilton, removed from the scene and recognized to have been a major cause of the fatal division of the Federalist party, was now, however, no longer obeyed with the alacrity and constancy which had been his unquestioned due when Secretary of the Treasury.[15]

On February 11, Speaker Sedgwick called the House to order and the balloting began. Each of the sixteen state delegations had one vote, decided by the majority preference of the representatives composing that delegation. These gentlemen would place their votes in their state ballot box and a teller would count the votes and place a duplicate of

---

13. (cont.)

speaking well of him on one occasion as late as 1796, had by 1797–1798 turned against him, disgusted with his morals and politics. Throughout the winter of 1800–1801 he made no attempt to portray Burr in any other light than as the lesser of two evils.

14. Hamilton, *Works of Hamilton*, VI, 521.

15. Sedgwick believed at the end of January that the disposition to prefer Burr had so increased that it had "become virtually unanimous." Sedgwick to Theodore Jr., January 30, 1801. *S.P.*, M.H.S.

The personally highly honorable Charles Cotesworth Pinckney wrote Sedgwick that he thought "the meditated arrangement of the Federalists with respect to the Election, political & judicious." Pinckney to Sedgwick, February 12, 1801. *S.P.*, **M.H.S.**

their result into each of the two general ballot boxes. After these had been mutually checked for accuracy, Sedgwick would announce the way each state had voted and whether or not either of the two candidates had yet received the necessary majority of nine states. Thirty-five times they voted, and without decision. Though Sedgwick had insisted that the House be not exposed in its deliberations to a noisy gallery, and had ordered his old bête noire Samuel Harrison Smith of the *National Intelligencer*, summarily out of the chamber, the Jeffersonians saw to it that their chief and their friends were kept well informed of the course of the struggle. Many rumors of Federalist usurpation and armed Republican retaliation circulated Washington and excitement steadily mounted. In the Capitol ill representatives were carried into adjoining committee rooms so no vote would be lost on either side,[16] and "doubtful" members were strenuously courted and threatened on both sides. If Otis and Sedgwick bullied Representative Bayard to remain true to Burr—as the *Aurora For The Country* claimed—there is reason to believe that the vote of Congressman Craik of Maryland was determined by the threat of his wife that she would divorce him if he did not vote for Jefferson.[17]

The main hope of the Burrites lay in wearing the Jeffersonians down until they consented to accept Burr or a Federalist-controlled interregnum; or until they at least gave extensive and specific promises of good behavior in return for the election of Jefferson. All their plans, however, depended upon the active co-operation of Aaron Burr. An unusual timidity and indecision, a passing appreciation of the impossibility of his position as an unwanted President, a fear of alienating Republican support, a sense of propriety, a sudden spasm of patriotism and conscience: one or more of these conditions or analyses had caused the enigmatic Burr to feel or pretend shock at the invitation of the Federalists. His conduct proved fatal to the hopes and intrigues of Sedgwick

16. Sedgwick aided the request of Representative Nicholson of Maryland to be allowed the privilege of giving his vote in such an adjacent room. Sedgwick to Mr. Dennis, February 22, 1801. (Copy) S.P., M.H.S.

Nicholson, a strong Jeffersonian, assured himself a modicum of immortality by bringing his sickbed with him to the House, despite a driving snow, thereby preventing the loss of Maryland to Burr.

17. *Aurora For The Country*, February 23, 1801; John C. Miller, *The Federalist Era, 1789–1801* (New York, 1960), 271. See, too, Richard Stockton to Sedgwick, February 18, 1801. S.P., M.H.S.

Duane, editor of the *Aurora*, was, of course, passionately Republican and very anti-Sedgwick. Sedgwick in his eyes was always playing "the principal *buffa*." See, especially, issue of February 17, 1801.

and his friends. The Burr boom collapsed; the bandwagon received no fresh recruits. By February 16, Sedgwick was ready to declare that as a result of Burr's fateful timidity, "the gigg is up." [18]

This gloomy prophecy had been inspired by the decision of James A. Bayard, sole delegate of Delaware, to shift his vote to Jefferson. When Bayard announced this decision at a caucus of the House Federalists on the morning of February 16, he was made the object of abuse so vehement that he finally consented to a compromise arrangement of sorts. It was agreed that Bayard and certain Federalist congressmen from Maryland, Vermont, and South Carolina would absent themselves or put in blank pieces of paper on the next ballot. This would give Jefferson the votes of Maryland and Vermont and so the necessary majority, while allowing the Federalists the cold comfort of avoiding any positive participation in this hateful result. The thirty-sixth ballot, cast on February 17, 1801, saw Jefferson obtain the votes of ten states, and Theodore Sedgwick had the galling task of announcing the Virginian's election as third President of the United States.[19]

Sedgwick, revolted at the thought of attending Jefferson's inauguration, hurriedly prepared to leave Washington. The Federalists, the saviors and protectors of the country, were no longer to control the nation's destiny.[20] What could be ahead, he reflected, but disaster?

Boarding the stagecoach at four in the morning on March 4, 1801, Sedgwick's gloom was probably alleviated not at all when he discovered that among his fellow passengers was John Adams—equally determined to escape the humiliation of witnessing Jefferson's inaugural. One wonders if Sedgwick and Adams passed a single word during the long cold journey north. Probably not, but each must have thought often of the other and blamed him for the fall of the Federalist régime.

The Federalists had indeed been defeated, but Federalism itself and its great accomplishments over the last twelve years were not to be erased or forgotten. The role which the Federalists had been destined to

18. Sedgwick to Theodore Jr., February 16, 1801. S.P., M.H.S. The "gigg" for Sedgwick was the actual election of Burr, rather than the prevention of any election at all or the substitution of the Chief Justice as President pro tempore.

19. Morton Borden, The Federalism of James A. Bayard (New York, 1954), 90–95; Miller, The Federalist Era, 1789–1801, 272–273.

For certain alleged promises given Senator Smith of Maryland by Jefferson and their supposed effect on Bayard, see Noble E. Cunningham, The Jeffersonian Republicans (Chapel Hill, 1957), 245–246.

20. Aurora For The Country declared (February 20, 1801): "the Revolution of 1776 is now, and for the first time arrived at its completion. . . . The reign of terror and corrupt government is at an end."

play they had played well, but it was of necessity one that called for an early exit. The Federalists had put the credit of the nation on a firm basis, created the machinery of government, and established vital precedents in all its spheres. They had reinvigorated commerce, designed a system of internal taxes, suppressed insurrection, and strengthened the nation's defenses. They prevented what would have been a disastrous war with England from materializing and brought French depredations on our commerce to a virtual halt, while maintaining a necessary diplomatic policy of isolation and neutrality. In short, the Federalists made a transitory and uncertain experiment secure and permanent. They helped create "a more perfect union," and a national sentiment conducive to the permanence of that Union. Vanquished by their own errors and internecine jealousies, and made obsolete by their very success, this party of great leaders now saw its custodianship of the new nation come to an abrupt close. It was not to be expected that they would accept this defeat gracefully. Men like Sedgwick felt that they had fought the king only to lose their freedom to the mob.

Sedgwick's own evaluation of his national political career and of the administrations to which he had so proudly contributed is perhaps best revealed in his *Farewell* to his Berkshire constituents in June, 1800, on the occasion of his refusing another congressional term. After declaring that the first part of his life was, "in unison with my countrymen, devoted to effect a revolution the most singular and the most important, which probably the world has ever known," and the latter part devoted "to render that revolution truly beneficial," Sedgwick went into a long explanation of the necessity for a strong, effective government. "To men enlightened, as are the inhabitants of New-England, it need not be observed, that inestimably precious as is liberty, it can, in no way be secured, but by the protection of government—a government of sufficient energy to controul the inordinate exercise of passions directed to self gratification." This energy had to be the result of one of two things: military force or public confidence. Our government was based on the latter. "Remove that foundation and it enevitably tumbles into ruins." Previous experiments in governments of confidence had failed and given way to governments of force. They had failed because of "the wicked arts of the profligate and ambitious." Chief among these "wicked arts" had been the flattering of popular prejudices and the inflammation of the turbulent passions of an ignorant mob. Unless this country was inspired with wisdom and cool reason, predictions that our republican experiment would also fail would be verified only too soon.

The government with which, for the last twelve years, he had had

the honor to be associated, had had to contend with difficulties which
could not have been expected. Who could have foreseen that we would
have such emergency expenses as were entailed in the suppression of two
insurrections, the purchase of peace with the Barbary pirates, and the
fortification of our ports and harbors and reconstruction of our navy
against the strong likelihood of a war with the plundering French? Despite all these extraordinary expenses, however, the government—the
Federalist administration—had restored credit, both public and private.
The national debt had been reduced and our navigation "infinitely extended." "But what . . . [was] infinitely more dear to humanity, under
circumstances of extreme irritation, such . . . [had] been the temper,
the moderation and the magnanimity of the government, that peace . . .
[had] been preserved . . . [we had] kept ourselves separated, from
the scenes of horror" which had desolated Europe. The conduct of our
government had been such that all men—"our own degenerate citizens,
and Jacobin renegadoes from other countries among us excepted"—
spoke of it in terms of respect and honor. Was not this a glorious reverse
of the situation of this country in 1789? One should not forget, moreover,
that these reforms and advantages had been produced and effected
"without one act of tyranny or oppression."

Why had not all these magnificent contributions of the present
government won it the protection of the people against the malignant
enterprise of its enemies? Was it not that many of our citizens—he did
not speak of New England which was still "essentially sound"—had
been duped by the wicked arts of the Republicans? These honorless men
had malignantly slandered the character of those whom they believed
possessed of the public confidence, and had miserably misrepresented
the measures of the government. The present was a time of fearful
danger. He prayed that he might be mistaken in the conception he held
of its magnitude. He felt obliged, however, as one of the last acts of his
public life, solemnly to declare his conviction of the peril that lay ahead
for the nation if its citizens were not awakened to the dire consequences
inherent in the philosophy of Jefferson. In closing, he could only wish
his constituents—electors of the First Western District—the purest happiness, and express the hope that they might in the future be served with
"as much fidelity" as they had in the past.[21]

It was both a heartfelt farewell and a prime example of forthright
politicking. His Berkshire opponents quite naturally concentrated on

21. *The Western Star,* June 4, 1800. Reprinted in the *Albany Centinel,* June 20,
1800.

the latter aspect. In a virulent pamphlet entitled *The Honorable Mr. Sedgwick's Political Last Will and Testament, With the Inventory and Appraisal of the Legacies Therein Bequested*,[22] they attacked, with heavy-handed irony, the character, deeds, and recommendations of their retiring enemy.

Thanking Speaker Sedgwick for his fine address, the Republican writer declared that perhaps it was just as well he was retiring, as it was generally understood that the sphere of his influence was considerably narrowed by some late measures of the President, and his "re election rendered somewhat problematical" by the increasing growth of Republicanism among the people. It would be unfair to oppose any longer Sedgwick's "known habitual wish for retirement to the shades of private life." It was, of course, eminently proper that such a change in the political world "be solemnly and seasonably proclaimed, [in order] that the people might have time to acquire a sufficient fund of philosophy to support the shock."

The address was timely, pertinent, and boldly inventive. Mr. Sedgwick's "inventive merit" was illustrated by the fierce moderation and ostentatious modesty of the address, and by his attempt at flattering the people "with the idea of being above flattery." It must come as something of a surprise to many who had attended his electioneering clubs and caucuses, had ridden their horses into the ground on urgent electioneering expeditions, and had "incurred his eloquent reproofs for not voting for him or not exerting themselves properly in his favor," to find now that he had always been so reluctant to serve. How amazed, too, would be Loring Andrews, former editor of *The Western Star* and ill-fated suitor of Sedgwick's daughter Miss Frances, to discover that his patron was all the time simply a humble, unassuming, modest friend of all.[23] But his surprise would be as nothing when compared to that of certain men, "who, to their lasting mortification and regret, were once prevailed upon to turn the dubious scale of an election, in favor of our

22. Copies of this anonymous twenty-one-page pamphlet, printed "By a Republican Press" in 1800 (n.p.), are to be found in the Boston Athenaeum, the American Antiquarian Society, the Boston Public Library, and Houghton Library, Harvard University. The copy in the B.P.L. attributes the authorship to Barnabas Bidwell.

23.

[The sincerity of Sedgwick's professions] will be duly appreciated by his former printer, who served him faithfully with pen and type, about seven years, while the time seemed short, for the love he bore to Rachel; but, having, by

author, by procuring and destroying votes given for an opposite candidate, on their passage from the selectmen to the sheriff." [24]

The writer had to admit that he was rather confused by Mr. Sedgwick's use of the term "the government," when he meant Mr. Hamilton's political party. But in this Mr. Sedgwick was but one with his friends. All too successfully they had "palmed themselves upon the public as the government, and decried all disapprobation of their extravagant schemes, as antifederalism, disorganization and jacobinism. . . . To that super-federal anti-republican party, no doubt, one half the people are cordially opposed."

Mr. Sedgwick's attempt to compare the criticism which had been showered on him with that suffered by the illustrious Washington, and his attempt to conclude his puny public career with a farewell address like that of the General's, was as ridiculous as it was audacious. The criticism which he had received had been righteous criticism on the score of his "inordinate ambition, undue attachment to British interests and fashions," and his 'immoral and irreligious life." How, moreover, dared he to say that he and his friends had kept the country from the horrors of the war which was "desolating Europe"? Had President Adams allowed himself to be led by such men as Sedgwick, instead of "pursuing his own independent judgment," we should be allied with George III, and engaged in a bloody and needless war with France at this moment.

The entire address was, indeed, nothing but an example of mawkish, irrelevant, and dishonest politicking, by a man who was making his exit from the national legislative arena just twelve years too late. One could only conclude that Sedgwick's generous offer:

> Of a dumping settlement of personal abuses and resentments, is wisely calculated for reciprocal advantages; like that of a bankrupt who, owing almost everybody, and having very little due himself, shrewdly proposes to balance accounts with all the world, and com-

---

23. (cont.)
    removing his press out of his patron's district, into another state, become no longer necessary, was at last denied the expected and merited reward.

Last Will and Testament, 10. Actually Andrews did not leave Stockbridge until 1797, some months *after* Sedgwick had absolutely forbidden his daughter Frances to marry Andrews. Sedgwick seems to have felt that Andrews was rather "loose living," and definitely not his daughter's social equal.

24. This probably refers to the hotly contested congressional election of 1789, and was sheer canard, in so far as it imputed to Sedgwick responsibility for the improperly regulated and informal election proceedings of those times.

mence business anew, without the burden of old embarrassments. A composition, on such terms, is beneficial to the debtor, for it extinguishes debts, which he could never satisfy, and not detrimental to the creditors [voters of the First Western District] as it only discharges demands, which would not be paid and could not be collected. It is adviseable therefore, to execute mutual releases; and in order to avoid similar inconveniences in future, have no further commerce or connection whatever. Amen.

Such widely variant views of the conduct of the man and his party as are represented by the *Farewell* and the *Reply from a Republican Press* cannot be reconciled by melting them down in any one crucible of historical analysis. Besides their own inherent value as historical entertainment and illustration, however, they do tend to show how controversial a character Sedwick was, and how magnificently intolerant and self-deceiving politicians and political analysts were even then. In the present author's opinion, Sedgwick's national legislative career redounded on the whole to the benefit of the country he so loved. Allegations that he was an obedient toady to his party or to any particular national figure—whether that be Hamilton, Robert Morris,[25] or Pickering—are ill-based. His admiration for, and agreement with, Alexander Hamilton came not from a lack of independent understanding or personal confidence but from a common set of political standards, and from a basic agreement as to the direction of the course they wished America to take. Promoting the various components of Hamilton's financial system; helping prevent the defeat of the Jay Treaty; personally drafting scores of House and Senate bills which put flesh on the skeletal framework of the Constitution; notable in his insistence on maintaining the independence of the executive department; tireless in his efforts to protect the nation's defense and security, Theodore Sedgwick was, during his twelve years in Congress, a capable and faithful public servant.

25. See *Aurora For The Country,* September 12, 1800, where Morris is labeled "the extraordinary chairman of *Sedgwick* in Congress."

AFTER THE REVOLUTION: A FEDERALIST IN THE ERA OF JEFFERSON

XVI

Sedgwick as a Political Spectator, 1801–1813

The aristocracy of virtue is destroyed.
Theodore Sedgwick [1]

ALTHOUGH Theodore Sedgwick never returned to politics after his solemn Farewell, he maintained an ardent interest in the political welfare of his country and the electoral fortunes of his party to the very end of his life. The twelve allotted years remaining, however, witnessed the continued popularity and political success of the Jeffersonian System and held for Sedgwick, the politician, little but bitterness and frustration. In his bitterness he typified the response of the New England Federalists to the domestic and foreign polices of Jefferson and Madison. His frustration symbolized that of his party in all sections.

Jefferson's first administration was eminently successful and gave the opposition slight chance for fruitful attack. Jefferson wisely did not attempt to cancel or discard any of the major accomplishments of the late Federalist régime, but devoted himself to liberalizing certain of their features and to lessening the fiscal burden of the individual citizen. He was determined that the Revolution of 1800 be sufficiently gradual and temperate to obliterate any chance of a successful counterrevolution.

Jefferson's conciliatory tactics had little influence on the opinions of Theodore Sedgwick. When that Federalist read Jefferson's Inaugural Address, he advised Rufus King that the Federalists could take all credit for its moderate tone. By preferring even Burr, the Federalists had shown how they despised Jefferson and had so frightened that timid gentleman that he now was attempting to soothe and placate his enemies. This, of course, infuriated his followers, who for the last number of years had been taught to refer to the Federalists as monarchists and worse.[2]

As the months passed and it became evident that the conciliatory

1. Letter to Rufus King, December 14, 1801. King, *King*, IV, 34.
2. May 24, 1801. *Ibid.*, III, 456.

Jefferson remained a Republican, Sedgwick's contempt turned to angry despair. The replacement of Federalist officeholders with "furious democrats," he considered outrageous; and the repeal of the Judiciary Act of 1801, highly improper.[3] He could not understand why, with such actions on display, Democracy was not quite stamped out. Instead it was growing like a rank weed. One could almost see the corruption of New England spirit that was taking place. Thoughts of national honor and glory were quite outmoded; warm, generous, manly sentiment was no longer prized. Now everyone thought only of economy and decreasing the public burdens. "The aristocracy of virtue is destroyed; personal influence is at an end. No length nor degree of popular service, neither the most shining talents, nor the most . . . disinterested conduct, give anything like weight and authority to character."[4] Perhaps when the people saw the true meaning of Jefferson's plans to pamper state sovereignty, attack the navigation laws, and dissipate the resources of the Treasury, they might remember "those men whose wise counsels" had once "saved them from ruin," and place them in their rightful position of authority. At present, however, the people appeared to enjoy their delusion.[5]

Although Sedgwick did not possess great ability of self-analysis, he did entertain a healthy respect for his own mental and physical energies. He appreciated that political commentary alone would hardly satisfy, and soon after his retirement from the national capital set about to find an occupation that would enable him "to avoid the evils of idleness."[6] He appreciated that the role of gentleman farmer would soon pall and that a return to full-time legal practice in the local courts would be irritating both to mind and temper. He soon determined upon a judicial career and set in motion a campaign of suggestion and correspondence which secured his appointment in February, 1802, as associate justice of the Supreme Judicial Court of Massachusetts. For the remaining

3. At first Sedgwick had declared that such a repeal would be unfortunate, but not unconstitutional; "for that would imply that a rational reform of the judicial, under circumstances which might reasonably be expected, would be impracticable." Later he swung over to the party majority opinion that the repeal represented an "unconstitutional legislative usurpation." See Sedgwick to King, December 14, 1801 (*ibid.*, IV, 36) and February 20, 1802, *S.P.*, M.H.S.

4. Sedgwick to King, December 14, 1801. King, *King*, IV, 34.
5. See Sedgwick to King, February 20, 1802. (Copy) *S.P.*, M.H.S.
6. Sedgwick to King, June 15, 1802. King, *King*, IV, 139.

eleven years of his life he served—and served ably—on the Massachusetts bench.[7]

Between terms of that court he would occupy himself with speculation and with politics. These he would carefully distinguish. Business, in the form of speculations in the South Hadley Canal Company or the undeveloped lands of the Genesee Country, was an avocation; his dedication was to politics. As a speculator, he would invest in the economic future of America; as a political observer, he would proclaim a mounting sense of frustration respecting the political future of his country and his party.

Sedgwick gradually came to see himself as the Jeremiah of the Federalist party—destined to bewail, to scold, and to warn. If he preferred the judicial robe to the wooden yoke, he would not renounce the role of the stern and despairing prophet.

Throughout his years of judicial service and political exile Sedgwick would pursue a heavy political correspondence with such former colleagues as Rutledge of South Carolina, Tracy of Connecticut, Ross of Pennsylvania, Patterson of New Jersey, and Bayard of Delaware. To these men he would deliver himself of his opinions concerning the probable future of the nation and the proper tactics for his party. The Federalist minority in Congress should be "cool and dignified." They should allow the inherent instability of the unwieldy, heterogeneous Republican majority to take effect. They should continuously reveal the true designs of Jefferson's evil measures. Before long "our enlightened and virtuous citizens must be roused by the distress that their own folly will produce."[8]

He found a certain, if transitory, confirmation of his wishful thinking in the results of the Massachusetts state elections of 1802, in the con-

7. This "political portrait" omits discussion of the judicial career of Theodore Sedgwick, for that career, as it followed his years in Congress, has little relevance to Sedgwick's position as an example and spokesman of the Federalist position. It is of significance, however, in the judicial history of Massachusetts. Sedgwick—as judge and as judicial reformer—played a valuable role in preparing Massachusetts for the "new era" associated with the name of Theophilus Parsons. Supporting evidence for this judgment will be found in two articles by the author: "The Parsons-Sedgwick Feud and the Reform of the Massachusetts Judiciary," *Essex Institute Historical Collections*, April, 1956 (pp. 171–187); "Judge Sedgwick and Mumbet," *The Boston Bar Journal*, January, 1964 (pp. 12–19).

8. Uriah Tracy to Sedgwick, January 29, 1802. S.P., M.H.S.

Tracy did not agree with Sedgwick's prophecy. He did not believe "this Country . . . [could] be saved in any way,—a change of Govt. . . . [was] certain, and to that change we must wade in blood."

tinued Federal ardor of the New England clergy, and in the unenthusiastic response of New England to the acquisition of Louisiana,[9] but his initial belief that Mr. Jefferson would not be re-elected steadily weakened. The Republicans with all the public records available to them had, of course, been unable to prove any evidence of "peculation" by the Federalists, but the apathetic citizenry seemed to take no notice of this. Jefferson had been shrewd enough to maintain good relations with Britain, even securing a convention on the settlement of the old British debts; various lazy Federalists refused to stand for office; and in the struggle between the Burr and Clinton factions in New York there was no hope for the Federalists, whoever the victor.[10] It was, on balance, surely, a very gloomy picture.

Sedgwick, despite his aberration on the occasion of the electoral tie of 1800, was still in the good graces of Alexander Hamilton, and in firm agreement with Hamilton's advocacy of Federal organization and patience, and with his opposition to democrary *and secession*. Sedgwick did become sufficiently discouraged with the "innovations made in our original compact" to contemplate in 1804 the propriety of "a solemn protest" by all the New England Federalists, but he staunchly opposed any "abandonment of the Union." It might well fail, but its failure should be patently attributable to the Jeffersonians alone.

Sedgwick certainly never supported any scheme for a Northern Confederacy, headed by Aaron Burr, although he did favor the candidacy of that gentleman in the 1804 New York gubernatorial election.[11] With the defeat of Burr in this election and the consequent death of Alexander Hamilton at the hands of Burr (July, 1804), any plans of a Northern Confederacy—if Pickering, Griswold, Tracy, Hillhouse, and Plumer ever *concretely* planned such—quite disintegrated. The recently deceased Hamilton would have applauded the result; for he was an ardent opponent of any sectionalization of Federalist strength. In per-

---

9. Sedgwick appreciated the "great inconsistency" in Jefferson, the strict constructionist, proceeding to add an empire to the confines of the Union, with hardly a by-your-leave from the sixteen sovereign states. Sedgwick's opposition to the acquisition would undoubtedly have been less if the convention had not established that Louisiana would eventually be assimilated into the Union and thereby increase greatly the voting strength of the West, and conversely diminish that of New England.

10. Clintonianism though "neither democracy nor jacobinism" was based on a hatred of all things Federal, and the Burr party was composed of "all the needy and desperate adventurers in the community." Sedgwick to King, August 24, 1802 (Copy) S.P., M.H.S.

11. See Thomas Dwight to Sedgwick, February 27, 1804. S.P., M.H.S.

haps the last letter he ever wrote, conscious of the possible fate that might await him on the Heights of Weehawken, Hamilton had addressed the Federalist party through his good friend Sedgwick as follows:

> I have had in hand for some time a long letter to you, explaining my view of the course and tendency of our Politics, and my intentions as to my own future conduct. . . . the letter is still considerably short of being finished— I write this now to satisfy you, that want of regard for you has not been the cause of my silence.
>
> I will here express but one sentiment, which is, that Dismemberment of an Empire will be a dear sacrifice of great position and advantage, without any counterballancing good; administering no relief to our real Disease; which is Democracy, the poison of which by a subdivision will only be the more concentered in each part, and consequently the more virulent. . . . God bless you [12]

To insist that Sedgwick refused to have a part in any secessionist plot [13] is not, of course, to say that he was in any sense resigned to the way political matters were going. The seduction of Massachusetts and Vermont by Jefferson in the presidential election of 1804 found him incredulous and depressed, and the quality of men chosen for the Massachusetts General Court led him to great excesses of sarcasm. "Learning and genius not only are not necessary," he observed, "but by our masters the sovereign people are absolutely reprobated & denounced as disqualifications of the character of Legislator."

During Jefferson's second term Sedgwick tried to assume an attitude of stolid martyrship. He refused to be surprised by anything the Democratic devils did, either nationally or in his beloved, if faithless, Massachusetts. Sedgwick's disdainful calm did not hold, however, when relations between the administration and the British navy reached such a position that Jefferson proceeded to institute "his damned embargo."

Sedgwick and the Federalist party, in general, were to varying extents, Anglophiles. They believed in the benefits of trade and the promotion of commerce, and our trade and commerce were indissolubly intertwined with British markets, British exports, and the British navy.

12. Hamilton to Sedgwick, July 11, 1804. M.H.S. (in safe).

On the twelfth, Hamilton seems to have addressed a short note to his wife, but the letter to Sedgwick was the last political communication he ever wrote. Hamilton and Sedgwick were planning to spend part of the summer in one another's company at Lebanon Springs.

13. Henry Adams appears to place Sedgwick among the disunionists of 1804, the believers in "disunion as a conservative necessity." There is little evidence for believing that Sedgwick, lover of dramatic exaggeration, favored secession in 1804. Adams, *History of the United States*, II, 188.

They had hated the égalitarian designs of the French Revolution and they now feared the world-conquering imperialism of Napoleon; Britain had fought the one to a draw and was locked in a death-struggle with the other. Granted she had been disgracefully abrupt in certain of her Orders in Council concerning neutral trade, we should still be eternally grateful that she had elected to fight for all the world the battle for law, order, and freedom from Napoleonic domination. The American trade forbidden by the British admiralty was not legitimate trade; if England had not been at war with all Europe it would never possibly have come our way. Its disruption was, therefore, not a proper cause for enmity. Conciliatory diplomacy on our part might well bring England back to a more reasonable position as concerned our trade with Europe. In any case we should remember she was fighting for her life, and that such a struggle was necessarily not conducive to agreeable behavior.

England's actions in impressing our seamen were disgraceful, but the weak national government of Mr. Jefferson had done little or nothing to discourage desertion by British sailors. We had attempted to retain all the advantages of neutrality without accepting any of its responsibilities. Consequently, we had been at the mercy of both England and France, especially France. If this country wished to become pugnacious with any European power, France was by far the most justifiable object of our wrath.

If Sedgwick and his party had been in control during the years 1805–1808, it is certain that they would have maintained and increased the military power of the United States, and quite possible that they would have promoted an alliance with England and a war with France. Sedgwick would have considered such a dignified, lucid policy protective of both our commercial interests and national honor. The administration in power, however, was that of Thomas Jefferson, a man unburdened with any predilection for Britain or the profits of American merchants. Mr. Jefferson decided on an economic substitute for war, the Embargo (December, 1807).

The only decent thing Sedgwick could say about the "French-inspired embargo" was that it might prove a political boomerang for the Republicans in the presidential election of 1808. To that election Sedgwick had pointed for several years. As it neared he realized that there was slight chance of a Federalist victory. He had had enough, though, of surreptitious Federalist support for disgruntled factions of the opposition. We should go it alone, he wrote Harrison Gray Otis, supporting Pinckney and King to the bitter end. The Massachusetts electors, who would surely be "federal men," must be "activated by principle alone," refusing to cast a single vote for Clinton, even if it seemed certain that only the latter and the apostate Madison had chance of election. If the Federalists conducted themselves with prudence and undeviating honesty, "causes which are now in operation and which cannot be controuled by the democrats," rendered it virtually certain that they would be successful in 1812. But should they now lend themselves "to the Clinton faction, that bright prospect would instantly disappear." He could not "endure the humiliating idea that those who alone from education, fortune, character, and principle are entitled to command should voluntarily arrange themselves under the banner of a party in all respects inferior, and in many odious, to them." [14] Hastily dismissing all memories of his support of Burr in February, 1801, Sedgwick was now for absolute integrity in all political associations. The Federalists should gain strength by securing converts to their faith in its full, undiluted form. They should promote constant interchange of sentiments between the various sections; they should institute committees of correspondence; [15] and they should rebuild their state organizations.

After the Federalist defeat in the presidential election of 1808, Sedgwick became increasingly bitter. Free from the restraining advice of Hamilton, and goaded by the ever more imminent prospect of war with England, Sedgwick increasingly lost sight of the great vision of *national* strength and unity which had proudly described his party in its years of power, and with other New England Federalists became steadily

14. Sedgwick to Otis, June 6, 1808. *H. G. Otis Papers*, M.H.S.
Otis and several other Federalist leaders favored supporting the once-hated Mr. Clinton. The Bostonian caustically replied to Sedgwick that "however desirable it is, to preserve the consistency & dignity of our party, it is of more *consequence to save the country*." Otis to Sedgwick, June 23, 1808. *S.P.*, M.H.S.
15. Sedgwick's desires in this respect had some effect. Thomas Fitzsimons wrote him, July 10, 1808, as follows:

> Some time ago, a Communication was received from Mr. Otis informing that a Committee of members of the legislature of your state to whose hands the management of the Federal business should be intrusted was recd. here. that Committee proposed that on the 2nd Tuesday in August there should be a Meeting at New York of one or two Confidential Agents from the Federal party in all the states E. of Virginia, and it was recommended to persons in this City to have such Conferees appointed and to Correspond with persons of like disciples [*sic*] as well in the Western part of this state as in the states of Delaware & Maryland—this has accordingly been done. . . .
> Thus you see your wish thus far has been realized.

S.P., M.H.S.

more provincial and intemperate. Where once he spoke of the glory of the Union, he now thought chiefly of the security of New England. A strong sectional bias once again dictated his political opinions and desires, especially where the European war and American foreign policy were concerned.

The Republicans, Sedgwick kept insisting, were "insidious in their conduct toward England, subservient to france, and heartily inimical to the essential interest of this part of the united states." Certainly all his friends in Massachusetts wished to see the Union preserved if it could be done without ruin to New England, "but the opinion is becoming more and more prevalent," that such might prove impossible. Secession was surely a hazardous solution, but submission "of every thing dear and valuable" was not to be expected.[16] The crisis was not far distant unless the administration stopped short in its mad career.

The Non-Intercourse Act (1809), forbidding trade with England and France, was almost as insane a measure as the Embargo. Macon's first bill, forbidding importation of foreign goods except in American bottoms, was most inept, and his "Bill #2" (May, 1810), simply an attempt to bribe one power into right conduct by promising to damage and harm its rival. Madison was constantly alternating between feeble complaints and empty threats, and, in consequence, the country was being sucked into the maelstrom of war, weak, unarmed, and divided.

By 1812 Sedgwick was quite disgusted with the lack of vigor displayed by the dwindling band of Federalists in Washington. Writing Harmanus Bleecker, a representative from New York, he warned that in a popular government no party could maintain its ground merely by acting on the defensive. The Federalists should introduce specific resolutions denouncing the Madisonian system and detailing proper national policies for the better "understanding of the people." [17] "Keep up a continued agition [sic]. There are no other means by which lost popularity can be reacquired." The Federalist congressmen should review the history of this country and describe the way in which our high and elevated situation had been degraded once common sense and experience were replaced by "phylosophy" and theory. They should explain how "if the intention of [the] federalists had . . . been permitted to progress, and had continued untill the time of the embargo, we should have been at that time, far beyond the possibility of insult from any nation on earth." The amount of revenue shamefully abandoned by the Republicans could have been, without hardship to a single individual

16. Sedgwick to Theodore Jr., February 4, 1809. *S.P.*, M.H.S.
17. January 4, 1812. *S.P.*, M.H.S.

in the community, the means of ample military defense. The deceitful Madison did not, he believe, wish war, but by his folly and base lust for popularity he would very probably embroil the nation in a bloody conflict. The British could not be expected to understand that demagogues and democrats did not always mean what they said, and would probably commit some act that would render war unavoidable. Should war come, he would despair for the welfare of the country. "A war with England [was] . . . inseperable from an intimate connexion with France; and a connexion with France must operate our irretreviable ruin." This being so, he could not understand why certain Federalist congressmen lent their support to the warlike measures of the administration. War was too great a price to pay for the privilege of discarding the burdens of neutrality, and the British, when they saw both American parties united in passing retaliatory legislation, would naturally think there was no chance of peace with the United States.

France was, of course, our real enemy. We had suffered much greater injuries at her hands. Napoleon's repeal of the Berlin and Milan decrees was but a farce. We had little benefit from commercial intercourse with France or with her dependencies. Whereas England in case of war could "inflict upon us severe chastisement," we were "completely without the reach of the vengeance of france, and should be defended against it by the omnipotence of the british navy." It would be disastrous if, despite such undeniable facts, we leagued with France against England. The Federalists in Congress should expose "the meanness, the bareness and partiality of the administration," before it was too late.[18]

Despite his detailed advice, the majority of the Federalist representatives and senators in Congress continued to exhibit, in Sedgwick's view, insufficient force and spirit. In Massachusetts, however, things were improving. Caleb Strong had unseated Elbridge Gerry in the gubernatorial election in the spring of 1812, and the new governor and state legislature responded nobly when the dread contingency of war with England became sobering fact. The General Court sent a memorial to Congress (June 5, 1812) opposing a declaration of war, and Strong subsequently refused to obey the request of the President to call out the state militia. Sedgwick, after some thought, heartily applauded Strong's stand. As the nation suffered no invasion or insurrection, nor any example of concerted violation of federal law—the three situations listed in the Federal Constitution as prerequisites to such a request by the President—Sedgwick was of the opinion that the Massachusetts

18. Sedgwick to Bleecker, January 23, 1812. *S.P.*, M.H.S.

militia should not have been called out. Furthermore, he admired the Governor's blunt forthrightness, declaring: "I am sure that upon this occasion it was the best policy to declare the truth, because no war can be successfully carried on to which New England, or what is the same thing Massa. & Connecticut are opposed; and this Madison & Co know as well as we do." [19] Sedgwick's hopes of thwarting Mr. Madison's War, and forcing the administration to "retrace their steps," came to naught. The declaration of war of June 18, 1812, was followed surely if slowly by a second contest of arms with King George III.

Sedgwick lived for only seven months after the commencement of the struggle. He seems never to have changed his belief that the war was unnecessary, and the result of party considerations and an unjust desire for the annexation of Canada. His views were, in short, those of his party, as expressed in the Address of the Federalist Members of Congress (June, 1812). Ill at home during the fall of 1812, Sedgwick mulled over the sad state of the Union. He rued the day when the South had been allowed to count three-fifths of its slaves for purposes of representation; hoped for the victory of "Clinton and Peace" over "Madison and War" in the coming presidential election; and praised the Berkshire Association of Congregational Churches for proclaiming a day of fast and penance. When with the re-election of Madison it became apparent that the war was to be fought as well as declared, Sedgwick was both grieved and bitter. Though he prayed for an American victory, he labelled the war as "clearly unjust."

Sedgwick did not favor secession by the New England states, but he firmly believed that the states had a right to hold conventions and, by their protests, attempt to check "our vile administration in their career of mischief." Emergencies such as the present "authorise[d] revolutionary measures." [20] If Sedgwick had been alive at the time of the Hartford Convention he would probably have approved of that meeting and, if a participant, attempted to prevent any concrete declaration of secessionist intent and to utilize the convention as a club to frighten the administration into a negotiated peace with Great Britain.

Viewed in a political light, the years 1801–1813 were for Theodore Sedgwick neither happy nor constructive. In measure, he found relief from the frustrations of political exclusion in his labors as judge and in

19. Sedgwick to H. D. Sedgwick, July 3, 9, 1812. *S.P.*, M.H.S. As one of the judges of the Massachusetts Supreme Court, Sedgwick concurred in an advisory opinion upholding Governor Strong's refusal.
20. Sedgwick to H. D. Sedgwick, August 23, 1812. *Ibid.*

the concerns of family and home. But even here events finally conspired to diminish the sense of confidence and self-pleasure that had so long served to inspire and console him.

His beloved wife Pamela, a victim of periodic melancholia, was in 1804 the victim of a severe attack of mental depression and was for a time completely irrational. She had by the next year recovered her sanity but would remain a semi-invalid until her death, September 20, 1807. Throughout thirty-three years of married life Pamela Dwight Sedgwick had been almost reverently devoted to her husband, and Sedgwick, if less selfless and dedicated in his devotion, had been her sincere admirer. His clumsy attempts to console her during her periods of mental depression witnessed a side of his nature little suspected by his political opponents,[21] and in his anguish at her death he briefly dropped all pretensions of reserve and self control.

Despite the devoted attentions of his unmarried children,[22] the "mansion" in Stockbridge was no longer a source of pride but a symbol of loss. His friends urged him to marry again; to give the "mansion" a new mistress. In November, 1808, the lonely widower took as his third wife Miss Penelope Russell of Boston. From the beginning he harbored doubts as to "the probable success of the alliance."[23] Those doubts were all too early realized, as his new wife proved the victim of a "delicate constitution" and consequently irritable temper. In marriage as in politics, it appeared impossible to recapture the past.

One further loss remained. With the years 1811–1812 Sedgwick began to suffer from severe attacks of gout and an increasingly severe asthmatic condition. In November, 1812, he forced himself to make the journey to Boston and sit with the court at the Suffolk County term. After presiding but a few days, however, he contracted what was probably bronchial pneumonia and was obliged to retire to some rooms he had engaged near Bowdoin Square. There in Boston he suffered a pain-

---

21. See, especially, Sedgwick to Pamela, December 16, 1791; February 18, 1793; January 5, 1794; December 30, 1794; December 16, 1795; February 3, 1799, Papers of H. D. Sedgwick; Sedgwick to the Misses Sedgwick, February 27, 1794, Papers of H. D. Sedgwick, S.P., M.H.S.

22. Theodore and Pamela Sedgwick had ten children: Eliza Mason (1775–1827); a child, unnamed (born and died, March 27, 1777); Frances Pamela (1778–1842); Theodore Jr. (1780–1839); Catharine (1782–1783); Henry Dwight (1784–1785); Henry Dwight II (1785–1831); Robert (1787–1841); Catharine Maria (1789–1867); and Charles (1791–1856). Theodore Jr. would become in his later years an ardent Jacksonian; Catharine Maria was perhaps the most popular female novelist in America prior to the publication of *Uncle Tom's Cabin*.

23. See, especially, Sedgwick to Theodore Jr., October 20, 1808. S.P., M.H.S.

ful confinement of six weeks duration and there he died on Sunday, January 24, 1813.

Political differences of opinion were now forgotten as Massachusetts united to honor one of its most public-spirited sons. Both houses of the General Court passed unanimous resolutions, January 27, 1813, to attend the "funeral solemnities . . . as a token of their respect for the memory of an able judge and distinguished patriot," and the lawyers of the city voted to attend en masse, each to wear a crepe band on his left arm.[24] The funeral services, arranged by the Boston bar, were held at four o'clock on the afternoon of January 27, at Dr. Channing's church on Federal Street.[25] Sedgwick's relatives and close friends then proceeded to the place of interment where Sedgwick was laid to rest. The services at the church were attended by scores of eminent Bostonians, all of whom, as the writer of the *Massachusetts Reports* declared, wished to pay their respects "to the memory of a man, who, through a long and active life, had devoted his eminent talents, with undeviating fidelity, and unabated ardour, to the services of his country." [26]

Sedgwick's body was evidently soon transferred to Stockbridge, for in the Stockbridge cemetery there is a large circular plot reserved exclusively for the graves of the Judge and his descendants. In the center of this graveyard—or "Sedgwick Pie" as it is familiarly called—is a tall obelisk-like monument which marks the final resting place of Theodore Sedgwick, and to its right a smaller one denoting that of his second wife Pamela. From the nucleus formed by these two stones there extend six clearly demarcated pie-shaped sections. The descendants of each of Sedgwick's six married children are buried in their respective section, and all are buried with their feet pointing to the center of the "Pie," or to the Judge's monument. According to local legend the reason behind this uniformity is that upon the signal marking the Day of Resur-

24. *Thomas's Massachusetts Spy*, February 3, 1813; *Columbian Centinel*, January 27, 1813.

25. Shortly before his death, Sedgwick, probably upon the urging of his daughter, Catharine Maria had expressed a desire to receive the sacrament from the Unitarian minister, William Ellery Channing. In the words of his daughter, Mr. Channing, on the ninth of January, "in the most tender and affecting manner administered the sacrament to him." Catharine M. Sedgwick to Mrs. Theodore Sedgwick Jr., January 12, 1813. S.P., M.H.S.

Sensing his approaching death, Sedgwick had probably been struck with the thought that his secular commitments had rather overshadowed all others. He had always considered himself a Christian and had spasmodically attended the Congregational church in Stockbridge, but he had always placed his reliance for salvation on "good works."

26. Memorandum of Dudley Atkins Tyng in 9 Mass. 215 (1813).

rection all descendants will automatically rise in position "facing the Judge," the much revered founder of their family. Whether this is actual historic fact is hard to determine, but, fact or fancy, it is an arrangement that the Judge himself would most probably have considered eminently suitable.

Whatever Sedgwick's specific position on the Day of Resurrection, his place in history must rest on his very real services to state and nation. On such a basis his right to the title of Patriot would seem secure. His activities as commissary agent during the Revolution and the legislative apprenticeship he served in both the General Court and the Confederation Congress brought him deserved prominence. His advocacy of the rights of Loyalists and his efforts in behalf of Negro emancipation in Massachusetts surely are to his credit. As a judge on the Massachusetts Supreme Court, Theodore Sedgwick was instrumental in reforming the administration and manners of that institution.

His greatest contribution, however, was made during his twelve years of service in the national Congress. Not a great statesman, he was an able legislator and politician, and in his motives and designs most representative of the dominant, majority wing of the Federalist party. A party "regular," Sedgwick was by no means a mere party "hack." He was recognized by both Hamiltonians and Jeffersonians as an influential political figure, a capable debater, and a tireless committeeman. The close friend and intimate confidant of nearly all the major Federalists, Sedgwick was Hamilton's chief lieutenant in the House during the funding and assumption contests, the outstanding administration figure in the debate on the Jay Treaty resolution of Mr. Livingston, and the senator most responsible for arming the nation in 1798 against the threat of war with France.

His bitter quarrel with Adams, his promotion of the Alien and Sedition Acts, and his efforts to elect Burr as President were separately and in combination highly unwise, but in each instance he was working for what he believed to be the best interests of the nation. Not unlike the party of which he was so proud a member, Sedgwick was often and concurrently high-minded and shortsighted.

Though not a complicated individual, Theodore Sedgwick was not without elements of the paradoxical. Often arrogant to his inferiors, he was undeviatingly loyal to his friends and devoted to his family. A man of passionate temperament, he admired above all human traits self-control. Strongly ambitious and anxious for fame, he respected principle and jealously guarded his reputation. A man of exemplary integrity in his personal dealings, he was not overscrupulous in his choice of political weapons. Tolerant if not casual in his religion, he was the zealot in politics. Risen from humble circumstances, he possessed an all-pervasive sense of class consciousness. Passionately devoted to his country, he did not trust the majority of his countrymen.

If Sedgwick was not a beloved figure, neither was he one that exhibited any great capacity for growth. One must not, however, exaggerate his political obduracy. If his was not a career marked by dramatic intellectual and professional development, neither was it an example of intellectual immobility. Initially the provincial, restricted to the horizons of his beloved Massachusetts, he gradually became an ardent nationalist. During his last years, when in political coventry, that nationalism would wane, yet not succomb. The proud champion of the powers of the Executive Branch at the time of the Jay Treaty, he later castigated John Adams for exercising his presidential discretion. The courageous defender of freedom of opinion during the Revolution, he later helped author the Alien and Sedition Acts and, still later, displayed a strong concern for individual liberty when a judge on the Massachusetts Supreme Court. For most of his political career the honest conservative—advocate of an effective national government, a responsible Executive, and an independent Judiciary; supporter of economic stability and progress, orderly change, and the security of property—his last years in Congress were marred by acts of illiberal extremism.

Sedgwick's fear of mobocracy and anarchy, his *noblesse oblige* patriotism, his confusion of partisanship and sedition are not easily understood or appreciated today. They were not unique, however. Here as always he reflected his party. Typical initially of the majority of his party's leaders and then but typical of that party's extremist wing, Theodore Sedgwick considered himself at all times the true FEDERALIST.

BIBLIOGRAPHY

Bibliography

THE following bibliography does not pretend to list all works of merit for the Federalist Period nor all books of that period with which the author is familiar. The *Harvard Guide to American History* (Cambridge, 1954) and the bibliographical essay at the conclusion of John C. Miller's excellent book, *The Federalist Era 1789–1801* (New York, 1960) make the first task unnecessary and the second would appear valueless. What follows is intended only to indicate the major sources for this biography and the author's opinion as to their importance for a biography of Theodore Sedgwick.

PRIMARY SOURCES

Among primary sources, the most significant are obviously the large body of Sedgwick Papers to be found in the Massachusetts Historical Society. These Papers have been completely and systematically examined for the first time in the writing of this biography. They constitute not only the chief source for a biography of Theodore Sedgwick, but offer illumination on such diverse topics as legal training and procedures in eighteenth century New England, changing agrarian patterns and land speculation in western Massachusetts, the supply of the Revolutionary army and early efforts at party organization in Massachusetts.

The Sedgwick Family Papers comprise 106 boxes arranged in several series and under various titles. Material dealing with the career of Theodore Sedgwick will be found in two series listed in his name and in certain boxes of Henry Dwight Sedgwick Papers; Minot-Sedgwick Papers; and Catharine Maria Sedgwick Papers. There are also in the possession of the Society, seven account books, three day books, and certain ledgers belonging to Theodore Sedgwick; other account books, journals, and letter books used both by Sedgwick and his eldest son, Theodore Jr.; the "Day Book of H. D. Sedgwick"; and several family Bibles.

Sedgwick material will also be found in the following manuscript collections at the Massachusetts Historical Society, particularly for the years cited: Adams Papers (John Adams Papers, 1798–1800, microfilm); Nathan Dane Papers (1786–1787); Caleb Davis Papers (1781; 1785–1787); William

Heath Papers; Rufus King Papers (1787; 1798–1802); Henry Knox Papers (1798); Livingston Papers (1786); Norcross Papers (1772); Norton Papers (1794–1797); Harrison Gray Otis Papers (1799–1808); Timothy Pickering Papers (1785–1801); Shays Papers (1787); Taft Papers (1798–1799; 1804–1805); Washburn Papers (1788).

Manuscript material relating to the career of Theodore Sedgwick will also be found in the following repositories and collections: Library of Congress: Papers of Alexander Hamilton (1788; 1793; 1796–1803); Papers of Thomas Jefferson (1793); Papers of the Continental Congress (1786; 1788); William Loughton Smith Papers (1800); Joseph Story Papers (1807). Stockbridge (Massachusetts) Public Library: Sedgwick Family Papers; folder on Sedgwick's manservant, Agrippa Hull; map and card file concerning property distribution in Stockbridge in late eighteenth century. Massachusetts Archives (Capitol Building): Volumes CXC; CLXXXIX. Berkshire Athenaeum, Pittsfield, Massachusetts: Sedgwick Family Papers. Beverly (Massachusetts) Historical Society: Nathan Dane Papers. New Haven Colony Historical Society: Genealogical Notes of Hubert Sedgwick. New-York Historical Society: Rufus King Papers (1787; 1796–1803; 1808). New York Public Library: Emmet Collection. Also miscellaneous Sedgwick letters at: Houghton Library, Harvard University; Boston Athenaeum; the Historical Society of Pennsylvania; Henry E. Huntington Library and Art Gallery.

Printed Collections of Documents

The most essential collections of documents for a biography of Theodore Sedgwick are the *Journal of the Continental Congress, 1774–1789* (Washington, 1904–1937); *Annals of Congress*, I–X (Washington, 1834–1851); and the *Reports of Cases Argued and Determined in the Supreme Judicial Court of the Commonwealth of Massachusetts*, I–X (Boston, 1805–1814).

For his Massachusetts career the following were also useful: Edmund C. Burnett, ed., *Letters of Members of the Continental Congress* (8 vols., New York, 1921–1936); "Letters to Caleb Strong, 1786, 1800," *American Historical Review*, IV (1898–1899), 328–331; *Acts and Resolves of Massachusetts, 1780–1797*, I–IX (Boston, 1890–1896); Jeremy Belknap, "Minutes of the Debates in the Massachusetts Convention of 1788," Massachusetts Historical Society, *Proceedings*, III (1858), 296–304; Jacob E. Cooke, ed., *The Federalist* (Middletown, 1961); *Debates and Proceedings in the Convention of the Commonwealth of Massachusetts Held in The Year 1788* (Boston, 1856); Jonathan Elliot, *The Debates in the Several State Conventions on the Adoption of the Federal Constitution*, II (Washington, 1845); *Journal of the Convention For Framing a Constitution . . . 1779 . . . 1780* (Boston, 1832); *Journal of the House of Representatives*, III–IX (1782–1789). The latter is a longhand *ms.*, though not the original, and is to be found in the Massachusetts State Library.

For congressional and post-congressional years, the following documentary collections were consulted: *Congressional Register or History of the Proceedings and Debates of the First House of Representatives of the United States of America*, I–III (New York, 1789–1790); Department of State, *Bulletin of Bureau of Rolls and Library*, #6 (Washington, 1894); *The Executive Journal of the Senate*, II (1793–1799), (Washington, 1820); *The Journal of the House of Representatives*, I–III (1789–1801), (Washington, 1828); *American State Papers: Foreign Affairs*, I–II; J. D. Richardson, ed., *Compilation of the Messages and Papers of the Presidents*, I (Washington, 1897); Hunter Miller, ed., *Treaties and Other International Acts of the United States*, I (Washington, 1931); Henry Adams, *Documents Relating to New England Federalism, 1800–1815* (Boston, 1877).

Newspapers

The Western Star (sometimes *Andrews' Western Star*) was examined for the years, 1789–1813 and proved an extremely valuable source both for Sedgwick's efforts at political organization in Berkshire and for discerning the customs and concerns of Stockbridge, Massachusetts—the town he considered his "seat." Among other newspapers consulted were the following, for the dates indicated: *Albany Centinel*, June, 1800; *American Herald* (Boston), 1784–1788; *American Museum* (Philadelphia monthly), 1787, 1790; *Aurora For The Country* (Philadelphia), 1799–1801; *Berkshire Reporter* (Pittsfield, Massachusetts), 1807–1813; *Boston Gazette and County Journal*, June, 1788; *Columbian Centinel* (Boston), 1794, 1796, 1813; *Federal Spy* (Springfield, Massachusetts), 1792–1796; *Hampshire Chronicle* (Springfield), 1787–1796; *Independent Chronicle* (Boston), 1782–1789, 1800; *National Aegis* (Worcester, Massachusetts), 1801; *Philadelphia Daily Advertiser*, 1797; *Pittsfield Sun*, 1800–1801; *Thomas's Massachusetts Spy* (sometimes *Worcester Magazine*), 1783–1785, 1787–1788, 1800; *Vermont Gazette* (Bennington), January, 1789.

Contemporary Pamphlets

The well-known collection edited by Paul L. Ford, *Pamphlets on the Constitution of the United States, Published during Its Discussion by the People, 1787–88* (Brooklyn, 1888) provided valuable background for Sedgwick's role in the ratifying convention. So, too, did an anonymous pamphlet published in Hartford, Connecticut, in 1788: "Impartial Reason," *An Address to the Inhabitants of the County of Berkshire Respecting Their Present Opposition to Civil Government*.

The virulence of subsequent party warfare is well illustrated by the following three pamphlets by the buoyantly vituperative James T. Callender: *The Political Register; or Proceedings in the Session of Congress, Commencing, November 3d, 1794, and Ending March 3d, 1795* (Philadelphia, 1795); *The History of the United States for 1796; Including a Variety of Interesting*

Particulars Relative to the Federal Government Previous to That Period (Philadelphia, 1797); *Sedgwick & Co. or A Key to the Six Per Cent Cabinet* (Philadelphia, 1798). Similarly partisan and informative are an anonymous work purporting to give *An Explanation of the Late Proceedings of Congress Respecting the Official Conduct of the Secretary of the Treasury* (Philadelphia, 1793); Edmund Randolph's *Vindication of Edmund Randolph Written by Himself And Published in 1795* (Peter V. Daniel, ed), (Richmond, 1855); and John Williams (Anthony Pasquin, pseud.), *The Hamiltoniad: or an Extinguisher for the Royal Faction of New England . . . Being intended As A High-Heeled Shoe for All Limping Republicans* (Boston, 1804). Discussed in detail in the text is the anonymous anti-Sedgwick diatribe, *The Honourable Mr. Sedgwick's Political Last Will and Testament, With an Inventory and Appraisal of the Legacies Therein Bequested To the Electors of the first Western District of Massachusetts. . . .* (n.p., 1800). Neither a pamphlet nor anonymous, but useful, was the well-known *Sketches of Debates in the First Senate of the United States in 1789–90–91* by William Maclay (George W. Harris, ed.), (Harrisburg, 1880).

Collected Works

The collected works of many of the leading statesmen of the Federalist era are in the process of being newly and "definitively" edited. The research for this biography began several years ago, however, and the correspondence of such statesmen as Hamilton and Jefferson was first consulted in earlier editions of their works. Consequently, the John C. Hamilton and Henry Cabot Lodge editions of the works of Hamilton are cited, for example, as well as that of Syrett & Cooke which will soon supersede them.

John Adams: Charles F. Adams, ed., *The Works of John Adams* (10 vols., Boston, 1850–1856); Lester J. Cappon, ed., *The Adams-Jefferson Letters* (2 vols., Chapel Hill, 1959). (The monumental edition of the papers of the Adams Family now in preparation under the direction of Lyman Butterfield has not reached to date the political correspondence of John Adams' presidency.) Fisher Ames: Seth Ames, ed., *Works of Fisher Ames* (2 vols., Boston, 1854). Alexander Hamilton: John C. Hamilton, ed., *Works of Alexander Hamilton* (7 vols., New York, 1850–1851); Henry C. Lodge, ed., *The Works of Alexander Hamilton* (12 vols., New York, 1886); Harold C. Syrett; Jacob E. Cooke, eds., *The Papers of Alexander Hamilton* (7 vols. to date, New York, 1961–1963). John Jay: Henry P. Johnston, ed., *The Correspondence and Public Papers of John Jay* (4 vols., New York, 1890–1893). Thomas Jefferson: Paul L. Ford, ed., *Writings of Thomas Jefferson* (10 vols., New York, 1892–1899); Julian C. Boyd, ed., *Papers of Thomas Jefferson* (16 vols. to date, Princeton, 1950–1961). Rufus King: Charles R. King. ed., *The Life and Correspondence of Rufus King Comprising His Letters, Private and Official, His Public Documents and His Speeches* (6 vols., New York, 1894–1900). James Madison: *Letters and Other Writings of James Madison Fourth*

President of the United States (4 vols., Philadelphia, 1865); Gaillard Hunt, ed., *The Writings of James Madison* (8 vol., New York, 1900–1908). (A new and more complete edition of Madison's works is being prepared by William M. E. Rachal and William T. Hutchinson.) James Monroe: Stanislaus M. Hamilton, *The Writings of James Monroe* (7 vols., New York, 1898–1903). Gouverneur Morris: Anne C. Morris, ed., *The Diary and Letters of Gouverneur Morris* (2 vols., New York, 1888). George Washington: Worthington C. Ford, ed., *The Writings of George Washington* (14 vols., New York, 1889–1893). Oliver Wolcott: George Gibbs, *Memoirs of the Administrations of Washington and John Adams, Edited from the Papers of Oliver Wolcott, Secretary of the Treasury* (2 vols., New York, 1842). As an edition of Wolcott's papers this volume is quite deficient, but it contains a rich collection of documents of various kinds relating to the Federalist period.

Of interest to a student of Berkshire County and Theodore Sedgwick's "family life" are two collections of letters of his youngest daughter and son: Mary E. Dewey, ed., *Life and Letters of Catharine M. Sedgwick* (New York, 1871) and Catharine M. Sedgwick, ed., *Letters of Charles Sedgwick to His Family and Friends* (Boston, 1870).

SECONDARY SOURCES

General Histories

The following histories proved valuable in placing Sedgwick within the general social and political framework of his period:

For the Colonial and Confederation periods the outstanding works are those of Merrill Jensen: *The Articles of Confederation: An Interpretation of the Social-Constitutional History of the American Revolution, 1774–1781* (Madison, 1940) and *The New Nation: A History of the United States During the Confederation 1781–89* (New York, 1950), although as noted in the text the author cannot at all points agree with the revisionist theories of Professor Jensen. Also helpful were such older works as: George Bancroft, *History of the Formation of the Constitution of the United States of America* (2 vols., rev. ed., New York, 1883); John Fiske, *The Critical Period of American History 1783–1789* (Cambridge, 1889); Evarts B. Greene, *The Revolutionary Generation 1763–1790* (New York, 1943); Vernon L. Parrington, *The Colonial Mind, 1620–1800* (*Main Currents in American Thought*, I), (New York, 1927).

For the Federalist period the volume in the New American Nation series by John C. Miller, *The Federalist Era 1789–1801*, already cited, is surely the best one-volume survey. Of the many other general histories of the Federalist period and its immediate aftermath, the author would list the following as most helpful in writing this biography: John S. Bassett, *The Federalist System 1789–1801* (New York, 1908); Charles A. Beard, *Economic Origins of Jeffersonian Democracy* (New York, 1915); Claude G. Bowers, *Jefferson and Hamilton: The Struggle for Democracy in America* (Boston, 1925); Henry J.

Ford, *Washington and His Colleagues* (New Haven, 1920); Richard Hildreth, *The History of the United States of America* (6 vols., rev. ed., New York, 1856); John A. Krout and Dixon R. Fox, *The Completion of Independence, 1790–1830* (New York, 1944); John B. McMasters, *A History of the People of the United States* (8 vols., New York, 1883-1913); Nathan Schachner, *The Founding Fathers* (New York, 1954); Leonard D. White, *The Federalists: A Study in Administrative History* (New York, 1948) and *The Jeffersonians* (New York, 1951).

In a category of its own may be placed the classic study of the presidencies of Jefferson and Madison by Henry Adams, *History of the United States of America* (9 vols., New York, 1889–1891).

State Histories

Whatever its present ailments, the Commonwealth of Massachusetts cannot plead historical neglect. Studies of the Bay State for the years of Sedgwick's political life are both numerous and of a high standard of excellence. In many ways the most satisfactory and scholarly study of Massachusetts political and economic history for this period is that of Oscar and Mary Handlin, *Commonwealth A Study of the Role of Government in the American Economy: Massachusetts, 1774–1861* (New York, 1947). The Handlins have also contributed a brilliant dissection of the confused state of parties and factions in post-Revolutionary Massachusetts, "Radicals and Conservatives in Massachusetts After Independence," *The New England Quarterly*, XVII (1944), 343–355.

Two multi-volume state histories were consulted: John S. Barry, *The History of Massachusetts* (3 vols., Boston, 1855–1857) and Albert B. Hart, ed., *Commonwealth History of Massachusetts* (5 vols., New York, 1927–1930); the latter of which is far superior. The essential economic background for the changing social and political scene in Massachusetts in the last half of the eighteenth century may be secured, with some difficulty, from William B. Weeden, *Economic and Social History of New England 1620–1789* (2 vols., Boston, 1890–1891), supplementing this work with that of the Handlins already cited and that of Ralph V. Harlow, *Economic Conditions in Massachusetts During the American Revolution* (Cambridge, 1918).

Three of the most suggestive general analyses of eighteenth century Massachusetts history are Brooks Adams, *The Emancipation of Massachusetts* (Boston, 1887); Harry A. Cushing, *The Transition From Provincial To Commonwealth Government in Massachusetts* (New York, 1896); James Truslow Adams, *New England in the Republic 1776–1850* (Boston, 1926). None is recent, nor as yet superseded. Two occasionally conflicting but equally stimulating studies of Massachusetts society and politics are Robert E. Brown, *Middle-Class Democracy and the Revolution in Massachusetts, 1691–1780* (Ithaca, 1955) and Elisha P. Douglas, *Rebels and Democrats. . . .* (Chapel

Hill, 1955). Professor Brown's thesis concerning the democratic quality of society and government in colonial Massachusetts is subject to qualification, but his book is both lively and significant. That the "Berkshire Constitutionalists" and others did not consider Massachusetts sufficiently democratic or equalitarian is shown by the old, much-used, and never-published doctoral dissertation of Fred E. Haynes, "The Struggle for the Constitution in Massachusetts, 1775–1780" (Harvard University Archives).

Such special topics as nominating procedures for members of the Massachusetts legislature in the 1770's and commissary operations in the Revolution are discussed by Frederick W. Dallinger, *Nominations for Elective Office in the United States* (New York, 1897) and Robert A. East, *Business Enterprise in the American Revolutionary Era* (New York, 1938). For the story of the ratification of the Federal Constitution in Massachusetts, and the social and political divisions it reflected, the model essay by Robert A. East, "The Massachusetts Conservatives in the Critical Period," *The Era of the American Revolution* (Richard B. Morris, ed.), (New York, 1948) was helpful, as was Samuel B. Harding's older analysis, *The Contest Over the Ratification of the Federal Constitution in the State of Massachusetts* (New York, 1896) and Charles Warren's charmingly written *Elbridge Gerry, James Warren, Mercy Warren and the Ratification of the Federal Constitution in Massachusetts* (Boston, 1932).

Berkshire County Studies

The best historical introduction to Sedgwick's home county is undoubtedly the recent study by Richard D. Birdsall, *Berkshire County: A Cultural History* (New Haven, 1959); the best general guide is *The Berkshire Hills*, a work of the Federal Writers Project of the Works Progress Administration (New York, 1939). Among the older histories the following all offered some anecdote or description that proved useful: Thomas Allen, *An Historical Sketch of the County of Berkshire and Town of Pittsfield* (Boston, 1808), the work of a political opponent of Theodore Sedgwick; Hamilton Child, *Gazeteer of Berkshire County, Mass. 1725–1885* (Syracuse, 1885); Rollins H. Cooke, ed., *Historic Homes and Institutions and Genealogical and Personal Memoirs of Berkshire County, Massachusetts* (2 vols., New York, 1908); David D. Field, ed., *A History of The County of Berkshire, Massachusetts* (Pittsfield, 1829); Josiah G. Holland, *History of Western Massachusetts* (2 vols., Springfield, 1855).

Of the town histories, perhaps the best and surely the best written is Sarah C. Sedgwick and Christina S. Marquand, *Stockbridge 1739–1939: A Chronicle* (Great Barrington, 1939). It offers an excellent description of the pioneer beginnings of the town of Stockbridge and its changes and transition during the residence of Theodore Sedgwick, and proved to be a valuable source. To a lesser extent so did: Electa F. Jones *Stockbridge Past and Present or Records of An Old Mission Station* (Springfield, 1854); Joseph E. Smith, *The History of Pittsfield (Berkshire County), Massachusetts, 1734–1876* (2 vols., Boston, 1869–1876); Charles J. Taylor, *History of Great Barrington (Berkshire County), Massachusetts* (Great Barrington, 1882).

Special studies of some aspect of Berkshire's social and intellectual life that proved useful in tracing the activities of the Sedgwick family were: Berkshire Association of Congregational Ministers, *Proceedings at the Centennial Commemoration of the Organization of the Berkshire Association of Congregational Ministers* (Boston, 1864); Harland H. Ballard, "A Forgotten Fraternity," Berkshire Historical and Scientific Society, *Collections*, III (1899–1913), 279–298; Richard D. Birdsall, "William Cullen Bryant and Catherine Sedgwick—Their Debt to Berkshire," *The New England Quarterly*, XXVIII (1959), 349–371; Katharine M. Abbott, *Old Paths and Legends of the New England Border* (New York, 1907); Harry M. Lydenberg, *The Berkshire Republican Library at Stockbridge 1794–1818* (Worcester, 1941). The most interesting description of Sedgwick's "mansion" is to be found in the account of the French emigré, the Duc La Rochefoucauld Liancourt, *Travels through the United States of North America . . . in the Years 1795, 1796, and 1797* (2 vols., London, 1799).

Biographies

As the research for this book began several years ago it is not always the newest biography that has been most used or useful. As with "Collected Works," it is consequently necessary in some cases to list not merely the latest "Life" but all that have provided references and information. This is especially true respecting biographies of Hamilton. Undoubtedly the best is the recently completed two-volume work by Broadus Mitchell (New York, 1957; 1962) but also useful in varying ways were John C. Hamilton, *History of the Republic of the United States of America As Traced in the Writings of Alexander Hamilton and Of His Contemporaries* (6 vols., New York, 1859); Louis M. Hacker, *Alexander Hamilton in the American Tradition* (New York, 1957); John C. Miller, *Alexander Hamilton, Portrait in Paradox* (New York, 1959); Nathan Schachner, *Alexander Hamilton* (New York, 1946).

Professor Dumas Malone is engaged in writing the definitive biography of Thomas Jefferson, three volumes of which have already appeared. The second, *Jefferson and the Rights of Man* (Boston, 1951) offers an interesting analysis on the causes for the famous breach with Hamilton, but for this work more useful were: Gilbert Chinard, *Thomas Jefferson: The Apostle of Americanism* (Boston, 1929) and Nathan Schachner, *Thomas Jefferson: A Biography* (2 vols., New York, 1951). An old and eulogistic *Life of Thomas Jefferson* by Henry S. Randall (3 vols., New York, 1858) provided two references to Sedgwick in Jefferson's correspondence not uncovered elsewhere.

Page Smith has written a much-praised two-volume study of *John Adams* (New York, 1962), which quotes largely and skillfully from the rich collection of Adams letters, but perhaps the most satisfactory analysis of that difficult personality is still that of Gilbert Chinard, *Honest John Adams* (Boston, 1933).

For the last and greatest figure of the Big Four of the Federalist era, the best biography is perhaps G. W. Stephenson and W. H. Dunn, *George Washington* (2 vols., New York, 1940).

Among statesmen of the period of the next rank, the following biographies of Sedgwick's Federalist colleagues were helpful: Albert J. Beveridge, *The Life of John Marshall* (4 vols., Boston, 1916–1919); Morton Bordon, *The Federalism of James A. Bayard* (New York, 1955); George A. Boyd, *Elias Boudinot, Patriot and Statesman* (Princeton, 1952); William P. Cresson, *Francis Dana: A Puritan Diplomat At the Court of Catherine the Great* (New York, 1930); Henry Cabot Lodge, *Life and Letters of George Cabot* (Boston, 1877); Samuel E. Morison, *The Life and Letters of Harrison Gray Otis, Federalist 1765–1848* (2 vols., Boston, 1913); Theophilus Parsons, *Memoir of Theophilus Parsons* (Boston, 1861); Octavius Pickering and Charles W. Upham, *The Life of Timothy Pickering* (4 vols., New York, 1867–1873); Howard Swiggett, *The Extraordinary Mr. Morris* (New York, 1952); Henry C. Van Schaack, *Life of Peter Van Schaack, LL.D.* (New York, 1842). There is as yet no satisfactory biography of Rufus King. Robert Ernst and James G. King are presently preparing one. The "life" of Charles R. King, already cited, is a collection of letters, not a biography. A slender essay on King's early years will be found in the *Essex Institute Historical Collections* for October, 1960: Richard E. Welch Jr., "Rufus King: The Formative Years, 1767–1788."

Biographies of Sedgwick's Republican opponents are equally numerous and should probably begin with those of James Madison, whom Sedgwick deemed his chief opponent throughout the 1790's. The old life by William C. Rives, *History of the Life and Times of James Madison* (3 vols., Boston, 1859–1868), has been superseded by the well-written if somewhat disputatious five-volume life by Irving Brant, *James Madison* (Indianapolis, 1948–1956). Among other biographies of men subject to the copious censure of Sedgwick are the following: Henry Adams, *John Randolph* (Boston, 1889) and *Life of Albert Gallatin* (Philadelphia, 1880); Dice R. Anderson, *William Branch Giles* (Menasha, Wisconsin, 1915); James T. Austin, *The Life of Elbridge Gerry* (2 vols., Boston, 1828–1829); William P. Cresson, *James Monroe* (Chapel Hill, 1946); William E. Dodd, *The Life of Nathaniel Macon* (Raleigh, 1903); James Parton, *The Life and Times of Aaron Burr* (New York, 1858); Nathan Schachner, *Aaron Burr* (New York, 1937); Paul A. Wallace, *The Muhlenbergs of Pennsylvania* (Philadelphia, 1950).

Biographical notes and memoirs of Sedgwick's family and ancestors include: Mary E. Dewey, *Life and Letters of Catharine M. Sedgwick*, already cited; Theodore B. Gold, *Historical Records of the Town of Cornwall, Litchfield County, Connecticut* (Hartford, 1877); Nathaniel Goodwin, *Genealogical Notes or Contributions to the Family History of Some of the First Settlers. . . .* (Hartford, 1856); Henry D. Sedgwick, "Robert Sedgwick," Colonial Society of Massachusetts, *Transactions*, III (1895–1897), 156–173 and "The Sedgwicks of Berkshire," Berkshire Historical and Scientific Society *Collections*, III (1899–1913), 89–106; Hubert M. Sedgwick, *A Sedg-*

wick Genealogy (New Haven, 1961); L. Hasbrouck von Sahler, "Two Distinguished Members of the Sedgwick Family—Robert and Theodore," *The New York Genealogical and Biographical Record,* XXXII (1901), 104–108.

In addition to the above works there were many others consulted that proved of value respecting some particular activity or period of Sedgwick's career. These are listed below under various self-explanatory headings:

Legal and Judicial Career:
Thomas C. Amory, *Life of James Sullivan* (2 vols., Boston, 1859).
Jeremy Belknap, "Answers to Queries Respecting Slavery," Massachusetts Historical Society, *Collections,* 1st Series, IV (1795), 193–211.
George Bliss, *Address to Members of the Bar, 1826* (Springfield, 1827).
Andrew McFarland Davis, "The Confiscatory Laws of Massachusetts," Colonial Society of Massachusetts, *Transactions,* VIII (1902–1904), 50–72.
William T. Davis, *History of Judiciary of Massachusetts* (Boston, 1911).
Frank W. Grinnell, "The Constitutional History of the Supreme Judicial Court of Massachusetts From the Revolution to 1813," *Massachusetts Law Quarterly,* II (1917), 359–552.
Mark A. Howe Jr., *Readings in American Legal History* (Cambridge, Mass., 1949).
George H. Moore, *Notes on the History of Slavery in Massachusetts* (New York, 1866).
John B. Pierce Jr., "Sketch of the Judicial Career of Theodore Sedgwick" (unpublished seminar paper, Harvard Law School Library).
William F. Poole, *Anti-Slavery Opinion before the Year 1800* (Cincinnati, 1873).
Lemuel Shaw, *Address Delivered Before the Bar of Berkshire On the Occasion of His First Taking His Seat as Chief Justice . . . 1830* (Boston, 1831).
William Sullivan, *Address to Members of the Bar of Suffolk . . . March 1824* (Boston, 1825).
Charles Warren, *A History of the American Bar* (Boston, 1911).
Emory Washburn, "The Extinction of Slavery in Massachusetts," Massachusetts Historical Society, *Collections,* 4th Series IV (1858), 333–346.
Emory Washburn, *Sketches of Judicial History of Massachusetts From 1630 To the Revolution in 1775* (Boston, 1840).
Richard E. Welch Jr. "The Parsons-Sedgwick Feud and the Reform of the Massachusetts Judiciary," *Essex Institute Historical Collections,* April, 1956, 171–187.
Richard E. Welch Jr., "Mumbet and Judge Sedgwick: A Footnote to the Early History of Massachusetts Justice," *Boston Bar Journal,* January, 1964, 12–19.

Revolutionary Period (Continental Congress and Shays' Rebellion):
Charles J. Bullock, *The Finances of the United States from 1775 to 1789* (Madison, 1895).
Edmund C. Burnett, *The Continental Congress* (New York, 1941).
Albert Farnsworth, "Causes of Shays' Rebellion," *Massachusetts Law Quarterly,* May, 1927.
Louis C. Hatch, *The Administration of the Revolutionary Army* (New York, 1904).
George R. Minot, *The History of the Insurrection in Massachusetts, In the Year MDCCLXXXVI and the Rebellion Consequent Thereon.* (Worcester, 1788). A contemporary source and an important one.
Allan Nevins, *The American States During and After the Revolution, 1775-1789* (New York, 1924).
Lorenzo Sabine, *Biographical Sketches of Loyalists of the American Revolution with An Historical Essay* (2 vols., Boston, 1864).
Marion I. Starkey, *A Little Rebellion* (Boston, 1955). A lively account of Shays' Rebellion, less persuasive in its analysis of causation than the old account of Joseph Warren.
William G. Sumner, *The Financiers and Finances of the American Revolution* (2 vols., New York, 1891).
Robert J. Taylor, *Western Massachusetts in the Revolution* (Providence, 1954). Concise and scholarly; the best study of the subject.
Joseph P. Warren, "The Shays Rebellion" (Unpublished doctoral dissertation, 1902, Harvard University Archives).
D. M. Wilcox, "An Episode of Shays's Rebellion," *Magazine of History,* XXII (1916), 100-107.
Edward Bellamy, *Duke of Stockbridge* (Boston, 1901). An historical novel, laid in Berkshire County during the period of Shays' Rebellion, and an excellent one.

Formation and Ratification of Federal Constitution:
Charles A. Beard, *An Economic Interpretation of the Constitution of the United States* (New York, 1913). First a book, then a bible, and now the subject of near-constant attack.
Robert E. Brown, *Charles Beard and the Constitution: A Critical Analysis of "An Economic Interpretation of the Constitution"* (Princeton, 1956). Without doubt a "critical analysis" and, in part, very effective.
Orin G. Libby, *Geographic Distribution of the Vote on the Ratification of the Constitution* (Madison, Wisconsin, 1894).
Forrest McDonald, *We the People: The Economic Origins of the Constitution* (Chicago, 1958). Critical both of Beard and of Robert Brown's criticism of Beard.
Jackson T. Main, *The Anti-Federalists* (Chapel Hill, 1961). Persuasively

revives older view respecting importance of *economic* background and suspicions of the Anti-Federalists.

Origin and Rise of Political Parties:

Joseph Charles, *The Origins of the American Party System* (Chapel Hill, 1956). Provocative analysis, strongly anti-Hamiltonian.

Noble E. Cunningham Jr., *The Jeffersonian Republicans: The Formation of Party Organization, 1789–1801* (Chapel Hill, 1957). A major contribution.

Carl R. Fish, *The Civil Services and the Patronage* (New York, 1904).

Rufus W. Griswold, *The Republican Court or American Society in the Days of Washington* (New York, 1855). Contains certain anecdotes reflective of the transition from factions to parties.

Homer C. Hockett, "Federalism And The West," *Essays in American History Dedicated To Frederick Jackson Turner* (New York, 1910).

Richard Hofstadter, *The American Political Tradition And the Men Who Made It* (New York, 1948).

Gaillard Hunt, "Office-Seeking during Washington's Administration," *American Historical Review*, I (1895–1896), 270–283.

Orin G. Libby, "Political Factions in Washington's Administration," *The Quarterly Journal of the University of North Dakota*, III (1913–1914), 293–318.

Orin G. Libby, "A Sketch Of The Early Political Parties in the United States," *The Quarterly Journal of the University of North Dakota*, II (1911–1912), 205–242.

Eugene P. Link, *Democratic-Republican Societies, 1790–1800* (New York, 1942).

Samuel Eliot Morison, "The First National Nominating Convention, 1808," *American Historical Review*, XVII (1911–1912), 744–763.

Anson E. Morse, *The Federalist Party in Massachusetts to the Year 1800* (Princeton, 1909).

William A. Robinson, *Jeffersonian Democracy in New England* (New Haven, 1916).

Leland D. Baldwin, *Whisky Rebels* (Pittsburgh, 1939).

Jacob E. Cooke, "The Whisky Insurrection: A Re-evaluation," *Pennsylvania History*, XXX, No. 3 (July, 1963), 316–346.

Federalist Extremism and Federalist Division:

Frank M. Anderson, "Contemporary Opinion of the Kentucky and Virginia Resolutions," *American Historical Review*, V (1899–1900), 45–63; 225–252.

Frank M. Anderson, "The Enforcement of the Alien and Sedition Laws," American Historical Association, *Annual Report for the year 1912*, 115–126.

Manning J. Dauer, *The Adams Federalists* (Baltimore, 1953). Professor Dauer may perhaps date too early the division between the High and Moderate Federalists, but no student of the Federalist party can afford to ignore this work. The appendices alone place them deeply in his debt.
Stephen G. Kurtz, *The Presidency of John Adams* (Philadelphia, 1957). Professor Kurtz emphasizes the struggle over the command of the army in 1798 and appears to feel that the High Federalists were fairly basely motivated in their demands for military preparations and alien and sedition acts.
Leonard W. Levy, *Legacy of Suppression: Freedom of Speech and Press in Early American History* (Cambridge, 1960).
John C. Miller, *Crisis in Freedom: The Alien and Sedition Laws* (Boston, 1951).
Anson D. Morse, "Causes and Consequences of the Party Revolution of 1800," American Historical Association, *Annual Report for the year 1894*, 531–539.
James Morton Smith, *Freedom's Fetters: The Alien and Sedition Laws and American Civil Liberties* (Ithaca, 1956). The most thorough study of the subject.

Economic Thought and Policies of the Federal Decade:
Henry C. Adams, *Taxation in the United States, 1789–1816* (Baltimore, 1884).
Joseph Dorfman, *The Economic Mind in American Civilization, 1606–1865* (3 vols., New York, 1946).
E. James Ferguson, *The Power of the Purse* (Chapel Hill, 1961). The best analysis of Hamilton's Financial System and a brilliant piece of writing.
Paul Studenski and Herman E. Krooss, *Financial History of the United States* (New York, 1952).
Curtis P. Nettels, *The Emergence of a National Economy, 1775–1815* (New York, 1962).

Foreign Relations:
Gardner W. Allen, *Our Naval War With France* (Boston, 1909).
Samuel F. Bemis, *Jay's Treaty A Study in Commerce and Diplomacy* (New York, 1923).
Samuel F. Bemis, ed., *The American Secretaries of State and Their Diplomacy* (10 vols., New York, 1927–1929).
Irving Brant, "Edmund Randolph, Not Guilty!", *William and Mary Quarterly*, Third Series, VII (1950), 180–198.
Alexander DeConde, *Entangling Alliance: Politics and Diplomacy under George Washington* (Durham, North Carolina, 1958). A careful piece of scholarship marred by a seeming determination to reduce Washington to a Hamiltonian puppet.

Charles D. Hazen, *Contemporary American Opinion of the French Revolution* (Baltimore, 1897).

Walter W. Jennings, *The American Embargo 1807–1809* (Iowa City, n.d.)

Bradford Perkins, *The First Rapprochement: England and the United States, 1795–1805* (Philadelphia, 1955). Much praised and deservedly so.

Vernon G. Setser, *The Commercial Reciprocity Policy of the United States 1774–1829* (Philadelphia, 1937).

Charles M. Thomas, *American Neutrality In 1793: A Study in Cabinet Government* (New York, 1931).

Arthur P. Whitaker, *The Mississippi Question 1795–1803* (New York, 1934).

Speakership of the House of Representatives:

Mary P. Follett, *The Speaker of the House of Representatives* (New York, 1896).

Henry B. Fuller, *The Speakers of the House* (Boston, 1909).

Speeches Delivered in the House of Representatives January 19, 1888 on the Presentation By The State of Massachusetts To The National Government of Portraits of Ex-Speakers Sedgwick, Varnum, and Banks. Washington, 1888.

INDEX

Index